Judicial Impeachment

JUDICIAL IMPEACHMENT

NONE CALLED FOR JUSTICE

Mary L. Volcansek

University of Illinois Press
Urbana and Chicago

This book is printed on acid-free paper.

Library of Congress Cataloging-in-Publication Data

Volcansek, Mary L., 1948–
    Judicial impeachment : none called for justice / Mary L. Volcansek.
        p.   cm.
    Includes bibliographical references (p.   ) and index.
    ISBN 0-252-01961-X (cl : acid-free paper)
    1. Claiborne, Harry Eugene—Impeachment. 2. Hastings, Alcee L.—
Impeachment. 3. Nixon, Walter L., 1928-   —Impeachment.
4. Judges—United States—Discipline—History. I. Title.
    KF8782.C53V65   1993
    347.73'14—dc20
    [347.30714]   92-16002
                                                                CIP

For "H" and the Kits

None called for justice, nor any pleadeth for truth;
they trust in vanity, and speak lies; they conceive mischief and
bring forth inequity.

—Isaiah 59:4

For, as thou urgest justice, be assured
Thou shalt have justice, more than thou desirest.

—*The Merchant of Venice*, Act IV, Scene 1

Contents

Acknowledgments

Many people contributed to the research for this book, most of them, unfortunately, anonymous employees in court clerks' offices, newspaper libraries, interlibrary loan, and the Library of Congress. Their conscientious and cheerful cooperation was essential. A few who helped are known and deserve mention, in particular, Alan Baron, Samuel Krislov, Orlando Perez, Becky Salokar, Kenneth Thompson, and Russell Wheeler. A special note of thanks is also due to John Reich. My greatest appreciation is reserved for my husband, Harry Antrim, without whom this book would never have been written. The errors, of course, remain my responsibility.

1

New Approaches
to an Old Problem

On October 9, 1986, the president pro tempore posed the question to the assembled Senate: "How say you: Is the respondent guilty or not guilty?" Those words had not been heard in the Senate chamber since the impeachment of Judge Halsted Ritter in 1936, but would resound twice more in the next three years, as senators assumed their roles in a political drama with antecedents in the fourteenth-century trial of Lord William Latimer and Richard Lyons in the British House of Lords.

Hundreds of impeachment resolutions have been introduced into the House of Representatives over the years, and some sixty or more were sufficiently serious that investigations were ordered. Before 1986, however, only thirteen actual impeachments were passed by the House and forwarded to the Senate for trial. Of those, four, all involving federal judges, resulted in convictions by the requisite two-thirds majority in the upper chamber. The sparing use of impeachment and trial over two hundred years of American history changed in the 1980s, and three federal judges were impeached, tried, and removed in as many years. Those cases brought the total of the judges actually convicted to seven of the twelve who had been impeached. The rusty machinery for impeachment and trial was dusted off and streamlined to cope with the new flurry of charges against miscreant federal judges.

What changed impeachment and made it almost an annual congressional event? A number of answers have been proffered, but none are wholly satisfying in the complex legal and political milieu that surrounds the process. This book will consider the impeachment and removal of U.S. judges Harry Claiborne, Alcee Hastings, and Walter

Nixon and attempt to unravel the threads that tie their convictions to a process first devised in medieval England. Because much scholarship on impeachment has either ignored "relevant historical evidence" or relied "on an incomplete or unclear historical record,"[1] I intend not only to analyze the implications of these three impeachments but also to provide a clear picture of the events and circumstances surrounding them. What happened in these cases has obvious implications for judicial independence as well as for the accountability of judges and the legitimacy of the system.

Traditionally in Britain, as well as on the continent and in the colonies, the judiciary was dependent upon the monarch, and until 1761, British judges served only so long as the ruler who appointed them survived.[2] Separation of the judiciary from both the executive and the legislative branches of government was a novel concept, proposed in Baron de Montesquieu's *Spirit of the Laws* (1748) but not put into practice until the U.S. Constitution became effective in 1789.[3] Indeed, Alexander Hamilton argued that the most viable means of ensuring the independence of the judiciary from the other powers of government was "permanency in office."[4] Independence protects the liberties of individual litigants and presumably the sanctity of constitutional guarantees in the face of majority sentiments. An unaccountable judiciary can block, at least temporarily, democratic wishes and therefore run counter to democracy. Thus, accountability is essential to ensure the legitimacy of the courts and of the regime itself. If, however, accountability hinges upon partisan whims or politics, more broadly defined, the majority triumphs, and independence is jeopardized.

Much has been made of the inherent tensions between accountability and independence for judges. Despite the relative newness of the concept, many have come to regard independence as the sine qua non of judging. Theodore Becker, for example, cites independence as one of the basic criteria for the very existence of a court,[5] a position Henry Lummis echoes: "The moment a decision is controlled or affected by the opinion of others or by any form of external influence or pressure, that moment the judge ceases to exist."[6] Independence, of course, implies impartiality toward the parties to the case; but when the judging function becomes part of the government structure, some, most notably Martin Shapiro, argue that independence becomes only the most deviant case. Independent judiciaries are not, he asserts, a universal attribute of judges, but conventional wisdom in the United States holds that judges must be in a position to decide against the wishes of other powers and to do so without fear of retaliation.[7] The entire debate over how best to name judges has been couched in the context of preferring independence to accountability or the reverse. Opponents of any form of election for judges assert that the heart of the judicial function is at peril if judges have political obligations, are seen as politicians, and are subject to a popular critique of essentially technical performance.[8] Life tenure is, therefore, essential to liberate judges "from the fear that public officials adversely affected by their decisions might remove judges whose decisions are contrary to their interests."[9] The judicial independence position is an eloquently argued one, but implicit in it is the basic assumption that independence is not to be preserved in the case of a corrupt, inept, or partisan jurist. The question is, How to remove the unethical judge?

Impeachment has long been seen as an imperfect tool because of its susceptibility to partisan manipulation. For Alexander Hamilton, impeachable offenses were inherently political, "as they relate chiefly in injuries done immediately to the society itself."[10] Although impeachment had been practiced in the American colonies and some variations adopted in several state constitutions,[11] the system in the Constitution essentially follows the British model. The significant elements of the process first observed in 1376 — presentment by the House of Commons and trial by the Lords — are reflected in the American constitutional scheme.

Early Practices

Finding an equilibrium between the competing goals of judicial independence and judicial responsibility has long taxed the genius of constitutional architects. The drafters of state constitutions experimented periodically with alternatives to the national system of life tenure, with removal only by impeachment, and their efforts reflect the conviction expressed by Chief Justice John Marshall that "the greatest scourge an angry Heaven ever inflicted upon an ungrateful and sinning people was an ignorant, a corrupt, or a dependent judiciary."[12]

Early state constitutions drew little upon the British system of executive appointment of judges; in no state in 1776 was the governor directly responsible for naming jurists. In the 1776 constitutions of Maryland, Massachusetts, New Hampshire, New York, and Pennsylvania, the governor could appoint judges with the advice and consent of a council, usually consisting of five to nine people elected by the legislature from among its own membership. Connecticut, Delaware, Georgia, New Jersey, North Carolina, South Carolina, and Virginia all provided that judges would be elected by the legislature.[13] Each of the original state constitutions that preceded passage of the current national one made judges removable through impeachment, limited terms of office, or address by two-thirds of the legislature. Provisions for life tenure "had a slightly hollow ring in those states in which a judge could be removed for any reason, simply by a two-thirds vote of a bicameral legislature."[14] Virtually every state constitution still provides for impeachment of state judges, but that traditional approach has been a failure "in all but the most egregious cases," largely because it encroaches on the legislative agenda.[15] As a result, most states have adopted supplementary or alternative schemes. "Address" by the legislature gained currency for a period, and in 1936 twenty-eight states allowed removal in that manner. That number, however, had dwindled to nineteen by 1982, and, like impeachment, address was rarely used.[16]

The American states, particularly in the twentieth century, were innovative in their efforts to control judicial misconduct and disability. California was the first to create judicial conduct organizations to monitor judicial behavior, and forty-seven other states had followed suit by 1983. Those reforming states now typically have involved their supreme courts, court administrators, judicial conduct organizations, and judges' associations in matters related to misbehavior or inability to serve.[17] Judicial conduct commissions, normally composed of a mix of lawyers and laypeople, hear evidence of judicial wrongdoing and can recommend removal, but the states' highest courts or legislatures usually retain the ultimate decision. Popular recall elections are also possible in certain states, a practice of direct democracy that is not without its critics and, like impeachment, used infrequently.[18]

While the states have experimented with alternatives to impeachment and have devised various avenues to check wrongdoing by judges, the national government has maintained impeachment in its original form. The cumbersome nature of the process has prompted debate off and on since the First Congress in 1791. At the conclusion of the trial of Supreme Court Justice Samuel Chase in 1805, Edmund Randolph proposed a constitutional amendment identical to one offered and rejected earlier at the Constitutional Convention. His recommendation was an adaptation of the then existing British system whereby judges could be removed by the executive upon address by both chambers of the legislative branch. All who had firsthand knowledge of the impeachment process found it clumsy, unwieldy, time-consuming, imprecise, and subject to partisan or other political influences. Impeachment, the argument went, should be reserved for major issues as a countervailing power of Congress against the executive should its officers abuse their powers; instead, the system has worked for "the ouster of dreary little judges for squalid misconduct."[19]

The Constitution mentions impeachment six times. Article II, section 4 defines the scope of impeachment as extending to "the President, Vice President, and all civil officers of the United States," who can be removed from office by impeachment and conviction of "Treason, Bribery, or other high Crimes and Misdemeanors."[20] The role of the House as accuser is defined in Article I, section 2, and the power of the Senate to try is treated in the next section; penalties are, in that provision, limited to removal and disqualification.[21] Article II prohibits presidential pardons in cases of impeachment, and Article III, in guaranteeing trial by jury, excludes cases of impeachment. Even divorced from a concrete case, these provisions were not without controversy, and their application to specific individuals has tended to obfuscate, not clarify, subsequent debate.

The essentially political or, more aptly, partisan character of impeachment was noted from the outset and acknowledged, even by Alexander Hamilton in his defense of the proposed constitution. The prosecution of impeachments, he wrote, "will seldom fail to agitate the passions of the whole community, and to divide it into parties more or less friendly or inimical to the accused." Consequently, the guilt or innocence of the parties will be less important in determining the outcome than the "comparative strength of the parties."[22] Jefferson later echoed Hamilton's fears and, when responding to the first congressional experience with impeachment, wrote to James Madison that "impeachment has been an engine more of passion than justice."[23]

Impeachment was rarely used in the United States, and the few cases that led to Senate trials are so disparate that little settled law or practice can be gleaned from them. The results, moreover, have typically been muddied by partisanship or politics in a more narrow sense, leaving the search for clear precedents or even guideposts wholly unsatisfying. The first impeachment, that of the alcoholic and mentally deranged

John Pickering in 1804, led to a conviction in the Senate on all four articles forwarded by the House. The verdict of guilt was for the ambiguous offense of high crimes and misdemeanors. Pickering's behavior on the bench, although injudicious and unseemly, hardly fit the alternatives of treason or bribery. The vote was along strictly partisan lines,[24] and almost simultaneous with that action, the Jeffersonians in the House passed eight articles of impeachment against Federalist Supreme Court Justice Samuel Chase. The justice, a flamboyant and controversial figure throughout his public life, was also charged with high crimes and misdemeanors for his highhanded treatment of defendants charged under the Alien and Sedition Acts. He was, however, acquitted on all charges,[25] and returned to the Court, where he served, although often ill with gout, until his death in 1811.[26] Following Pickering's removal and Chase's acquittal, ten other judges were impeached by the House of Representatives. As in the first two instances, all were tried before the Senate on the rather elastic offense of high crimes and misdemeanors.

President Andrew Johnson and Secretary of State William Belknap, both of whom the Senate acquitted, were the only nonjurists whom the House accused formally. James Peck, a district court judge from Missouri, was acquitted in 1831 of charges that he abused the contempt power. Charles Swayne (1904) and Harold Louderback (1933) were likewise exonerated by the upper chamber when the House brought charges. George English was impeached in 1926 but resigned before the Senate could try the case. The practical effect of resignation was to halt the process, but, in a strict constitutional sense, a trial before the Senate remained possible. Present removal and future disqualification are separate acts, and resignation does not absolutely end the threat, but Congress has never successfully tried anyone after resignation.[27] Only three other judges—West Humphreys, Robert Archbald, and Halsted Ritter—were convicted in Senate trials and removed from office before 1986. Humphreys was removed in 1862 for supporting secession and holding office under the Confederacy, while Robert Archbald of the commerce court was convicted in 1912 of abuse of power. Halsted Ritter was, oddly enough, found not guilty on six articles that alleged specific acts of misconduct but convicted on a summary article of bringing his court "into scandal and disrepute, to the prejudice of said court, and public confidence in the administration of justice therein."[28]

Because of the unique features of each case and the historical context in which they occurred, there are few solid precedents regarding impeachment. Those impeachments resulting in convictions are not particularly instructive because no defense was even presented in either the Pickering or Humphreys cases. The convictions of Archbald and Ritter are not helpful because of the ambiguous outcomes and puzzling contradictions between acquittals on some articles and convictions on others. None of the few instances of impeachment shed much light on the meaning of "high crimes and misdemeanors" in the Constitution, although four judges committed them according to two-thirds of the Senate. The infractions apparently need not be criminal offenses, and, indeed, none were.[29] Drawing upon the American experience, a more precise statement is not possible. Consensus on what constitutes impeachable offenses seems to reject the rather open-ended definition that Gerald Ford offered when he was House minority leader : "whatever a majority of the House of Representatives considers it to be at a given moment in history."[30] Charles Black, in an attempt to lend somewhat greater specificity to the concept, suggested that impeachable offenses are ones that "are rather obviously wrong, whether or not 'criminal,'" and are sufficiently serious to make "dangerous the continuance in power of their perpetrator."[31] That admittedly general statement captures how unsettled the question remained in 1936 after eleven officials were impeached, but only four federal judges were convicted.

Although no U.S. judge was impeached for fifty years after Halsted Ritter, others, most notably Supreme Court justices Abe Fortas and William O. Douglas, were investigated by Congress. Douglas was the object of congressional inquiry, or at least resolutions proposing impeachment, on three occasions: in 1953 for granting a stay of execution in the case of Julius and Ethel Rosenberg; in 1957 for marrying for the fourth time; and in 1970 for general, undefined impeachable offenses. All came to naught. Fortas was investigated initially in conjunction with Lyndon Johnson's proposal to elevate him from associate to chief justice upon Earl Warren's retirement. The nomination failed, but more and more revelations of possible conflicts of interest surfaced, and by May 1968, even senators of his own party were calling for his resignation. The Justice Department found no "smoking gun," and impeachment was not the immediate issue. Fortas, nonetheless, resigned, explaining that "while he had done nothing improper, he thought that in view of the outcry in the press, it would be in the best interest of the court for him to resign." He later said that "there wasn't any choice for a man of honor."[32]

Congress came to rely upon judges acting with honor when their behavior became the focus of congressional inquiry. At least twelve resigned before investigations were transformed into impeachments.[33] Only major political actors were threatened with impeachment after the Ritter case in 1936. No articles of impeachment were voted except in the case of President Richard Nixon, and errant judges no longer were brought to the bar of the Senate to answer for their actions.

In the interval between the trial of Halsted Ritter and those of Claiborne, Hastings, and Nixon in the late 1980s, a new issue further complicated the monitoring of judicial behavior. Can a sitting judge or other civil officer liable to impeachment be prosecuted before impeachment? Although impeachable offenses need not be criminal, what happens if a judge indulges in criminal behavior? Article I, section 3(7) does not preclude criminal prosecution in addition to impeachment and removal; it states, "but the convicted Party shall nevertheless be liable and subject to Indictment, Trial, Judgment and Punishment according to the law."

Former Illinois governor and incumbent U.S. Circuit Judge Otto Kerner and the former director of the Illinois Department of Revenue were convicted in 1973 for conspiring to commit bribery and mail fraud, for income tax evasion, and for making false statements to the Internal Revenue Service in connection with manipulating horse-racing dates. Kerner was also convicted of perjury. The allegations covered the time that Kerner was governor and extended to his tenure as a federal judge. He argued that, based on Articles I and II of the Constitution, he could only be removed through impeachment. Because trial and conviction on criminal charges amounted to removal from office, he maintained that criminal prosecution was a judicial usurpation of congressional prerogatives.

In deciding the case, the U.S. Court of Appeals for the Seventh Circuit concluded that holding a federal office did not bar criminal prosecutions, for "protection of tenure is not a license to commit a crime or a forgiveness of crimes committed before taking office."[34] The appellate court based its opinion on a series of historical events ranging from actions by the First Congress in 1790 to House positions in 1796 and the 1802 repeal of the Judiciary Act of 1801. Although the Supreme Court had never decided a case involving a federal judge, the court of appeals relied on tangential cases in which the justices had upheld the conviction of a sitting senator (*Burton v. U.S.*); limited congressional immunity under the speech and debate clause (*U.S. v. Brewster* and *Gravel v. U.S.*); and sanctioned criminal prosecutions of judges, legislators, and executive officers in general (*O'Shea v. Littleton*). The Seventh Circuit Court further found that the separation of powers doctrine was no barrier and even went so far as to suggest that because of the "political overtones" of impeachment, judicial independence was actually better protected in courts of law, where the "issues are heard in a calm and reasoned manner and are subject to the rules of evidence, the presumption of innocence, and other safeguards."[35] When Kerner resigned from office, the House of Representatives took the same option that it had with George English and chose not to pursue impeachment.

The Judicial Conduct Act of 1980

Many states had substituted other methods for disciplining wayward judges, and consensus held that the impeachment process, especially as it related to federal judges, was unsatisfactory. The Constitution had established a structure that fostered judicial independence, decentralization, and individualism, making judges virtually autonomous in all actions.[36] Encroaching upon the activities of judges was interpreted as tampering with judicial independence. However, the system also permitted abuses to become entrenched. The first real attempt to integrate the federal judiciary, at least administratively, can be traced to 1914, when Chief Justice William Howard Taft proposed that some central person, court, or group of judges be empowered to monitor the business of lower courts. Eight years later, Congress created the Judicial Conference, composed at that time of the chief justice of the Supreme Court and the senior judges in each of the nine circuits. The conference was empowered to adjust judicial assignments.[37] This was the first step in a process that would eventually allow judges to admonish one another, albeit with penalties short of actual removal from office.

Administration of the federal judiciary began to take a clearer form in 1939, when federal judges themselves offered reform proposals, perhaps contrived largely out of fear of such incursions on their independence as Franklin Roosevelt's failed court-packing plan of 1937. The Administrative Office Act of 1939 primarily intended to separate management of the federal judiciary from the executive branch through creation of the Administrative Office of the U.S. Courts, under the supervision of the Judicial Conference. Circuit councils composed of the appeals court judges were established to facilitate intracircuit communications, to supervise the work of judges, and, in certain circumstances, to discipline their peers. The act specifically authorized the councils to define and control judicial assignments, including scheduling of judges' vacations, requiring judges to act on cases too long held "under advisement," and setting standards of judicial ethics. The councils, within this broad jurisdiction, were prohibited only from issuing "irrational or unreasonable directives" to trial court judges.[38]

The role of the circuit councils in monitoring judges was made more explicit in the revision of the Judicial Code in 1948, wherein councils were authorized to issue direct orders instead of generalized directives. With this new authority, the councils could freeze judges' caseloads until backlogs were cleared, assign judges to virtually nonexistent jurisdictions, and certify judges' physical or mental disability. The councils, through the last option, essentially created judicial vacancies that could be filled with new appointees. The mere threat of such sanctions seemed as effective as their implementation.[39] Under the new code, more than one jurist was relieved of his or her caseload because of alleged improprieties or incompetence, and the Supreme Court upheld council actions.[40]

A major test of the authority of judicial councils arose in the case of Stephen Chandler, U.S. district judge for the Western District of Oklahoma. The judicial council of the Third Circuit was, for more than four years, involved in a running controversy with Chandler over his attitude and conduct. The council noted specifically that Chandler had been the defendant in a criminal case and the respondent, while a judge, in civil litigation. He had also refused, when petitioned, to recuse himself from related cases. When the council, on December 13, 1965, relieved Chandler of all judicial duties, he countered that the council order infringed on "his constitutional powers as a judge" and usurped the "impeachment power, committed by the Constitution to the Congress exclusively."[41] The Supreme Court, without reaching the question of separation of powers, decided that Chandler had not made a case for the "extraordinary relief of mandamus or prohibition" that he requested. The majority opinion did note, however, that the refusal of a single judge to accept the council's reasonable procedures did not mean that "the extraordinary machinery of impeachment is the only recourse."[42] Only the separate opinions of Justices John Harlan (concurring) and Hugo L. Black and William O. Douglas (dissenting) addressed the constitutionality of the scheme that allowed judges to discipline their peers.

Even as the saga of Judge Chandler continued in the courts, Congress began consideration of other, more effective methods for managing federal judges. In 1965, a Senate subcommittee under the leadership of Joseph Tydings began a study of possible judicial reforms, including how to remove unfit judges. Proposed legislation dragged through the committee system in one form or another without being enacted, even though the Fortas controversy in 1969 temporarily gave the topic of judicial reform some impetus. The Tydings bill proposed a form of judicial discipline that would be administered by a Commission on Judicial Disabilities and Tenure composed of five judges appointed by the chief justice.[43] It sought to expand the approach of the 1939 Administrative Office Act by extending the logic that judges ought to be responsible for monitoring themselves. Judges should be able to sidestep the unwieldy mechanism of impeachment by pressuring or persuading unfit colleagues to resign.

A new round of judicial discipline discussions began in Congress in 1975, when Senator Sam Nunn introduced his Judicial Tenure Act. The original version of the Nunn bill met with a series of criticisms. Senator Sam Ervin had, for example, referred to the body of judges proposed to review the behavior of their brothers and sisters on the bench as "a hazing commission."[44] Although that bill did not become law immediately, it prompted judicial reassessment as the Judicial Conference instructed judicial councils at the circuit level to devise their own procedures for handling misconduct complaints. The Nunn bill survived and, although altered and modified in conference committee, finally passed in 1980 over some serious objections. Senator Howell Heflin, for example, opposed the bill because under the Constitution "the Judiciary was given no power, either express or implied, to police its own members."[45] Senator Charles Mathias characterized the bill as being of "dubious constitutionality, unnecessary, and unwise as a matter of public policy." Impeachment, he added, "is the sole constitutionally permissible method of *disciplining* federal judges."[46] Senator Paul Laxalt noted other problems, called the law unnecessary, and voiced his fear that "it will chill the independence of the Federal Judiciary."[47] These same arguments would be raised again by judges whose behavior was investigated by a judicial council, particularly by Judge Alcee Hastings, who, although acquitted in a criminal trial, was nevertheless investigated by his judicial council. Jimmy Carter, despite the constitutional arguments against it, signed the bill on October 15, 1980.[48]

The new Judicial Councils Reform and Judicial Conduct and Disability Act of 1980 (hereafter referred to as the Judicial Conduct Act) altered dramatically how judicial misconduct would be addressed. Membership on judicial councils had previously been restricted to appellate court judges, who could issue orders to their colleagues on the lower district courts. That system had, for obvious reasons, been unpopular with jurists on the inferior courts, and their grievance was redressed in the new system by placing trial court judges on the circuit councils.

The act permits anyone to file a complaint against a district or circuit court judge, as well as a magistrate or bankruptcy judge, for "conduct prejudicial to the effective and expeditious administration of the business of the courts," including allegations of mental or physical disability. A copy of the complaint is filed with the appropriate circuit court and is first reviewed by the chief judge of the circuit, or by the senior circuit judge should the chief judge be the object of the complaint. It is simultaneously sent to the accused judge. Expeditious review by the chief judge is mandated; he or she may dismiss the complaint if it relates directly to the merits of a specific decision or is deemed "frivolous," or end the proceeding if proper corrective action has been taken. When the chief judge of the circuit cannot address a complaint simply, it is referred to a special committee of district and circuit judges whom the chief judge appoints. The committee conducts an investigation and reports its findings to the judicial council for the circuit. The committee may recommend that the circuit council certify disability, that the judge under investigation be urged to retire voluntarily, that the judge's caseload be frozen temporarily, that the judge be privately or publicly reprimanded or censured, or that some other action be taken.

A judicial council is expressly denied the power to remove a judicial official, but, if its investigation produces evidence that such action is warranted, may refer the complaint to the Judicial Conference. This is also the prescribed route should a judicial council be unable to resolve the issue. The Judicial Conference likewise may not remove a judge. If it decides that impeachment is warranted, however, that finding and all records of the case may be certified to the House of Representatives. A judge who is the object of a complaint may appeal decisions of the chief judge of the circuit to the judicial council or to the Judicial Conference. All disciplinary proceedings are, moreover, totally confidential unless necessary for impeachment or trial, or unless the judge under investigation and the appropriate investigating body concur in writing to release documents.[49]

A number of questions were immediately raised about how the Judicial Conduct Act would operate. Issues of definition were prominent in this regard, for example, What constitutes a quorum, or a disability, or a proper complainant? Other terms, such as "conduct prejudicial to the efficient and expeditious administration of the courts," "misconduct," and "expeditiously," were alleged to be too vague to be meaningful. The actual process for conducting an investigation was not clearly delineated, nor was the procedure for appeals. The limits of public disclosure were also not specified.[50] Such ambiguities were not just niggling questions for abstract debate. The Ninth Judicial Circuit, believing the act was directed only at minor infractions, did not act upon the behavior of Judge Harry Claiborne, even after his conviction in a criminal court.[51]

Under the terms of the 1980 act, judicial councils are charged with curtailing judicial misbehavior that falls short of impeachable offenses. There have been no shortage of complaints; 1,586 were filed from 1983 through 1989, an average of more than two hundred each year. Of those, the chief judges of the circuits dismissed 1,224, and the circuit councils dismissed another 290. The overwhelming majority of the complaints that the chief judges dismissed related directly to the merits of a case; only thirty-four were dismissed as "frivolous." The chief judges or the circuit councils only took action in fifty-four cases.[52] The councils publicly censured one judge, privately censured another, and issued a private warning to two more. The recommendations that impeachment might be warranted in the cases of Alcee Hastings and Walter Nixon also resulted in public actions. Because of the confidentiality that shrouds the process, the corrective actions taken fifty-four times by chief judges—and the precise nature of those remedies—are unspecified. At least eleven judges, however, chose to retire after judicial conduct complaints were filed. When complaints were received, presumably others took senior status or reduced workloads because of deteriorating physical or mental health. Some, who perhaps had alcohol or psychological problems, may have agreed to seek appropriate help. Because these remedies might, however, have been accomplished informally without the necessity of formal complaints, it is difficult to evaluate the meaningfulness of the Judicial Conduct Act.[53] Only in the case of Alcee Hastings is it evident that impeachment and trial might not have occurred were the procedures not in place.

The act must, in any event, be regarded as a new variable in the impeachment equation, one that did not exist when Pickering, Chase, and the others were called to answer the Senate. How those cases might have been altered were the law in place must remain in the realm of speculation. After the law was implemented, though, the House impeached three U.S. judges; the Judicial Conduct Act standing alone could hardly explain those impeachments. The act was invoked actively in one case, passively in another, and ignored in the third. In each instance, the judges involved were first the focus of criminal investigations. How other judges chose to treat the outcomes of criminal procedures is instructive in predicting the future use of the Judicial Conduct Act.

Politics, Crime, and Prosecutorial Zeal

None would seriously argue that a judge who has committed treason, accepted a bribe, or acted in a felonious manner should be protected by the shield of judicial independence. The very legitimacy of political authority and the government system would be at risk were such behavior accepted or even tolerated. Legitimacy hangs on the ability of the system "to engender and maintain the belief that the existing political institutions are the most appropriate ones for the society."[54] It depends on perceptions and beliefs and is at risk when those who allocate the rewards and sanction offenders are seen as unprincipled or venal. Maintaining an aura of uprightness on the bench has become more compelling as the realist school debunked the myth of judges' finding law and recognized the penetration of extralegal influences in judicial decision making. Law and judges need to be seen as dispassionate in a world where politicians are suspect. They are the guardians of the belief that law governs the rulers as well as the ruled.

The dilemma, of course, rests in how to purge unethical jurists. No simple solution emerges, for all schemes, short of the constitutionally prescribed one of impeachment, can smack of interference with judicial independence. Where should the responsibility lie for instigating proceedings against a judge? Justice Douglas, himself at times at the center of impeachment inquiries in the House, wrote a scathing dissent regarding the treatment of Judge Chandler in 1970. The Constitution, he argued, does not enable "one group of federal judges to censor or discipline any federal judge" or to "declare him inefficient and strip him of his power," Douglas asserted, although "if they break a law, they can be prosecuted."[55] His colleague Justice Black, also dissenting, concurred that judges, "like other people, can be tried, convicted and punished for crimes."[56] Judges Claiborne, Hastings, and Nixon were all subject to criminal prosecutions by the Justice Department. The catalyst for their impeachment and removal did not begin through a complaint filed with the circuit court, but through the scrutiny of the Public Integrity Section of the Justice Department.

Congress responded to the need for additional federal judges in 1978 by creating 152 new district court positions, increasing the number of judges to almost six hundred. Jimmy Carter benefited from such largesse and filled more judicial vacancies than any president before him—202 district court judges and 56 appeals court judges.[57] Ronald Reagan was able to appoint even more, 290 at the district court level and 78 at the circuit level.[58] One line of reasoning suggests that these increases alone may have diluted the quality of the bench—the more judges there are, the more bad apples are likely to slip through.[59] That argument may have some general validity, but only two judges who faced criminal prosecutions were appointed during the era of a rapidly expanding judiciary. The third was one of the 122 judicial appointments that Lyndon Johnson made in five years, and none were Reagan appointees.

The selection process that the Reagan Justice Department used may, nonetheless, be instructive in understanding how so many judges' misconduct came to light in such a short time. The Justice Department under Edwin L. Meese, III, took a singular approach to its role, whether screening potential judicial nominees, plotting a strategy for argument before the Supreme Court, or selecting emphases for investigation. Meese's Justice Department has been described as "a battleship, Klaxons blaring and guns ablaze," for Meese was anxious to launch a conservative agenda and succeeded in giving the department considerable muscle to that end.[60] The Office of Legal Policy, not the deputy attorney general, was the center of judicial selection activity as the commitment to nominate only those whose philosophies were in harmony with the president's became increasingly obvious. That meant appointing individuals who opposed the status quo positions of the Supreme Court on school prayer, abortion, equal protection, and rights of the criminally accused. The screening process was, for the first time, honed to a science; candidates' court decisions, articles, and speeches were analyzed for ideological content, and all potential candidates were subjected to intensive personal interviews.[61] Analysis of the people Reagan nominated leads to the conclusion that Attorney General William French Smith, during Reagan's first term, was as dedicated to finding appointees who shared the president's social agenda as was his successor, Edwin Meese. The primary difference apparently lies in the style and openness with which the selection process was pursued.[62]

The importance of the Justice Department's strategy on judicial selection cannot be divorced from the department's view of judges who already occupied the federal bench. Richard Thornburg, when head of the criminal division of the Justice Department under the Ford administration, had in 1976 created a special division, the Public Integrity Section. This unit was designed to investigate and prosecute criminal activities of public officials in order to root out corruption. The three judges who faced impeachment charges in the 1980s alleged that the Public Integrity Section had targeted them for investigation. All three were, after all, Democratic appointees, and both Hastings and Claiborne were vocal advocates of liberal policies.

To employ the criminal process to harass or prosecute public officials for their political persuasions would be but a twist on the standard argument that impeachment is a political tool to rid government service of the undesirable as well as the dangerous. That the impeachments of John Pickering and Samuel Chase were instigated by irritated Jeffersonians, with the complicity of the president, is now rather widely accepted.[63] Eight resignations and five impeachments between 1903 and 1936 have also been labeled as an attempt by the Democratic party to remove Republican jurists and to embarrass the dominant Republicans.[64] Overt political maneuvering would not be an unprecedented use of impeachment or criminal investigation. Richard Nixon, while in the White House, had not been above such antics. The Internal Revenue Service was the primary tool he chose to intimidate "enemies," including Democratic National Committee chair Lawrence O'Brien. When CBS correspondent Daniel Schorr offended the Nixon administration, moreover, twenty-five of his friends, relatives, and employers were interviewed by FBI agents within seven hours.[65] Although only anecdotal evidence exists, there is more than a strong suggestion that other presidents also used the FBI for political purposes.[66]

The enforcement arm of the executive branch potentially has a long and powerful reach, and its muscles can be flexed. All presidents, naturally, have those whom they dislike and whose policy or ideological positions are in opposition to the administration's. Prosecutorial harassment and tax audits may not be the typical means of handling such disagreements, but the possibility, nonetheless, is present. Such tactics ideally would force resignation. The costs—financial, professional, and personal—of defending against a criminal charge can deter mavericks on the bench. If accused, surely a judge would leave the office in advance of impeachment. Should resignation not occur, the Justice Department may, by prosecuting judges, set an agenda for Congress. A criminal conviction virtually guarantees that Congress must take some action against the misbehaving judge. The Judicial Conduct Act simply introduces another element into the equation that, conceivably, also could vindicate a judge wrongly prosecuted or discipline a judge incorrectly acquitted.

Motivations, besides obvious ideological or partisan ones, for such prosecutions are plausible. Individuals or teams of prosecutors can be excessively zealous in either their desire to achieve political ends or to further their own ambitions. The lines between rigorous investigation and prosecutorial misconduct are easily crossed when an assistant U.S. attorney becomes intent on pursuing wrongdoing by a major figure; convicting a federal judge is the stuff that launches a legal career. Such inducements may have played a part in the prosecutions of Claiborne, Hastings, and Nixon, particularly in light of the shady characters who originally implicated each judge and the very nature of the crimes for which convictions were won. Junior attorneys in the Justice Department were the trigger for impeachment proceedings.

The susceptibility or immunity of public figures in any branch of government to criminal prosecution is blurred by the separation of powers doctrine, and neither the Constitution nor the case law of the Supreme Court offers adequate clarifications on the limits of criminal liability for people in public office. Protections for sitting officials are left vague at best, ambiguous at worst. Because the president is the head of the enforcement arm of the government, he is cloaked in a kind of immunity because he controls the apparatus of investigation and prosecution. The charges levied against Richard Nixon present the only concrete instance in which the extent of a president's immunity has been tested, but his resignation and subsequent pardon by Gerald Ford rendered the topic moot.

The Supreme Court has trod lightly in the realm of immunity and liability for sitting federal officers. In 1906, it upheld the constitutionality of the trial and conviction of Senator Joseph Burton for accepting payment for his efforts with the Postal Department on behalf of a client. Burton, however, alleged that his criminal prosecution violated the separation of powers doctrine. Because the Constitution, in Article I, section 5, provides that "each House shall be the Judge of the . . . Qualifications of its own Members," Burton contended that he, as a senator, could not be tried for violation of a law made by Congress. The Court, on the other hand, concluded that there was no bar to governmental protection of every department "against such evils, indeed against everything from whatever source it proceeds that tends or may tend to corruption or inefficiency in the management of public affairs."[67] Parameters of congressional attempts to "judge" the qualifications of its own members were limited expressly to constitutional requirements of age, citizenship, and residence.[68]

The criminal liability of a sitting judge had never been addressed by the Supreme Court but was decided by the court of appeals when Otto Kerner was convicted. Although Kerner argued that an incumbent judge could be removed only by impeachment, the appeals court ruled that the impeachment clause "does not mean that a judge may not be indicted and tried without impeachment first."[69] That decision was treated as the controlling precedent in the 1980s when Alcee Hastings and Harry Claiborne raised constitutional challenges to their criminal prosecutions. The Supreme Court, now as then, denied *certiorari* when petitioned to review each case. The closest the Court has ventured into the issue of official immunity was in the 1974 case of *O'Shea v. Littleton*, which is cited as approving the liability of government officials.[70]

Politics and Practice

The paucity of authoritative legal pronouncements on the topic of criminal liability of sitting judges prior to impeachment allows custom and practice to govern. Criminal investigations of sitting federal judges have, thankfully, not been common occurrences, although Martin Manton in 1939 and Otto Kerner in 1974 were each tried and convicted of criminal behavior. However, impeachment was avoided when both resigned: Manton before the trial commenced, and Kerner only after his conviction was affirmed on appeal. Harry Claiborne and Walter Nixon, although convicted of felonies, demanded impeachment and trial. Apart from their assertions of innocence, their publicly stated motives fail to explain fully their willingness to persist through the ordeal of impeachment. What became of Justice Fortas's sentiment that an honorable man must resign and that there are no other options for a man of conscience? Why would Claiborne, Nixon, and even Hastings risk the added public humiliation of impeachment, not to mention the emotional and financial strains that accompany extended legal battles?

Claiborne, Hastings, and Nixon portrayed themselves as victims of vendettas, although their claims did not carry sufficient weight with the Senate to save them. The political side of impeachment has certainly colored the process since its inception in medieval England. "Political animus," according to Raoul Berger, is inherent in impeachment, for it is "the nature of the beast."[71] Berger, without explicitly making the connection, notes that federal judges, clothed with life tenure, have no "inducement to become tools of unpopular Presidential policy."[72] Administration policy, however, might be more readily attainable if judges were made to fear criminal prosecution that would lead to impeachment. Appellate judges noted the uses to which impeachment can be put and said that the "political overtones" of the process made trying judges in courts of law preferable.[73]

When Congress passed the Judicial Conduct Act of 1980, it thought it had created a mechanism for monitoring better judicial behavior; at the same time, it released itself from the business of impeaching judges. The extent to which the former goal has been achieved is unclear, while the second aim obviously has not followed. How did Congress, under these circumstances, adapt to the unexpected turn of events, the House to its grand jury role and the Senate to its place as judge and jury? The cases of Harry Claiborne, Alcee Hastings, and Walter Nixon are, from the perspectives of politics and practice, more than studies in judicial misconduct. The events leading to their Senate convictions allow evaluation of how law enforcement, the Judicial Conduct Act, impeachment, and politics all fit together. All four factors had not previously intersected, but in these three cases they formed an interlocking relationship that will undoubtedly shade the debate over accountability versus independence.

Notes

1. Gerhardt, "The Constitutional Limits to Impeachment," 5.
2. Haynes, *The Selection and Tenure of Judges*, 79.
3. Montesquieu, *Spirit of the Laws*, 152.
4. Hamilton, *The Federalist, No. 78*, 505.
5. Becker, *Comparative Judicial Politics*, 13.
6. Lummis, *The Trial Judge*, 10.
7. Shapiro, *Courts*, 20.
8. Volcansek, "The Effects of Judicial-Selection Reform: What We Know and What We Do Not," in *The Analysis of Judicial Reform*, ed. Dubois, 79.
9. Drinan, "Judicial Appointments for Life," 1103.
10. Hamilton, *The Federalist, No. 65*, 423–44.
11. Hoffer and Hull, *Impeachment in America, 1635–1805*.
12. As quoted in *O'Donoghue v. United States*, 289 U.S. 516, at 532 (1932).
13. Poore, *The Federal and State Constitutions*, 1288–1412.
14. Volcansek and Lafon, *Judicial Selection*, 36.
15. Perlstein and Goldman, "Judicial Discipline Commissions," in *The Analysis of Judicial Reform*, ed. Dubois, 93.
16. Comisky and Patterson, *The Judiciary*, 150.
17. Gardiner, "Preventing Judicial Misconduct," 113.
18. Abraham, *The Judicial Process*, 48–49.
19. Berger, *Impeachment*, 3.
20. The original wording of that clause was restricted to acts of treason and bribery, but on September 8, 1787, George Mason introduced a third offense, "maladministration," alluding specifically to the British parliamentary inquiry of Warren Hastings: "Treason as defined in the Constitution will not reach many great and dangerous offenses. Hastings is not guilty of Treason. Attempts to subvert the Constitution may not be Treason as above defined. . . . [I]t is the more necessary to extend: the power of impeachments. He moved to add after 'bribery' 'of maladministration.' " Because of the vagaries of the term "maladministration," the phrase "other high crimes and misdemeanors" was substituted. Farrand, ed., *The Records of the Federal Convention of 1787*, 2:550.
21. In Britain, the penalties that the House of Lords could impose extended even to execution.
22. Hamilton, *The Federalist, No. 65*, 424.

23. As quoted in Johnson, *Foundations of Power*, 207.

24. *Trial of John Pickering, Judge of the New Hampshire District*, 62–63.

25. The Jeffersonian Republicans might have expected to convict, but they broke ranks and the two-thirds majority (twenty-three votes) required to convict were not obtained on any charge. Smith and Lloyd, *The Trial of Samuel Chase*, 2:493.

26. Once John Marshall became chief justice of the Supreme Court, he kept the writing of most major decisions to himself. Other justices wrote primarily in those cases in which Marshall did not participate. Chase, however, is noted for his opinions in *Calder v. Bull, Ware v. Hylton,* and *Hylton v. United States*. Humphrey, "The Impeachment of Samuel Chase," 831.

27. Gerhardt, "Constitutional Limits," 95.

28. *Journal of the Senate*, April 17, 1936, 506–12.

29. *Impeachment Inquiry Hearings before the Committee on the Judiciary,* 3:280–83.

30. *Congressional Record*, April 15, 1970, H-3113–14.

31. Black, *Impeachment*, 39–40.

32. Murphy, *Fortas*, 566–73.

33. Thomas Irwin resigned in 1859, as did Mark Delahay and Charles T. Sherman in 1873, and Edward Durrell and Richard Busteed in 1875. Borkin, *The Corrupt Judge*, 219–58. Resignations were also the route taken in the early twentieth century by Cornelius Hanford, Alston Dayton, Daniel Thew Wright, Frank Cooper, Francis Winslow, James A. Lowell, Joseph W. Molyneaus, and Samuel Alschuler. Ten Broek, "Partisan Politics and Federal Judgeship Impeachment," 185.

34. *U.S. v. Isaacs and Kerner*, 493 F.2d 1124, at 1142 (1973).

35. Ibid., at 1144.

36. Fish, *Federal Judicial Administration*, 7.

37. Ibid., 30–35.

38. Ibid., 157. For a thorough explanation of the process by which the Administrative Office Act was passed, see chapter 4. The important role that Circuit Court Judge Martin Manton, who later would resign prior to his felony conviction, played in securing the new law is also described there.

39. Ibid., 419.

40. *LaBuy v. Howes Leather Company*, 325 U.S. 249 (1956).

41. *Chandler v. Judicial Council*, 398 U.S. 74, at 82 (1970).

42. Ibid., at 85.

43. For an in-depth discussion of the proposals and debates surrounding judicial reform in the 1960s, see Holloman, "The Judicial Reform Act," 128–50.

44. Ibid., 144.

45. Heflin, "Additional Views," 4334.

46. Mathias, "Additional Views," 4336–37.

47. Laxalt, "Additional Views," 4342.

48. See Neisser, "The New Federal Judicial Discipline Act," 146, which provides a concise summary of the events leading to passage of the law.

49. P.L. 96–458, 94 *Stat.* 2035 (1980). See also the discussion in *U.S. Code and Administrative News* (1980), 4315–31.

50. Neisser, "The New Federal Judicial Discipline Act," 143–60.

51. Burbank, "Politics and Progress," 13–23.

52. Figures taken from *Annual Report of the Director of the Administrative Office of the U.S. Courts* (1988), 97 and *Annual Report of the Director of the Administrative Office of the U.S. Courts* (1989), 93–95.

53. Fitzpatrick, "Misconduct and Disability of Federal Judges," 283.

54. Lipset, *Political Man*, 64.

55. *Chandler v. Judicial Council*, 398 U.S. 74, at 137 and 140 (1970).

56. Ibid., at 141–42.

57. Goldman, "Carter's Judicial Appointments," 346.

58. Goldman, "Reagan's Judicial Legacy," 318.

59. One explanation for the increased impeachment activity is simply the number of judges, for "it is likely that as the number of our federal judges increases, we will have more cases of judicial misconduct." Heflin, "The Impeachment Process," 125.

60. Wines, "Shaking up Justice," 48, 84.

61. Goldman says that, "arguably, the Reagan administration was engaged in the most systematic judicial philosophical screening of judicial candidates ever seen in the nation's history, surpassing Franklin Roosevelt's administration." "Reagan's Judicial Legacy," 319–20.

62. Ibid., 327.

63. See, for example, Johnson, *Foundations of Power*, 209.

64. Ten Broek, "Partisan Politics and Federal Judgeship Impeachment," 185–88.

65. White, *Breach of Faith*, 152–53.

66. In an unpublished memo, written by William Sullivan and given to the Senate Watergate Investigating Committee by John Dean, the comment was made that the facts "would put the current [Nixon] administration in a very favorable light" when compared to previous ones. Wise, *The American Police State*, 292. For a more elaborate version of political uses of both the IRS and the FBI, see chapters 9 and 10.

67. *Burton v. U.S.*, 202 U.S. 344, at 369 (1906).

68. *Powell v. McCormack*, 395 U.S. 486 (1969). Berger argues that the decision of the Court in *Powell* establishes a precedent for judicial review

of convictions by the Senate in impeachment cases, for the same verb, *judge*, is found in the description of impeachment as is used in the qualifications clause. Berger, "Impeachment for High Crimes and Misdemeanors," 443–49. No such response, however, has occurred, and the logic of cases since *Isaacs and Kerner* implicitly rejects that thrust.

69. *U.S. v. Isaacs and Kerner,* 493 F.2d 1124, at 1142 (1973).

70. *O'Shea* involved a state judge in Cairo, Illinois, who was named in a civil suit for systematically violating the civil rights of citizens through his practices of bond and jury fee setting and sentencing. The issue did not confront directly the criminal liability of federal jurists. The Court in *O'Shea*, nonetheless, maintained that "the performance of the duties of judicial, legislative, or executive officers" does not require or contemplate "the immunization of otherwise criminal deprivations of constitutional rights." *O'Shea v. Littleton*, 414 U.S. 488, at 503 (1974).

71. Berger, "Impeachment for High Crimes and Misdemeanors," 437.

72. Ibid., 442.

73. *U.S. v. Isaacs and Kerner,* 493 F.2d 1124, at 1144 (1974).

2

Claiborne: Investigations and Trials

Harry Eugene Claiborne, U.S. district judge in Nevada, was vigorously pursued by federal prosecutors through two trials until a conviction was secured on charges peripheral to the initial investigation. No federal judge had, once pronounced guilty, continued on the bench, but Claiborne refused to resign. He contended that he was not guilty and wanted to expose the base tactics that the FBI and the Justice Department had used against him. He was, he claimed, targeted for prosecution on charges that stemmed from wholly unreliable and self-serving sources. He was the victim of federal agents.

Judge Bruce Thompson of Nevada resigned from the federal bench in August 1978.[1] Congress had created 152 new district judgeships for Jimmy Carter to fill that year, but a number, like Thompson's, came to the president by virtue of normal attrition. Claiborne, an attorney with thirty years of experience as a criminal defense lawyer, was recommended by James Gamill, who had the concurrence of Senator Howard Cannon. Claiborne would later claim that his nomination had caused some consternation in the Justice Department and the FBI,[2] however the recommendation forwarded to President Carter in late July noted simply that "all necessary checks have been completed" and that "Attorney General Bell recommends the appointment."[3] Harry Claiborne, after a pro forma confirmation hearing in the Senate, was invested as a U.S. district judge on September 1, 1978.

Claiborne was sixty-one when he became a federal judge after a long legal career in Nevada.[4] For three years he was an assistant district attorney but resigned to enter politics. His campaign for assemblyman of Clark County was successful, but his career as a political candidate ended after one term and a defeat in his bid for the Nevada senate. For the next thirty years he had a private legal career, first a general practice and then one specialized in criminal defense.[5] A hazard of the criminal defense attorney's trade is unseemly clients and among those whom Claiborne defended were Joseph and Sally Conforte, owners and operators of an almost legendary brothel, the Mustang Ranch. Claiborne defended the Confortes on a Mann Act charge and later was on Sally Conforte's defense team in a tax evasion case. That relationship was the catalyst for events that ultimately resulted in Claiborne's removal.

The existence of a "feud" between the federal judges in Nevada and the FBI was apparent by the spring of 1980, when District Judge Roger Foley ordered U.S. marshals to Justice Department Strike Force offices, where cartoons were seized that satirized both Judges Foley and Claiborne as being puppets of organized crime.[6] Claiborne, shortly thereafter, became the focus of FBI investigations and four separate grand jury inquiries. That pattern formed the core of his persistent defense that he was targeted for prosecution.

How could a federal judge, sitting for only two years, have provoked the ire of the FBI and Justice Department to the point that they would pursue a "vendetta" against him? The wrath of the Strike Force was incurred, according to Claiborne, because of a series of decisions in his first years on the bench. He had, for example, dismissed a firebombing case brought by the Strike Force against a union official and granted an injunction to protect a major hotel, whose owners were allegedly tied to organized crime. He threatened to jail an IRS agent and a U.S. prosecutor for failure to return money seized, according to the judge, illegally. The issue, however, that won the greatest animus of the government was his reponse to wiretapping. He and other federal judges often questioned the propriety of government requests for wiretaps based solely on information supplied by "confidential sources." Claiborne went so far as to declare to reporters that the U.S. prosecutors were "rotten bastards who think everybody in Nevada is a crook."[7]

Prosecutors, including the House managers who conducted his prosecution before the Senate, argued that allegations of "targeting" are irrelevant if indeed Claiborne was guilty of criminal acts. Claiborne's defenders, on the other hand, countered that he was singled out because the "crime" for which he is convicted is ordinarily not the subject of a criminal prosecution. His case was handled differently, the argument went, because he had antagonized the Justice Department and its law enforcement arm.

The bribery case hinged on the believability of Joe Conforte and his lawyer Stanley Brown, supported only by ambiguous tape-recorded conversations. A jury, through seventeen days of testimony, measured the two against Claiborne, and the verdict was a hopeless deadlock. Prosecutors dropped the bribery charges and went, instead, for their fallback position, false statements on income tax returns. A verdict was forthcoming in the second trial—guilty on two counts. The case against Claiborne rested on details of taxes and income. These sometimes tedious points and the subtle variations they assumed in different forums constitute the core of the case against Harry Claiborne.

Claiborne's Accuser

The first of several grand jury investigations of Claiborne began shortly after the judge's public declaration of outrage at the U.S. Strike Force. The Las Vegas grand jury met in the spring of 1980 and probed Claiborne's activities as a private attorney before going on the bench. That grand jury focused on allegations that Claiborne had hired a private investigator, Eddie LaRue, to conduct illegal wiretaps. LaRue was indicted and later acquitted, but no indictment was forthcoming against Claiborne.[8] Two more grand juries in Portland, Oregon, heard allegations against Claiborne and focused on bribery, but he was not indicted in either case, probably because his chief accuser, Joseph Conforte, remained a fugitive in Brazil.[9]

Conforte had entered the prostitution business in 1953; since 1967 he had owned the Mustang Ranch near Reno.[10] When he and his wife, Sally, were convicted in U.S. Court of evading employment taxes, Claiborne had served on Mrs. Conforte's defense team.[11] The Confortes' original sentences were vacated on appeal, and resentencing was scheduled for December 23, 1980. Conforte faced a probable five-year sentence, a bribery charge in Nevada, and a sizable ($19.5 million) tax bill. The night before his sentencing hearing, he drove to Mexico, but before fleeing the country, he called the head of the Justice Department Strike Force in Las Vegas and told him "that I had been screwed, I don't feel I have it coming to me. . . . I said, 'I could give you some information on Judge Harry Claiborne.' I said, 'If you want him, I will give him to you in a platter.' "[12]

The next year, Conforte left Mexico and moved to Rio de Janeiro, where he remained for almost three years. Life as a fugitive had drawbacks, however, and in the summer of 1981 he began a round of negotiations with federal agents. The FBI had initiated contacts through Conforte's bodyguard, John Colletti, who relayed to Conforte the promise that discussions would be beneficial. After several telephone conversations, a meeting was arranged that November in Rio between Conforte and agents of the FBI and IRS. Another meeting followed in 1983, this time in Acapulco, with the FBI officials; Steven Shaw, the chief prosecutor in the case against Claiborne; and Peter Perry, who represented Conforte. A third, still-inconclusive, meeting was held in Costa Rica in November 1983.

Shortly thereafter, an agreement was concluded between Conforte and the U.S. government whereby Conforte would return to the United States and testify "candidly and truthfully in all court proceedings" against Judge Harry Claiborne.[13] In return, Conforte's sentence was reduced from five years to fifteen months, commencing upon his return to the United States. Any other convictions or plea agreements were to run concurrently. The Justice Department pledged, moreover, to "assist" in reaching plea agreements in the bribery case pending in Nevada and in the case for flight. Conforte was granted immunity from prosecution for anything about which he might testify, but the agreement excluded tax or other financial liabilities.[14]

The charges of bail-jumping and flight, which can carry a five-year sentence, were eventually dismissed, and Conforte was given an eighteen-month concurrent sentence on Nevada charges for bribery (ten-year maximum sentence) and under the habitual criminal law (maximum life sentence).[15] His tax liability was reduced by $12 million, to $7.3 million,[16] but the tax settlement, he insisted, was not related to his testimony against Claiborne.[17]

Conforte testified before a Reno grand jury, the fourth to consider allegations against Claiborne, on December 7, 1983, and the indictment returned the same day charged Claiborne with the following felonies: bribery of a public official, wire fraud, influencing or injuring a federal official, making and filing false tax returns, and making false statements on judicial ethics disclosure. The trial that began on March 12, 1984, involved ninety witnesses and more than a hundred exhibits; the transcript consumed more than four thousand pages.

Bribery Charges

The central charge against Claiborne was that he took one bribe from Joe Conforte and solicited another because he could not maintain the life-style that had been possible on his $300,000 annual income as a private attorney but was prohibitive on his judicial salary of $50,000.[18] Count I alleged that Claiborne had accepted a $30,000 bribe from Conforte in the fall of 1978. FBI agents had attempted to serve subpoenas on some of the prostitutes employed by the Mustang Ranch, and the ranch was devastated, Conforte explained, "because girls in that profession, any time they have anything to do with police or courts or investigations, they get all excited." Within half an hour of the incident, "half of the crew . . . were gone."[19] Conforte argued that Claiborne had clearly solicited and accepted a bribe regarding the subpoenas in December 1978. Stanley Brown, he said, relayed a message that Claiborne wanted to talk to him and would call on the evening of December 11, a Monday night, Conforte recalled, because he was watching a professional football game. A meeting was arranged, according to Conforte, for the next night.[20] Conforte, in anticipation of the rendezvous, went to a friend's apartment, borrowed her car because his was a conspicious stretch limosine, and drove alone to Claiborne's apartment building, "a big place, that's all I can tell you." He rang the buzzer, was electronically admitted, and "Judge Claiborne was standing at least one flight up," waving.[21] Conforte could not remember on which floor the apartment was but recalled going into the kitchen, "a combination of kitchen and dining area, . . .like a hole in here and a there's a table here like a bench, a table bench." Claiborne was, he said, in the kitchen, and the two men faced each other over the counter, but Conforte could see into the kitchen, where the stove and the sink were side by side.[22] The defense later countered with testimony that Claiborne's apartment, Number 318, had no open counter, and the sink and the stove were on opposite sides of the kitchen.[23]

Conforte said that he and the judge exchanged small talk before Claiborne wrote on a yellow legal pad, "I need $30,000 and don't worry about your case." Conforte, because he had two cases pending, wrote back, "which case?" Claiborne responded, still using the legal pad, "the subpoenas." "I don't have it with me," Conforte claimed he wrote, "I will bring it tomorrow," and Claiborne nodded in assent. Then the judge, according to Conforte, tore the page off the legal pad, together with others bearing impressions, lit them, and threw the remains in the sink. Conforte said that he asked for Claiborne's telephone number and was given a business card on the back of which the judge wrote his private number.[24] Conforte produced the card in court, with some scratched-over writing, where he said he had obliterated the numbers to protect Claiborne.[25]

Conforte testified that on December 12, 1978, he collected receipts from the ranch (all of which were in cash or traveler's checks) and supplemented them with cash from safe deposit boxes at the Bank of Commerce and Nevada National Bank.[26] He went to the same friend's apartment, where he put $30,000 in $100 bills in his pockets and again borrowed her car. He said he arrived at Claiborne's between eight and nine, and "thirty seconds after we got into the door I picked up the money and handed it over to him." Conforte wrote on the yellow pad, "you are a very smart person to deal with me directly instead of going through with Stan Brown." Claiborne responded with "a strange look, but nothing else." Conforte then tore off the pages, ripped them, and gave the pieces to Claiborne.[27] He was satisfied with his investment because the subpoenas stopped.

Claiborne's defense was that none of what Conforte described could possibly have occurred. The indictment alleged that Claiborne "on or about December 14, 1978 and December 15, 1978" received $30,000 from Conforte, but Conforte had been in New York on December 12 to have his passport renewed.[28] The defense, moreover, pointed to records from Conforte's banks that showed he had entered the safe deposit box only once that week, at 5:00 P.M. on December 15, 1978. The bribe could not have occurred on December 15, however, because Claiborne had flown to Las Vegas that afternoon to attend a Lung Association dinner.[29]

The prosecution countered that on December 13, 1978, the day after Conforte claimed the bribe was paid, Claiborne bought a $14,000 Datsun 280Z as a gift for a girl friend and wrote a check for the full purchase price.[30] No evidence was presented, however, that the judge made any substantial deposit, certainly not $30,000 in cash, to cover that check. A hearing on the subpoenas served on the employees of the Mustang Ranch was held before Judge Claiborne the next day, and when the case was finally resolved in October 1979, it was in favor of the government and against Conforte. The prosecution, however, contended that Claiborne, by granting several stays in the case, allowed it to become stale and, in effect, killed it. Claiborne had, within the allotted time, ruled on the motions and argued that subsequent delays were caused by the slowness of the government in submitting briefs and by its lack of resistance to continuances that the defense requested.[31]

The second bribery count was technically a wire fraud, which required that an interstate telephone call be made for the purpose of defrauding someone and that false statements were made as part of the fraud. The prosecution described it as "your run of the mill classic fraud situation where you have a flim-flam man who is telling some hapless victim that he can do something for him, that he knows he can't. And he gets that victim to pay him money."[32]

The suggestion that Claiborne was the flim-flam man, preying on Joe Conforte, revolved around a decision by the Ninth Circuit Court of Appeals in 1979 on Conforte's tax conviction. Conforte testified that in February 1979 Stanley Brown relayed a message that Claiborne wanted to see him about an "Idaho judge." Brown located Claiborne in Portland, Oregon, where the judge was trying a case. Conforte, the next day, took $50,000 and flew to Portland at five or six in the afternoon.[33] When he and his companion reached Portland, they were unable to rent a car and instead took a taxi to the downtown Hilton Hotel, which had no vacancies. Conforte said that he then called Claiborne at the Portland Motor Lodge, and Claiborne invited him to his room there. Conforte recommended instead that they meet in the morning and offered to call the judge at six to arrange specifics. Conforte and his companion then took the taxi back to the airport, where the taxi driver recommended that they might find a rental car, and around eleven that night the pair settled into a "fleabag" hotel and asked the clerk to wake them at 5 or 5:15 in the morning. The following morning Conforte went to the Portland Motor Lodge and "cased" it. He then called the judge and suggested that they meet in the motel's garage.

Their conversation, according to Conforte, was rather direct:

> Conforte: Harry, I hear that Stan was telling me that you have a buddy, a judge from Idaho that you are going to assign my case to.
> Claiborne: Yes, I think we can take care of that, but in case we can't we're going to win the appeal.
> Conforte: That's great. That's great news.
> Claiborne: How much do you want to pay? How much can you pay?

Conforte: The sky's the limit.
Claiborne: We need $100,000 to get things started.
Conforte: Harry, I don't have $100,000. I have $50,000.
Claiborne: That will get things going.
Conforte: Harry, do you need any expense money?[34]

Conforte added that when Claiborne gave a "nodding look," he took the $50,000 from his pockets and put it in Claiborne's, adding another $5,000 for expenses.[35] That Conforte flew to Reno that afternoon was confirmed by members of the University of Nevada basketball team, who were also on the flight.[36]

Judge Claiborne did not deny that he met Conforte that day, but his version of the encounter was vastly different. The judge claimed that he was approaching the steps of the Portland courthouse shortly before nine in the morning when he heard Conforte hailing him. The two men entered an elevator with another couple, who remembered Conforte's "receding hairline and stinky cigar." Claiborne said that he and Conforte talked for about fifteen minutes in the hallway, and that Conforte was angry and discussed firing his New York lawyers. The entire conversation, in Claiborne's rendering, was in a hallway; no money changed hands.[37] The glitch in that account was that Conforte's rental car was ticketed for a parking violation outside his hotel at 9:04 that morning.[38]

The defense countered with testimony by Claiborne's secretary, Judy Ahlstrom, that Stanley Brown could not have told Conforte where the judge was staying because the judge had to check out of the Hilton Hotel on March 6 and did not know where he would be lodging the next night. He had brought his suitcase to the courthouse and, when he returned Brown's call, did not yet have an accommodation. Only later was a vacancy found at the Portland Motor Lodge. The defense also discredited Conforte's story with records indicating that he was at his safe deposit box twice on March 7, one time at five in the afternoon, making it impossible for him to have taken the 5:05 flight to Portland. Conforte, according to the defense theory that matched rental car records, arrived in Portland at 10:23 P.M. and rented a car at eleven. This was bolstered by the absence of any taxi records confirming a lengthy trip into town and back to the airport or testimony from anyone at the hotel that Conforte was awakened at 5:30.[39]

Conforte's tax case was argued before the Ninth Circuit Court of Appeals on May 16, 1979, before Judges Edmund Palmieri, Anthony

Kennedy, and Thomas Tang, and oral arguments led observers to believe that Conforte would win. Early in June, while Claiborne was trying a case in California with the same Judge Kennedy, he called Stanley Brown and supposedly asked that Conforte contact him. This was the crucial interstate telephone call that made the charge one of wire fraud because it was designed as part of the scheme to defraud Conforte. When Conforte returned the call, he was told that "it's in the bag," and the code phrase "the sky's the limit" was repeated. Claiborne did apparently inquire of Kennedy when a decision might be forthcoming in the case,[40] but he and Judge Kennedy differed on the circumstances of that inquiry.

Conforte was comforted by Claiborne's call but still asked Stanley Brown to talk with him. That conversation, according to Brown, took place in Claiborne's darkened and deserted courtroom, where Claiborne said that Judge Kennedy had confirmed that Conforte's case would be reversed. Two other similar conversations between Claiborne and Brown supposedly followed later in the year. In one, Claiborne allegedly told Brown that he had stayed with Judge Palmieri, who also said that Conforte would win the appeal. The prosecution contended that Claiborne had not talked to either judge, but rather that these comments were offered to ensure that when Conforte won the case, Claiborne would be credited. On April 30, 1980, the Ninth Circuit, to everyone's surprise, affirmed the trial court conviction.[41]

Other than Brown's testimony, there was only one piece of evidence that any of these conversations ever occurred,[42] a taped telephone call that Brown initiated to Claiborne in 1982, after he had been called before the Portland grand jury. That conversation began with the judge commenting that he was sick with a sore throat. Brown asked, "Can you talk?" and Claiborne responded, "Can you get down here tonight?" Brown said he could not but needed to talk.[43] The crucial comment was made by Claiborne: "Any arrangements I ever had with him, I mean it was between me and him." The prosecution interpreted that remark as relating to the bribe Conforte paid in Portland,[44] whereas the defense version suggested that it referred to legal fees.[45] Brown's other damning remark in the taped conversation was, "I don't know what he [Conforte] said about the rumors that you heard during the course of the appeal and how in the [expletive deleted] am I going to explain those if they, if he's told them about that." Claiborne's explanation was, "I don't know what he was talking about," and he claimed that he called Brown back later to ask the point of that statement.[46]

The bribery counts both hinged on the contradictory testimony of Joseph Conforte, his lawyer Stanley Brown, and Harry Claiborne. What little independent verification of their stories existed depended upon others' memories of events five years earlier. The prosecution argued that Conforte had no reason to lie, that his plea arrangement was unaffected by Claiborne's fate; the defense offered Conforte's life as a testament to his lack of credibility. Stanley Brown, according to Claiborne's team, just followed his standard practice of living off Joe Conforte, earning "five to $10,000 a month plus expenses, that's why they're here to tell the story."[47] Claiborne's motive for lying was obvious, and, as prosecutor Steven Shaw put it, "we are dealing with an intelligent criminal defendant."[48]

Obstruction of Justice

The third count against Claiborne was obstruction of justice, an allegation that he tried to persuade Stanley Brown to lie before the Portland grand jury. Two conversations were pivotal to the charge, one with an attorney friend of both Brown and Claiborne, John Squire Drendel, in April 1982, and a second in Brown's office that July. Claiborne had supposedly sent word to Brown through Drendel, imploring him not to be interviewed by the FBI and asking about his knowledge of the bribes. Drendel testified, to no one's surprise, that Brown was lying.[49] The defense's other counter to the Brown allegations was that all of the calls and meetings between Brown and Claiborne, particularly those Brown taped, were initiated by Brown; Claiborne was merely trying to be helpful to an old friend. The contacts were essential, according to the defense theory, for Brown to convince Conforte of the story he had contrived about the fate of the tax appeal and his fees. However, Brown responded that he wrote a memorandum about each meeting immediately after it occurred. In one memorandum after the April 30 meeting, he quoted Claiborne as saying that "nothing went wrong in Portland," and that Claiborne whispered, "the fact that I thought it was going to be reversed was the length of time it took." Brown took that comment to mean "tell this story," but Claiborne never, according to anyone's version, directly said "lie about this to the grand jury."[50] Claiborne, in fact, claimed that in the same conversation he said, "It's a damn lie . . . ; you know I never said that I spoke to Judge Kennedy; you know I never told you that I was at Judge Palmieri's."[51]

The primary flaw in the charge of soliciting Brown's perjury was a recorded conversation on July 2, 1982, that was never produced in court because, the defense charged, "they didn't like what was on it."[52] Brown and Conforte were conning each other; Conforte used gimmicks to lure Brown to Rio to join him in the plot against Claiborne, and Brown claimed that he had conversations with Claiborne to continue to receive money from Conforte.[53] Even in a December 3, 1981, taped conversation between Conforte in Rio and Brown in Nevada, Brown said, "Look, Joe, I don't know that he got any dough, you're telling me that he got the dough. Ya know I don't know that he got any bribes, you told me that he got a bribe, but I don't know that for a fact."

In that same conversation, Conforte reminded Brown of his supposed conversation with another judge about Conforte's affairs. "Well, but, you told me that, the ah, eh, eh, did he see him once before?" Conforte suggested that perhaps it was Harry [Claiborne], not Brown, who had seen him, to which Brown responded: "God, I don't remember. . . . I think he said he did talk to him."[54] Nevertheless, Brown cooperated with the federal authorities as Conforte wished and gave testimony that corroborated Conforte's before the Portland grand jury and in Claiborne's criminal trial. The government submitted that Brown would not commit perjury for his client,[55] and that his testimony had "the ring of, the feel, the essence of truth about it."[56] The validity of the obstruction of justice charge similarly depended upon the contradictory testimony of Claiborne and Brown; there was no corroborating evidence.

The Tax Evasion Counts

Claiborne was charged with willfully making false statements on his tax returns in three separate years—1978, 1979, and 1980. The 1978 tax charge was contingent largely upon Claiborne's failure to report the $30,000 bribe and another $5,000 fee from Conforte. It also included fee checks from his former associates of $5,400 and $10,000 that were not reported as income. His unreported income for 1980 was larger, totaling $88,000 according to the government, and to conceal that amount, Claiborne supposedly changed tax preparers. His defense in each instance was that he relied on the person compiling his return and, in the first two years, signed blank returns.[57]

Much of the government case relied upon Claiborne's habit, one adopted since leaving private practice, of cashing checks at casinos so as not to "leave as clear a trail."[58] The judge argued, on the other hand, that cashing checks anywhere might or might not be followed for tax or accounting purposes.[59] Another motive for lying was that Claiborne's income had been reduced drastically since he had become a judge. The prosecution, to buttress this argument, cited an August 1980 letter about an unpaid fee to Harry Rothman, executor of the estate of a client of Claiborne's. Claiborne wrote that he was "desperate for money." He later said that he had likely exaggerated his situation, but "I had bought some property and I did need money."[60]

The government portrayed Claiborne as an expert on tax questions who had presided over at least ten tax cases in 1979 and 1980. As the prosecution questioned Claiborne about each case, he remembered most but said that some involved fraud or multiple counts of which the tax question was but one. Others resulted in guilty pleas and never reached trial. Claiborne even acknowledged that he "would be able to comprehend most of the ordinary tax problems," which was interpreted as meaning that the judge should readily have spotted irregularities on his own tax forms.

Most of the 1978 income in question, other than the alleged bribe from Conforte, came from a fee-splitting arrangement with former associates. Once Claiborne became a judge, he agreed to divide his accounts with associates if they were willing to collect them.[61] The approximately $20,000 was not declared as taxable income. The allegations for 1979 were more complex because two separate accounts were entangled. Early in 1980, Judge Claiborne had sought a mortgage and asked his tax preparer, Joseph Wright, to send letters to several potential lenders attesting to his income. Claiborne tallied his deposits for 1979 and transmitted a figure of $45,371.93 to Wright in early March for the mortgage letters. Later, when Wright began work on Claiborne's income taxes, he used that figure as a base. However, Claiborne told him that not all of those deposits were legal fees; some were matured certificates of deposit, interest payments, or other transactions. The final figure Wright used in tax calculations was considerably reduced ($22,332), whereas Claiborne's actual legal fee income was $41,000.

Claiborne explained that he was leaving town before the April 15 filing deadline and wrote another letter to Wright detailing the correct figure. That letter, together with his W-2 form and a check payable to the IRS for $8,000, were delivered to Wright's office on April 11. That Wright received the W-2 and the check was obvious, but the fate of the accompanying letter was not clear. The first, incorrect figures were used to compute Claiborne's tax liability, and Claiborne also used the same, lower figure when filing his judicial ethics disclosure. Wright testified once that he had seen the April 11 letter. On redirect examination, however, he said that Claiborne's files had been lost, and he had not seen the letter until Claiborne's lawyers showed it to him. Claiborne's defense for the 1979 return rested on the existence of the April 11 letter (defense exhibit no. 1), which, the prosecution said, "was made up after this investigation began."[62]

Judge Claiborne had a much higher fee income for the 1980 tax year; he received individual checks for $42,000, $37,500, and $7,000, as well as some for smaller amounts. Consequently, he faced a much larger tax bill. In fact, he estimated his taxes for the year at $42,847 and included a check for $22,030 with his request for an extension. The government made much of the fact that Claiborne, when facing this large tax bill, chose to change accountants and "discarded him [Wright] in favor of Jerry Watson."[63] The most controversial part of the 1980 tax year was the Schedule D prepared by the new accountant, Watson of Creative Tax Planning, a document drafted in pencil, with several scribbles on it. The essential elements were the figures of $250,000, $150,000, and $100,000 that were used to demonstrate a capital loss of $100,000 in Claiborne's law practice. The unreported legal fee income supposedly was included in the $150,000 figure as an asset, accounts receivable. Schedule D was used, according to Claiborne's tax preparer, as a means of taking a capital loss on the law practice that was abandoned. Therefore, no attempt was made to hide or conceal the judge's fee income. The government, on the other hand, viewed the schedule as an attempt to defraud the government a second time by claiming an unacceptable loss as well as not reporting all income.[64] Claiborne contended that for all three years in question, and with both tax preparers, he signed the returns and never examined them. Rather, when he signed the returns, he assumed that they "were true and correct . . . because of confidence I had in the people who were preparing it."[65] The prosecution summarized that explanation to argue "that the defendant had his head in the sand through this three-year period and deliberately avoided knowing the truth."[66] Claiborne had, according to the prosecution's version, fired Wright because of his integrity, begun cashing checks in casinos to conceal his income, and hired Watson to avoid paying his rightful share of taxes.

Ethics in Government Form

The final count was that Claiborne lied on his financial disclosure form in 1978 by concealing a $75,000 loan. If the judge had taken such a loan, he was legally bound to report it, however the very existence of the loan was disputed. On one of accountant Wright's worksheets for Claiborne's taxes for 1979, the figure $75,000 appears, with the notation beside it (and underscored twice) "not income"; below is written "borrowed to pay tax for 1977." According to Wright and Claiborne, the $75,000 notation referred to a deposit in Claiborne's account. Wright testified that he did not recall any conversation with Claiborne about the amount, although such a conversation had apparently occurred.[67] The timing of the deposit and Claiborne's payment of his 1977 taxes on August 31, 1978, did coincide.

The prosecution called Claiborne's explanation "the old Las Vegas shoebox defense,"[68] for the judge claimed that in 1972 a friend, Sidney Wyman, a since-deceased professional gambler, had given him $100,000 in a shoebox. Wyman had not, however, filed a gift tax return for the sum, as he had done for similar gifts to two other people.[69] Claiborne said that he had put money, still in the shoebox, in Teddy Binion's vault at the Horseshoe Casino, which Binion, the Horseshoe's owner, confirmed.[70] The money was deposited in Claiborne's bank account on August 31, 1978, and he wrote a check for approximately $76,000 to pay his 1977 taxes.[71] The government argued that the shoebox defense fell, simply because Claiborne had invested other funds in interest-accruing accounts and that $100,000 over six years would have made at least $25,000 in interest.[72] The defense, on the other hand, called the whole charge "a silly count," because there was absolutely no documentation about who made the loan or whether any part of the loan had been repaid—or indeed that the loan ever existed.[73]

Round Two

On April 5, 1984, the jury that had been at liberty throughout the trial was sequestered for deliberations. After two days, it asked to hear again the tape-recorded conversations, and the following day when Judge Hoffman inquired about progress, the jurors replied that they were "hopelessly deadlocked." A mistrial was declared, and a new one scheduled to commence on July 31, 1984.

The second trial began promptly as scheduled and was, in many ways, merely a replay of selected scenes from the first. Any drama of the first one was lost, for the real skirmishes coloring the outcome preceded the actual trial. Judge Walter E. Hoffman invited counsel for both sides to submit any motions and directed that the jury for the second trial would, unlike the first, be sequestered. The defense moved for Judge Hoffman to disqualify himself, but that motion was denied, as were defense motions for continuances, for an unsequestered jury, and most other requests.[74] Hoffman, however, granted with prejudice the critical prosecution motion to dismiss all of the charges against Claiborne that were connected with Joseph Conforte. The bribery, wire fraud, obstruction of justice, and 1978 tax charges were eliminated, leaving only the false statement charges on 1979 and 1980 tax returns and on the 1979 financial disclosure form. The government, for all its trouble with Conforte, gained only an indictment of Claiborne and nothing more. The owner of the Mustang Ranch did handsomely and won a reduced prison term, the dismissal of all other pending charges against him, and a significantly smaller tax bill.

The new trial began on schedule with jury selection on July 31, 1984, and the defense's fears about Judge Hoffman's continuing with the case were immediately realized. One prospective juror said he thought that Claiborne was guilty and his innocence would have to be proved. After the judge cautioned him about the presumption of innocence, the juror said he would serve impartially. Another member of the panel similarly said that she did not like Claiborne's appearance and had formed an opinion about the case from what she had read in the press. She, nevertheless, claimed that she could be objective as a juror. The defense challenged both jurors, but Judge Hoffman would not remove either for cause, and two peremptory challenges were required to delete them from the jury.[75]

The case lasted only nine days, and the witnesses were the same cast of characters. Two tax experts appeared, one each for the prosecution and the defense, and two tax preparers, Wright for 1979 and Watson for 1980. The defense portrayed Claiborne as "an outspoken protector of the little man,"[76] but one who may have been careless or negligent.[77] The prosecution, on the other hand, described him as will-fully cheating on his taxes and lying to save his own skin. The first trial had been a dual for credibility between Claiborne and Conforte, but in the second Claiborne's chief antagonist was his bookkeeper and tax preparer for thirty years, Jay Wright.

The 1979 Taxes

Wright, who had handled Claiborne's bookkeeping and taxes through the 1979 return filed in 1980, admitted that he had no current recollection of any of the conversations to which he testified and ac-knowledged that before the first trial he had spent about a hundred hours (and an additional seven before the second) preparing for his testimony with the aid of government lawyers.[78] Consequently, he was, according to the defense, simply parroting what the government had drilled him to say.

The existence of the disputed April 11, 1980, letter remained, as in the first trial, crucial to Claiborne's case. The correct total for Claiborne's fee income for 1979 was $41,072.93, and Claiborne claimed again that he had conveyed that figure to Wright in the letter (defense exhibit no. 1). The government argued vociferously that the whole case de-pended on "whether Jay Wright got defense exhibit 1; that is what it all comes down to, it's very simple."[79] If the letter had existed and had been conveyed to Wright, they insisted, he obviously would have used the more recent figures in the letters he sent to lending institutions in late May.[80]

Claiborne's secretary, Judy Ahlstrom, was his only counter, saying that she personally delivered the letter that correctly listed all of the judge's fee income.[81] Judge Claiborne testified that he went to Wright's office later on April 11, 1980, to deliver a second check for $2,500 to cover his estimated taxes for the next tax year and, while there, saw his letter of the same day.[82] The conclusion, according to the defense, was either that Wright had misplaced the letter or Claiborne and Ahl-strom were both perjurors.[83] Wright had, in the first trial, acknowledged that Claiborne's file had been misplaced, but he denied receipt of the letter in later testimony.

If Claiborne did write the April 11 letter and Ahlstrom did deliver it to Wright, why did Claiborne fail to notice the error when he signed the final tax return dated June 15, 1980? Claiborne's answer was simple.

He had signed a blank return in early May and dated it June 15 because he had been asked on May 1 to try a case in Los Angeles. If the case were a long one, as he anticipated, he would not be back in Las Vegas before the filing deadline in mid-June. Wright, he said, suggested that they handle the situation as they had previously. He would sign a blank form that Wright would complete and submit on time.[84]

Wright's logs indicated that he had worked on Claiborne's return on June 15 and 16 (the actual deadline), and the IRS received the return on June 17, 1980. Wright testified that Claiborne had signed a blank return but had questioned "whether we used it or not."[85] His calendar log, which indicated that he had worked two and three-quarters hours on Claiborne's return on June 16, was followed by the notation, "and he was in later."[86] Wright, therefore, inferred that Claiborne had signed the completed return. Wright was asked, however, if he was afraid that the IRS might gather up a number of returns he had filed to see if they, too, had been signed blank, for it is improper for a client to sign a blank form and not review the final return.[87]

The second tax count was based on Judge Claiborne's 1980 tax return, "an event in Judge Claiborne's life," according to his attorney's opening statement, "which he would like to relive if he had the opportunity."[88] The tax return itself was described as "an abortion or an aberration" because of the bizarre inclusion of Schedule D (the capital gain/loss statement) in which Claiborne's fee income for that year was supposedly buried. The defense position, however, was that despite Claiborne's careless selection of a tax preparer and Jerry Watson's ineptitude, the judge had made a full disclosure of his income and had not willfully erred in his tax calculation although the error netted him a refund of $44,256.

Claiborne explained his switch of tax preparers by saying that he was impressed by Jerry Watson, who "portrayed an image to me of professionalism."[89] He argued, moreover, that he did not discard Wright, who had a thriving practice and "needed me like he needed another head."[90] The prosecution, however, made much of the fact that Wright had charged Claiborne only $600 for tax preparation and general bookkeeping, whereas Watson had charged $2,000. Claiborne explained that when he received the bill, his "first reaction was that it was too high," but after a moment's reflection and recollection of "the huge amount of records that I took him," he concluded that "the bill was not exorbitant."[91]

The defense argued that Claiborne was not attempting to hide his income because he had filed his own extension for 1980, calculated for purposes of that return that he expected to incur a liability of $42,000, and included a check for half that amount ($20,818). The judge had further reported the full amount of his legal fees for the year, $88,500, on his judicial ethics form one month before sending his return to the Internal Revenue Service. The yellow sheets that the judge had given to Watson included all of his income, including the disputed legal fees along with deductions, expenses, and other figures for his taxes.[92] The prosecution again relied heavily on Claiborne's new practice of cashing checks in casinos as an indication of his intent to hide income, while Claiborne again explained that the change in routine was due to his altered circumstances, that when checks arrived, he cashed them for living expenses.[93]

The charge that Claiborne lied on his judicial ethics disclosure form in 1978 by failing to reveal a $75,000 loan was tagged the "afterthought count" by the defense but pursued nonetheless by the prosecution. Claiborne's August 31, 1978 deposit of $75,000 in $100 bills and the fact that he wrote a check for approximately the same amount to clear his income tax liability for the previous year were the bases for the charge. Unlike the first trial, however, the prosecution did not contest the fact that Claiborne had received a gift of $100,000 in cash from gambler Sid Wyman in 1972. Instead, it argued that the gift was not the same money that appeared in 1978.

Wright, the source of the information about the loan, had no recollection nor documentation about the events in question,[94] whereas Claiborne offered a rather simple explanation. On the last day before he became a judge, August 31, 1978, he had called Wright and was reminded of the outstanding tax bill. Wright brought the bill to Claiborne's office, and Claiborne said, "I am going to go over to the Horseshoe and get the money." Wright, the defense suggested, merely assumed that Claiborne intended to get a loan.[95] That he would not need to borrow money was obvious. Claiborne had more than $50,000 in his checking account at the time the $75,000 deposit was made. The entire charge rested on Wright's single unexplained notation on his worksheets.

The Verdict

The defense hammered the point that Judge Claiborne had been negligent and careless in his treatment of tax matters and in his choice of Jerry Watson to handle his 1980 return, but argued that negligence and carelessness were not crimes. The refrain was repeated, from opening arguments to final pleas, "shame on Judge Claiborne." Claiborne, nonetheless, had not willfully and knowingly made false statements to the IRS, had made a full disclosure to his tax preparers, and was merely the victim of errors they committed.

The prosecution, on the other hand, sketched a portrait of Judge Claiborne as a liar and a cheat. The crucial April 11, 1980 letter that correctly conveyed his income to Wright, was, according to the government, a forgery after the fact. Claiborne's admission that he had exaggerated his financial situation to pry fees owed him from Sid Wyman's estate was cited as but another example of his willingness to lie for money. "We have a defendant in this case," prosecutor Steven Shaw argued, "who treats the truth as his personal toy."[96] Claiborne's lack of awareness of Watson's scheme to avoid tax liabilities was "deliberate ignorance," and "if we do things in our lives and deliberately avoid the truth," Shaw contended, "we're responsible for those consequences."[97]

Within twenty-four hours the jury found Harry Claiborne guilty on both counts of making false statements on his tax returns but not guilty of making a false statement on the judicial ethics disclosure form. When sentencing followed shortly on October 2, 1984, both sides made the expected speeches and recommendations. Judge Hoffman, as is customary, invited Claiborne to make any comments. Claiborne, standing at the podium, began an eloquent statement that insisted on his innocence. "I do have remorse," he said. "Not for any illegal act that I have committed, because I have committed none. I am remorseful for any embarrassment that my indictment and my trial may have caused the judiciary which I served well and faithfully. For that, I am exceedingly remorseful."[98]

He went on to explain his philosophy that led him to stand up for the little people, the "little person that politicians talk about on the Fourth of July and quickly forget."[99] As he launched into an explanation of how these little people must confront the resources and power of the government to assert their rights, Judge Hoffman tersely interrupted him. Claiborne resumed his soliloquy of harassment by the government, asserting that "I am guilty of being reckless with my own personal affairs," but not of crimes.[100] Hoffman then pronounced the sentence: a $5,000 fine on each charge and a two-year prison sentence. Then

Harry Eugene Claiborne, U.S. district judge for the District of Nevada, did what no other federal judge in American history had done—he did not resign from office. He remained free on his own recognizance while pursuing appeals and retained his judicial title and stipend, even though a convicted felon.

Notes

1. Carter Presidential Library, Document FG53/ST28/A.
2. Claiborne claimed that he was approached by two acquaintances in the FBI, who told him "the bureau's investigation was the most exhaustive ever made of a nominee to the federal bench," because "the FBI didn't want a criminal lawyer from Nevada elevated to a judgeship . . . and was determined to find something in his past to stop him." Thompson and German, "The Impeachment of Judge Harry Claiborne," 10.
3. Carter Presidential Library, Document FG53/ST28/A.
4. Claiborne was a native of Arkansas and had attended Quachita Baptist University in Arkadelphia before entering a two-year program at Cumberland University School of Law in Lebanon, Tennessee. He finished his law degree in 1941 and entered military service, at the conclusion of which he settled in Las Vegas. Nevada had a one-year residence requirement for admission to the bar, so Claiborne became a policeman for two years while he studied for the bar examination.
5. *Senate Impeachment Trial Committee*, 924–25.
6. *U.S. v. Claiborne*, 781 F.2d 1327 (9th Cir. 1985), at 1328 (dissent of J. Reinhardt).
7. Thompson and German, "The Impeachment of Judge Harry Claiborne," 11–12.
8. Claiborne's attorney presented this argument before the subcommittee of the House Judiciary Committee that conducted hearings on Claiborne's impeachment. He, at that time, contended that before the trial began, LaRue was approached by representatives of the Public Integrity Section, who said, "Mr. LaRue, you are looking at getting 25 years if you are found guilty. If you will tell us that Judge Claiborne had you perform illegal wiretaps for him, everything will be dropped." *Conduct of Harry E. Claiborne*, 53–54.
9. *U.S. v. Claiborne*, 781 F.2d 1327 (9th Cir. 1986) at 1329.
10. In 1955 he opened the Triangle Ranch, followed by the Jolly Dolly Ranch in 1958, the Sands in 1959, the Starlight Ranch in 1967, and, finally, the Mustang Ranch, also opened in 1967. *U.S. v. Claiborne, Trial No. 1*, Transcript, Case No. 83–00057 (1984), 765–66.

11. The Confortes had failed to collect or pay employment taxes for "auxillary" personnel (nonprostitutes) for portions of 1974 and 1975. The total tax liability of $19.5 million resulted from the Conforte's contention that the earnings of auxiliary personnel were "tips," not wages, because they were paid from the so-called "tip fund" at the ranch. Earnings by the prostitutes were paid to the cashier, who returned to the prostitute one-half of her fees minus 10 percent. That 10 percent was placed into the tip fund, from which all auxiliary employees were paid according to a fixed scale. Any deficiency in the tip fund was covered by the Confortes. The Ninth Circuit Court of Appeals determined that money paid to the auxiliary employees "would be defined as a wage by lay people and tax experts alike." *U.S. v. Conforte*, 624 F.2d 869 (9th Cir. 1980), at 873.

12. *U.S. v. Claiborne, Trial No. 1*, Transcript, 899.

13. Ibid., 717–26.

14. Ibid., 1051–58.

15. Ibid., 1007–11.

16. Ibid., 1000–1006.

17. Ibid., 1047–48.

18. Ibid., 3514.

19. Ibid., 578–79.

20. Ibid., 587.

21. Ibid., 589–92.

22. Ibid., 833–41.

23. Ibid., 3589–90.

24. Ibid., 596–98.

25. Ibid., 601–2.

26. Conforte did most of his banking at the Security National Bank, but the IRS had attached the safe deposit boxes there. He used the safety deposit boxes at the Bank of Commerce and the Nevada National Bank because the IRS was unaware of them. Ibid., 604–7.

27. Ibid., 609–16.

28. Ibid., 885.

29. Ibid., 3584.

30. Ibid., 3201–6.

31. Ibid., 3206–12.

32. Ibid., 3527.

33. Ibid., 623.

34. This dialogue was created by excerpting quoted remarks from Conforte's testimony. Ibid., 639–41.

35. Ibid., 625–43.

36. Conforte testified that the basketball players asked him for passes

to the Mustang Ranch. "They always ask me," he explained, "I was kind of a Santa Claus to those kids." Ibid., 648.

37. Ibid., 3213–23, 3555–56, 3594–95.

38. Ibid., 3556.

39. Ibid., 3593–600.

40. Ibid., 1855.

41. Ibid., 3540–43.

42. Judge Claiborne testified that Brown had contrived the entire story, but "I doubt that whether he has completely made it up himself; he may have had a lot of help." Ibid., 3222.

43. Ibid., 3225.

44. Ibid., 3554.

45. Claiborne, in that conversation, was recorded as saying, "You never paid any of his fees to me, and, so, you, I mean, that's the way it is." Claiborne explained on the witness stand, "Stan Brown never paid me a quarter for Joe Conforte and any fee that I ever got from Joe Conforte in his life." The prosecution noted, however, that Brown transmitted a $5,000 fee from Conforte in October 1978. Claiborne distinguished that case from the normal practice because "Sally Conforte was my client. I talked to Stan Brown for my fee." Ibid., 3226–27.

46. Ibid., 3226–30.

47. Ibid., 3583.

48. Ibid., 3558.

49. Ibid., 3650.

50. Ibid., 3558.

51. Ibid., 3650.

52. Ibid., 3604, 3649.

53. Ibid., 3645.

54. Ibid., 987.

55. Ibid., 3656.

56. Ibid., 3663.

57. Ibid., 3560–63.

58. Ibid., 3280.

59. Claiborne actually used a somewhat folksy analogy: "if you saw an elephant's tracks in the snow, I mean one guy might see it and another might not." Ibid., 3281.

60. Ibid., 3288.

61. Ibid., 3243–44.

62. Ibid., 3262–63.

63. Ibid., 3266.

64. Prosecutor Hendricks walked Judge Claiborne through his 1978 tax return, in which the disposition of his law library, law office equipment,

and leasehold improvements were detailed. He had also questioned Claiborne closely about how he had established his own legal practice in 1947, with regard to research files, goodwill, and client list, all items that Watson testified were part of the $250,000 value he had assigned to the abandoned law practice. Ibid., 3239–47.

65. Ibid., 3270–73.
66. Ibid., 3560.
67. Ibid., 3623–25.
68. Ibid., 3566.
69. Ibid., 3679.
70. The prosecution referred to Binion as Mr. Raggio's "amusing witness," because Binion testified that Claiborne's treatment of the $100,000 "was just like Joe Conforte handled his cash." Ibid., 3680.
71. Ibid., 3188.
72. Ibid., 3680.
73. Ibid., 3605–7.
74. The first defense motion for recusal (No. 182) was entered on April 23 and denied a week later (No. 183). A supplementary request for recusal was filed on May 10 and denied on June 22; a second supplementary request was filed on June 25 but denied on July 10. The prosecution opposed recusal in each instance. Docket sheets of *U.S. v. Harry Eugene Claiborne*, Case No. 83–00057. The basis for the defense request was a link between the Claiborne case and the earlier Swanson-Lemberes case that allegedly resulted from a bizarre sting operation designed to remove all obstacles to Conforte's negotiations to testify against Claiborne. See Thompson and German, "The Swanson Sting," 14.
75. *U.S. v. Claiborne*, 765 F.2d 784, at 800 (9th Cir., 1985).
76. *U.S. v. Claiborne, Trial No. 2*, Transcript, Case No. CR-R-83–57 (1984), 20.
77. Ibid., 31.
78. Ibid., 1331–32.
79. Ibid., 1296.
80. Ibid., 1298–99.
81. Ibid., 1184.
82. Ibid., 1329.
83. Richard Johnston, for Claiborne, summarized the situation in closing arguments: "You would have to believe that the April 11th '80 letter which as I've said is the most critical piece of evidence in this case is a complete forgery, that it was made up after the fact and very cleverly fitted in with the check and the $2500 check and the date on the application for extension." Ibid., 1338.
84. Ibid., 1329.

85. Ibid., 177.

86. Ibid., 1190.

87. Goodman (ibid., 1195) pursued the question of when Wright had determined that the form that was submitted was not the one that was signed blank: "Goodman: 'When did you decide that it was not signed blank?' Wright: 'When I was reviewing my logbook.' Goodman: 'Well, is this during the seven hours plus that you spent with representatives of the Government preparing this morning?' Wright: 'Yes.' Goodman: 'They went over that with you?' Wright: 'Yes.' Goodman: 'Did they persuade you that the return was not signed blank?' Wright: 'No. I determined myself that I do not believe this return was signed blank.' "

88. Ibid., 32.

89. Ibid., 1019.

90. Ibid., 1020.

91. Ibid., 1026.

92. Ibid., 1342–43.

93. Ibid., 986.

94. Ibid., 1196.

95. Ibid., 37.

96. Ibid., 1388.

97. Ibid., 1383.

98. Ibid., 1520.

99. Ibid., 1523.

100. Ibid., 1526.

3

Claiborne's Case
in the Courts and Congress

When, on March 16, 1986, Harry Claiborne entered the federal penitentiary at Maxwell Air Force Base in Alabama, he was the first sitting U.S. judge ever to be incarcerated. He chose to fight his conviction in the courts and in Congress, and, thereby, added to both the law and practice of judicial accountability. The case law on immunity of federal judges had rested solely on *Isaacs and Kerner*, buttressed by analogy with pronouncements on immunity of other federal officials. The precedents provided only a bare outline, but Claiborne's appeals and those of Alcee Hastings, who had also been indicted, lent a concreteness previously lacking and also firmly established the status of *Isaacs* as the prevailing and unchallenged precedent.

Impeachment, however, remained the only avenue available to deny Claiborne the title and salary of his judicial office. Without a conviction before the Senate, he could even have returned to the bench when his sentence was completed. The House had brushed off the books and begun to reacquaint itself with impeachment in 1974 during the Watergate scandal, but Richard Nixon's resignation permitted Congress to relegate impeachment once more to the archives. Only Harry Claiborne's obstinacy forced Congress to confront, after fifty years of atrophy, the process of impeaching and trying a sitting federal officer. The wheels of the constitutional machinery were in disrepair, and Claiborne's criminal conviction suggested that shortcutting—or, more euphemistically, streamlining—the system was warranted. Claiborne's case became a dress rehearsal for those to follow, as both the House and Senate became familiar with their constitutional roles. The impeachment of Harry Claiborne established the norms that would govern similar situations as they arose.

The appeals and congressional testimony provided further evidence of prosecutorial mishandling, as what had been only vague contours of charges of overly zealous investigation became clearer. The confusion among judges about how the Judicial Conduct and Disability Act of 1980 should operate when a sitting judge is a defendant in a criminal trial was likewise highlighted. In the criminal trials, moreover, Harry Claiborne had remained a tough defense lawyer, but before Congress he emerged as a likable and sympathetic character.

The Appeals

Claiborne's first appeals preceded his trial and, had they been successful, would have blocked the criminal prosecutions. On January 3, 1984, a motion was filed to quash the indictment against him and to dismiss the proceedings, alleging that the Constitution prohibits the criminal prosecution of a sitting federal judge in advance of his removal from office. Walter Hoffman, the trial judge, denied the motion as frivolous and maintained that the trial would proceed as scheduled. Claiborne, later that month, appealed to the Ninth Circuit Court, which was represented by a special three-judge panel named by Chief Justice Warren Burger.

This first unsuccessful appeal was argued on February 24, 1984, and decided within days. Claiborne's argument was that Article III of the Constitution guarantees judges tenure for "life or good behavior," and Article II, section 4 gives Congress the sole right to remove judges by impeachment. The special appellate panel concluded, however, that the Constitution does not specifically preclude the executive branch from prosecuting federal judges for criminal behavior, and that the executive branch is charged, without an exception for federal jurists, "to take care that the laws be faithfully executed." The appeals judges based their claim on the *Isaacs and Kerner* case and on *U.S. v. Hastings* (1982). These cases, both decided by federal appeals courts, rebuffed virtually identical claims of immunity for federal judges. The assertion was rejected that a criminal prosecution was tantamount to removal from office and thereby a usurpation of the congressional power of impeachment. *Chandler v. Judicial Council* and hearings in the House of Representatives on the 1980 Judicial Conduct and Disability Act were both cited as supporting the expectation that "judges, like other people, are subject to criminal prosecution for their misdeeds."[1]

The appeals court likewise brushed aside arguments that subjecting judges to criminal prosecutions would interfere with judicial independence because, first, judges, like other individuals, enjoy protections from vindictive prosecution; second, the criminal process affords more safeguards than does a trial in Congress; and, finally, the executive branch, checked by free discussion in an open society, is not likely to abuse its authority.[2] Claiborne's final assertion—that if he were acquitted his impartiality would always be questioned in cases involving the federal government—was rejected because judges are presumed to be biased only in cases in which they have a personal or financial stake. The public, perhaps more importantly, would have little faith in a judiciary that is above the criminal law.[3] The decision of the specially appointed Ninth Circuit Court of Appeals was taken to the Supreme Court, but like *Isaacs and Kerner* and *Hastings, certiorari* was denied and the path cleared for Claiborne's trial.[4]

Because the post-conviction appeal presented an unusual dilemma for the Ninth Circuit, the twenty-five judges in the circuit were asked to vote on their course of action. There were two polls, one to determine if it would be appropriate to vote on calling an *en banc* hearing and a second on actually hearing the case. Nineteen judges indicated that there was nothing improper in voting on the question of an *en banc* appeal; six said that they would recuse themselves. Judge Reinhardt, of the Ninth Circuit, argued that "there can be no distinction drawn between the propriety of a judge's voting on a call for a hearing *en banc* and the propriety of a judge's hearing the appeal itself."[5] By his reasoning, there were, therefore, at least nineteen judges eligible to consider Claiborne's appeal. The second vote, however, was in the opposite direction. Consequently, a certificate of necessity was forwarded to Chief Justice Warren Burger, asking him to designate out-of-circuit judges to hear the case. Burger named another panel of three, which, according to Reinhardt, gave "the appearance that the judges designated are being hand-picked to decide the controversy" for there were no guidelines governing the selections.[6]

The second special panel heard arguments in the case in March 1985, and rejected all points in Claiborne's request for a new trial. The opinion by Judge Wilbur Pell dismissed Claiborne's contentions that provisions of judicial tenure in Article III of the Constitution and the requirements of impeachment in Article I immunized a federal judge from a criminal prosecution. All arguments that the grand jury proceedings were improper were also rejected, including allegations that Joseph Conforte had committed perjury, that tax information had been supplied to the grand jury in a non-tax case, and that presentation of the same evidence to three different grand juries divided the process. The judges further found that the evidence presented was sufficient to sustain a conviction, and that the litany of trial court errors Claiborne proposed did not justify a new trial. Pell concluded his opinion with a notation that other errors alleged by Claiborne, including that of selective prosecution and the extraordinary concessions made to secure Conforte's testimony, lacked sufficient basis in the record to warrant a new trial.[7]

The next year, three judges sitting in the Ninth Circuit (Warren Ferguson, Stephen Reinhardt, and Harry Pregerson) took the extraordinary act of registering dissents to the circuit's refusal to hear the case. Errors in the special panel's handling of the case and the absence of constraints on Burger's appointments were noted specifically. "This case is an unusual one in a number of respects," Judge Reinhardt urged, and "it raises serious questions about the fair and impartial administration of justice."[8] Having failed at the circuit level, Claiborne petitioned the U.S. Supreme Court, but the high court, as it has done in each case raising a tie between criminal liability and impeachment, declined review.[9] With appeals exhausted, Claiborne entered prison but declined to leave the federal judiciary voluntarily.

House Action

Claiborne's friends advised—even implored—him to resign, and his stubborn refusal to do so raised eyebrows in the press and commanded the attention of Congress. The syndicated columnist James J. Kilpatrick called the situation "preposterous, incredible, outrageous" and added that "if this eminent felon had one ounce of respect for the bench that he has disgraced by his criminal conduct, he would step down."[10] Claiborne, however, protested that he was innocent and was determined to seek a fair hearing. "I have to leave the heritage to my grandchildren," he explained, "and they have stripped everything that I could leave them . . . but courage."[11] He portrayed himself not only as a victim of prosecutorial misconduct, but also as a surrogate for others injured by overbearing government agents.[12] Whatever minor suspense may have been created by Judge Claiborne's failure to resign from office was dispelled when, on June 3, 1986, Chair of the House Judiciary Committee Peter Rodino introduced House Resolution 461: "*Resolved*, That Harry E. Claiborne, Judge of the United States District Court for the District of Nevada, is impeached of high crimes and misdemeanors." The resolution was referred to the Subcommittee on Courts, Civil Liberties and the Administration of Justice of the Committee on the Judiciary.

The subcommittee convened on June 19, 1986, with Representative Robert Kastenmeier presiding, to begin hearings on the impeachment resolution. Claiborne had resisted calls for resignation, in hopes, he claimed, of having a full exploration of his case, but the subcommittee had different ideas. A jury had already tried and convicted him; that fact, standing alone, warranted removal from office. Nor did the subcommittee want to commit the time that a full hearing of all of Claiborne's contentions would require. The decision, therefore, was made in advance and communicated to all witnesses that the hearings would be strictly limited to the two counts on which Claiborne was convicted—making and filing false statements on tax returns for 1979 and 1980. Because he had been convicted for these offenses already, the subcommittee only considered whether "Claiborne's conviction and incarceration constitute behavior incompatible with the duties and responsibilities of a Federal judicial officer."[13] The outcome, in other words, was foregone. Claiborne was brought to the hearings from prison facilities in Alabama, but he chose to return the same day because of the restricted scope of the inquiry.[14]

William C. Hendricks of the Public Integrity Section of the Justice Department sketched the government's case as it had been presented at the second trial: the 1979 return, the 1980 return, the switch in accountants, Claiborne's dire financial position in 1980, his practice of cashing checks at casinos, and, finally, calculations of the underpayment of income tax for two years. He also outlined the chronology of litigation from indictment through appeals. When any inquiries by committee members strayed to the first trial, Chairman Kastenmeir firmly redirected the hearing.[15] Kastenmeier's chiding to maintain those parameters did not deter some abbreviated allusions to the first trial in committee questions, but little interest in allegations of prosecutorial misconduct surfaced.

Circuit Court Judge Charles Wiggins was also called before the subcommittee to explain why the Ninth Judicial Circuit had taken no action against Claiborne after his conviction. Judges in that circuit, Wiggins explained, were under the impression that the 1980 Judicial Conduct Act was designed to handle litigant and lawyer complaints against judges, not charges of criminality. The Constitution, he emphasized, directs responsibility for impeachment to the legislative rather than the judicial branch.[16]

The only other presentation was that of Oscar Goodman, who had defended Judge Claiborne in both trials. He briefly summarized the evidence of prosecutorial misconduct and Claiborne's defenses for the errors in his tax returns. The whole hearing lasted only a day, and that time was punctuated by recesses for votes on the House floor and for lunch. The subcommittee heard all that was necessary and reconvened the following week to draft four articles of impeachment against Judge Claiborne. Each article charged him with committing high crimes and misdemeanors, underreporting of income taxes for 1979 and 1980, and making false statements on both the 1979 and 1980 returns. The fourth article alleged that Claiborne had failed to meet his oath of office to uphold the integrity of the bench and, thereby, brought disrepute upon the federal courts.[17] There was really no debate by the full committee on the first three articles, and all passed unanimously.[18] Kastenmeier explained that the fourth article, the one not predicated upon factual findings by a jury, was intended to demonstrate that Claiborne's misbehavior extended beyond criminal actions and to avoid sending the message that only criminal conduct was impeachable.[19] That article, however, brought objections because it might open the door for Claiborne to introduce all of his arguments about governmental misbehavior; Claiborne could, after all, be removed without it. Article IV, nonetheless, was also adopted unanimously by the subcommittee.

That consensus was echoed by the full House of Representatives when the articles were presented as a single amendment to H.R. 461 on July 22, 1986. The lower chamber voted 406 to zero to forward the articles to the Senate. The House then passed the necessary resolutions to inform the upper chamber officially, to appoint House managers to prosecute the case before the Senate, and to allocate funds for the prosecution. Formal conveyance of charges to the upper house and the naming of managers repeated the ritual that had been observed in England in a crude form as early as 1376.

The Senate Trial

The Senate machinery for impeaching federal officers had also grown rusty in the half century since Judge Halsted Ritter was tried, although some attention to and updating of procedures had occurred in 1974 when a trial for Richard Nixon seemed likely. The major innovation, adopted in 1935, was Rule 11, which allowed a committee to take evidence and report to the Senate as a whole. The utility of this device is obvious: all pending business of the Senate need not come to a halt while lengthy testimony is presented. Although available when Ritter was impeached, an evidentiary committee of the Senate had never been used.[20] Rule 11 was perpetuated, however, in amendments to Standing Rules of the Senate in August 1986 and was first used for the Claiborne trial.[21]

The solemnity of an impeachment trial, although sometimes lost later, was preserved at the outset. On August 6, the Senate interrupted debate to receive a delegation from the House led by Rodino. Some three dozen senators sat in silence as Rodino, speaking from the well of the Senate, read the four articles of impeachment against Claiborne and requested that the judge be brought to trial and removed from office. Although Claiborne's counsel objected to the committee system and demanded a trial before the full Senate, a twelve-member committee, headed by Republican Senator Charles Mathias of Maryland and equally divided between Republicans and Democrats, was appointed the next week.[22]

The Senate Impeachment Trial Committee convened on September 10, 1986, with most of the committee members present, along with nine representatives of the House and their counsel, Nicholas Chabraja, serving as the prosecution. After a brief skirmish over the parameters of the hearings, the House managers and Claiborne's counsel offered their opening statements.[23] Much of the hearings that followed merely replicated Claiborne's second trial, but some new twists and turns were introduced and earlier events were emphasized differently.

The House managers' star witness was Joseph Wright, Claiborne's long-time accountant, chief accuser in the second trial, and the person responsible for preparation of the 1979 tax return.[24] Wright, varying his statements but little from the second trial, explained the judge's extension on the 1979 return and the mortgage application letters. He used the figure of $45,371.93 in both cases. Claiborne later told him that fees only comprised $22,332.87 of the amount. The remainder, Claiborne said, was the result of a cashed certificate of deposit ($10,000), interest on that certificate ($622.17), interest income ($761.16 and $655.73), and proceeds from the sale of the judge's airplane ($11,000).[25] The fee income for that year that should have been reported was $41,072.93, and the discrepancy of $18,740.06 brought one conviction for filing false statements. Claiborne's defense continued to rest on his claim that on April 11, 1980, he had informed Wright of the full amount of fee income in the misplaced or fabricated letter of that date.[26] Both Wright and his wife had previously been unable to account for the letter but now swore it was never received.[27] Underreporting of income, however, Wright admitted, ran counter to Claiborne's policy of more than thirty years of resolving any such question in favor of the government.

New theories for the missing document were proposed when Wright was cross-examined: the document had been lost, or, in a more sinister version, removed from the files by government agents. The first theory was that the letter had either been lost when the Wrights moved their office in 1981 or in one of the several break-ins that occurred in the office during the last half of 1980. One of Wright's former employees testified about the possibility of documents being lost as a result of the burglaries, but Wright firmly asserted that "Mr. Claiborne's files, to my knowledge, were never touched."[28] He admitted that nothing of value was taken in any of the burglaries, and Claiborne's attorney then tried to suggest that because nothing was stolen, the break-ins were not the work of common burglars, but rather part of a government conspiracy against Claiborne. Neither the burglaries nor the hints of foul play elicited any interest from the senators.

Other than a photocopy, the only evidence of the existence of the April 11, 1980, letter from Claiborne, apart from his own assertions, was the testimony of Judy Ahlstrom. One of Wright's former employees testified that a woman identified as Judge Claiborne's secretary had been at the office that day, but he could not identify her at the hearings.[29] Ahlstrom testified much as she had in the criminal trials, but added that she had been "scared to death" by Judge Hoffman, whom, she felt, tried to imply she was lying. She said that he made such comments as "that isn't what you told me a few minutes ago, is it?"[30] The fate of the April 11 letter remained, as before, the precarious hook on which Claiborne's defense hung.

The House managers' case on the 1980 tax return was essentially the same as that presented by the prosecution at the second trial. The stakes, however, in terms of unpaid taxes were different than in the criminal trials, for now at issue were two new elements: $87,911.83 in unreported legal fees and unconventional tax treatment of capital gains in the sale of a house. According to the House managers' expert, the combination of the two resulted in underpayment of $73,443 in taxes.[31] The managers also strung together the same set of circumstances as the government prosecutors had earlier to suggest that, in addition to his dire financial circumstances, Claiborne acted willfully to evade taxes by changing preparers and cashing checks at casinos.

Judge Claiborne was forceful before the senators in his explanation of his decision in 1981 to change tax preparers. He said that Wright was brusque with him and seemed no longer to care about their relationship. Early in 1981, he explained again, he met Jerry Watson and arranged for preparation of his 1980 tax return, which the managers' expert had characterized as "grossly incorrect."[32] Ten pages or more of the Senate hearings transcripts are devoted to a detailed analysis by William L. Wilson, the House managers' expert and a certified public accountant, of what was wrong with the tax return. The major errors— for even simple arithmetic and directional calculations from line to line were frequently off—again related to the failure to include a Schedule C to report fee income and the unusual calculations on Schedule D for capital gains losses on Claiborne's former law practice. The new element introduced concerned how capital gains on the sale of Claiborne's residence were computed on Form 2119. The amount claimed should have been $214,812, rather than zero.[33]

Because the fact of underpayment was not contested, the focus of defense questions was standard Internal Revenue Service procedures for handling similar cases of underpayment. Put more directly, When does an error in computation that results in underpayment of taxes cease to be a civil matter and trigger criminal procedures? The "targeting" or selective prosecution claim was closest to the surface in this single question. Even according to the managers' expert, when Claiborne's return was selected by a manual survey by the IRS, it normally would have been sent for a field audit, but none was ever conducted on either the 1979 or 1980 returns. The related question was that of civil penalties versus criminal sanctions. Although there were variations, the threshold is typically 25 percent underpayment of taxes, but "there's no clear standard." In the Claiborne case, the 25 percent mark was passed when the sale of his house was added. According to the expert, the return would also likely be flagged for criminality because of the sum of money involved. Once the criminal division of the IRS becomes involved, however, the taxpayer is typically notified and the case proceeds through an administrative process before indictment. Wilson was willing to go that far but stopped short of speculating further about precise procedures followed in criminal tax cases. "Willfulness" is the key to criminality, and the taxpayer has "a good faith responsibility to consider the reasonableness of the results he's getting from his preparer," because "the taxpayer knows as well as anyone when a return is grossly in error."[34]

The key person in filing the much-maligned 1980 tax return, Jerry Watson, testified that although he had an initial interview with Claiborne, the actual preparation was done by his employee, Charlotte Travaglia. Watson was directly involved only in making a few calculations about the sale of the house. He, nevertheless, explained the theory behind the return and, more importantly, testified again that it reflected all income for the 1980 tax year because $88,500 in legal fees were actually covered in Schedule D.[35] An arbitrary value of $250,000 was assigned to the law practice, which was designated under the heading 1978;[36] a figure of $100,000 was deducted from that value in assigning a capital loss of $150,000 on the practice. According to Watson, the $100,000 consisted of "accounts receivable" in the amount of the questioned $88,500 in legal fees and the judge's law library, which had been donated to a university.

Watson's approach to tax preparation, he explained, was that mistakes caught by the IRS could be resolved in an office audit, an expectation consistent with Wilson's explanation about IRS procedures.[37] That an indictment was sought instead of a meeting with the taxpayer short-circuited Watson's whole system. Watson insisted that the understatement of income was caused by mistakes in his office, not by inaccurate information provided by Claiborne.[38] The judge, however, according to the House managers, should have been alerted that something was amiss when he received a tax refund of more than $44,000. It was the managers' own tax expert who provided an explanation, for none of the estimated tax payments of more than $20,000 that the judge made during the tax year were claimed on the return. "So if the taxpayer knew he was going to get a $20,927 refund and got a check for $44,000, he might well ask, 'What's the difference?' " and reach the reasonable conclusion, " 'Well, we didn't claim these several payments on the original return.' "[39]

Witness intimidation by federal agents, the new variable in the equation, was pursued by Claiborne's counsel and various senators. Watson was first contacted by IRS and FBI agents before the Oregon grand jury investigation and told that they were investigating the judge for accepting a bribe from Joe Conforte. The meeting was, in Watson's words, "particularly abusive" owing to his determination to comply with a subpoena by the grand jury and not to give copies of Claiborne's tax records directly to the agents.[40] Federal agents again visited him before the second grand jury appearance and made what Watson took as threats: "I remember them telling me that I was being made a fool of; that I was sticking my neck out—or 'going out on a limb'. . . that Judge Claiborne would saw that limb off for me."[41] Watson repeatedly asked the agents if he was a target of the grand jury or of any criminal investigation. The answer was always negative.

Even during his testimony before the Reno grand jury, Watson believed that the investigation focused on bribes or practicing law while on the bench. When he updated the judge on his grand jury experience, Claiborne recognized that Watson had failed to tell the grand jury about the $88,500 in legal fees. Watson testified that he contacted a lawyer, once the omission was pointed out, and sent a telegram to the grand jury correcting the mistake.[42] That day Watson suffered another disturbing visit from federal agents, who instructed him to write down two sections of the U.S. Code relating to conspiracy and fraud and said that he "had better become very familiar with these two items before you testify before the grand jury."[43] At his third grand jury appearance, Watson's lawyer was told that Watson himself was then a target of the investigation.[44] Watson said he "never testified without fear."[45] All three agents Watson named were called as defense witnesses, but each, not surprisingly, denied that any form of undue pressure had been placed upon Watson.[46]

Watson managed to undermine his own credibility when called before the committee a second time. He requested that he be dismissed from his subpoena, and when his plea was denied, he said that he had been advised to invoke his privilege under the Fifth Amendment. Only three days later, he reappeared, claiming to have just located "another yellow paper," one that had never been presented to any of the grand juries or in either Claiborne trial. No date was on the document, which Watson claimed was written by Judge Claiborne and listed dates, monetary amounts, and explanations of their sources. Watson stated that the newly found document was among the papers Claiborne provided for preparation of the 1980 tax return. Watson, in that context, also provided yet another version of the preparation of the 1980 return.[47] By the conclusion of Watson's second round of testimony, Senator Albert Gore felt obliged to comment on the existence of penalties for perjury.[48] None of the senators seemed inclined to quarrel with a former employee's comment: "I would not call him [Watson] intelligent."[49]

A series of character witnesses, including the judge's former law clerk, the publisher of a major Las Vegas newspaper, and a number of lawyers, briefly paraded before the committee, and all that was left was the testimony of the accused, Judge Harry Eugene Claiborne. The judge, in a calm and measured presentation over the three days that he answered the committee, readily pleaded "guilty to being careless with my own personal business" while steadfastly asserting that "I have done nothing wrong."[50] Claiborne explained that he knew he was under investigation by the FBI at the time he filed the 1979 tax return, a coincidence of events that would make lying about his income totally foolhardy. Claiborne testified that on April 8, 1980, a reporter stopped him and asked about the grand jury investigation, a fact confirmed in the next day's papers. Within three days he put together the information for Joseph Wright to complete his 1979 tax return. The implication, an obvious one, is that he would not make a conscious decision to lie on taxes while already under federal scrutiny.

The government's case on the 1980 return revolved, in part, on Claiborne's decision to switch tax preparers, because much had been made of Watson's incompetence throughout the hearings.[51] The other element about which Claiborne was questioned was the issue of "willfulness" in the understatement of taxes in both years. The House managers and Senator John Warner compiled lists of tax cases with which Claiborne was involved, either as a criminal defense lawyer or as a judge. Their transparent intent, like that of the prosecution in both trials, was to demonstrate that Claiborne was well-versed in tax law and could not have been readily deceived by incompetent tax preparers. Claiborne displayed an amazing recall for the specifics of the cases even though most had been decided six or seven years earlier, but his adroit memory did not substantiate his knowledge of tax law. Rather, it highlighted the point that many of the cases listed were only tangentially tax cases. He contended, moreover, that he brought in expert tax lawyers when tax issues were involved in the criminal cases for which he was a defense counsel.[52] Senator Orrin Hatch proposed to Claiborne that "you might have been an expert at that time for that particular case in those particular facts, and even on that particular law, but the minute the case was over, you would go on to another case; is that right?"[53]

The government had, in both trials, made much of the fact that Claiborne was in desperate need of money when he filed the faulty tax returns. That assertion was based solely on a letter he wrote to Frank Rothman requesting payment of fees. Claiborne, when asked, explained that the need was real, but the degree was exaggerated. "There was a 3-month period of time that I was in a serious financial bind," he admitted. He explained that he had sold his house and a piece of adjacent land and had purchased a second house. The sale of the first home collapsed, leaving him responsible for two residential properties. Because he was owed $37,500 by Sid Wyman's estate, he wrote to Frank Rothman to pry the money loose. "I did need money," but he added, "I do not think I was desperate for money."[54]

The final issue that the Senate committee raised with Claiborne was the procedure followed by the IRS in their investigation of his taxes, a subject relevant not only to the question of selective prosecution, but also to his tax preparer's assumption that any mistakes could be settled in the process of an audit. Senator David Pryor asked if Claiborne had ever been afforded an opportunity to discuss his taxes for 1979 or 1980 with the IRS. Claiborne replied that he never received a letter, an audit, or any other form of communication, but he was invited to testify before the grand jury and declined "on advice of counsel because of the leaks that had been coming out of the grand jury room as to all of its proceedings."[55] Claiborne's position remained that he was a victim, a target of an overly zealous or misdirected Justice Department; "they went after me . . . [and] I don't think I'm paranoid in that."[56] A war, he claimed, existed between the federal judges and the federal Strike Force in 1979. Fellow U.S. Judge Roger Foley was challenged by the Strike Force as biased and asked to recuse himself from cases, and Judge Bruce Thompson, according to Claiborne, referred to the chief counsel of the Strike Force as a schizophrenic. Soon three judges were refusing to hear any Strike Force cases, leaving only one federal judge in Nevada to try them; "it was not a good atmosphere."[57]

Claiborne succinctly captured what he saw as the issues that should govern his removal or retention: the independence of the federal judiciary, as well as his own innocence. The former issue he cast in terms of the relationship that should exist between prosecutors and judges, because "the biggest danger that I can see to the federal courts is if ever there be created a 'buddy' relationship between the federal judges and the executive branch of our government." His own innocence he justified rather simply: "if you honestly feel in your heart that I got a raw deal, and . . . that I in good faith disclosed all of my income to my tax preparers . . . therein is, as I see the choice that you have to make."[58]

After seven days of testimony, the Senate committee hearings came to a conclusion. The senators might have taken the easier route and granted a summary judgment based on Claiborne's conviction when the House had suggested, "your only decision is whether to impose the collateral consequence of barring him from any other office of high trust."[59] Claiborne, by most accounts, succeeded in raising the questions he intended, although no one seriously expected that he could avoid removal. Staffers and senators alike found Claiborne likable and lively, and even a very credible witness. Even so, "you can't have a convicted man on the bench."[60] Claiborne's attorney Oscar Goodman won considerable admiration for his smooth style and ability to maneuver testimony to make his points, even within the parameters established by the committee, whereas Nicholas Chabraja for the House came across as so arrogant that one house manager suggested that he needed "a humility bypass."[61]

Guilty of High Crimes and Misdemeanors

Scheduling Claiborne's trial for the full Senate became largely a logistical matter, although Claiborne filed a final flurry of legal motions to stay Senate action. They came to naught, as a federal district judge and an appeals court panel in the District of Columbia both concluded that the Senate could set its own rules for impeachment proceedings, and Chief Justice William Rehnquist denied the request for a stay mere hours before the final vote. Claiborne had also filed a motion for a full Senate trial that was denied after a two-hour closed session debate.

Votes on the motion split oddly, with Republicans and Democrats, liberals and conservatives, lining up on both sides. Claiborne had also asked to present additional witnesses to the full Senate, ones who had been barred from the committee hearings. Senate Majority Leader Robert Dole moved that no additional witnesses be heard, a motion that passed 61 to 32. Other motions, such as adoption of a standard of "beyond a reasonable doubt" for conviction were also rebuffed, first by presiding officer Vice President George Bush and then by a vote of 17 to 75. Hour-long presentations for each side by the House (Representative Peter Rodino and managers' counsel Chabraja) and Goodman for Claiborne drew a reasonable audience of forty to fifty senators. Claiborne addressed the Senate after Goodman, "primarily, I think, to let you see me." But he ended his statement with a summation that "what is involved is a sense of honesty and decency and . . . the independence of the American judiciary."[62]

The Senate gathered on October 9, 1986, withdrew into executive session, and closed the doors of the chamber. Even more senators attended those deliberations than the earlier presentations. The Senate, arranged to resemble a courtroom, reconvened, with the House managers and their counsel seated at a table in the well of the Senate on the right, and Claiborne and his defense team on the left. President pro tempore Strom Thurmond determined the presence of a quorum, and the sergeant at arms issued a proclamation akin to fourteenth-century British practice: "All persons are commanded to keep silent on pain of imprisonment while the House of Representatives is exhibiting to the Senate of the United States articles of impeachment against Judge Harry E. Claiborne."

Thurmond then put the question to the Senate before each roll-call vote: "Senators, how say you: Is the respondent, Harry E. Claiborne, guilty or not guilty?" On Article I, willful underpayment of 1979 taxes, the vote was 87 guilty to 10 not guilty, with one senator voting present; two senators were absent. The requisite two-thirds majority was achieved and Claiborne's removal assured, but the Senate continued through votes on the remaining three articles: Article II, underpayment of 1980 taxes, guilty by vote of 90 to 7; Article III, false statements on 1979 and 1980 taxes, not guilty by vote of 46 to 17; Article IV, bringing disrepute on the federal judiciary, guilty by vote of 89 to 8.[63] Voting took an hour, and the senators, in recognition of the solemnity of the occasion, each rose to pronounce their vote. Even the eighty-five-year-old Senator John Stennis, whose leg had been amputated the previous year, lifted himself on the arms of his wheelchair four times to cast his vote of guilty. The entire Senate sat in uncharacteristic silence as each of the roll calls was taken.[64]

U.S. marshals quickly escorted Claiborne from the Senate chambers once Majority Leader Dole sent an order to notify the House of Representatives and the president. Jeff Bingaman of New Mexico, who had also served on the evidentiary committee, then addressed the Senate to explain his votes of not guilty on all but one article, that addressing underpayment of taxes for 1980. His threshold question was the proper role for the Senate in impeachment decisions, in particular the use of a committee to gather evidence. Bingaman stated that in cases such as this, where findings of fact have been made in a court, the process was likely responsible, but not necessarily in other situations. Bingaman focused on the question of willfulness in the Claiborne case and stated his conclusion that "to make that type of independent determination of his state of mind, I believe it would be essential to hear witnesses and judge the credibility of those witnesses."[65] Other senators said that the process might set bad precedents because it suggested that criminal conviction was equivalent to impeachment and, conversely, that acquittal was tantamount an official being unimpeachable.[66]

The Aftermath

The Claiborne case, as the first impeachment and trial in more than half a century, was destined to have ripple effects beyond the removal of one judge from his office. Several senators vowed that in the next session they would seek an investigation of Justice Department tactics in the case, but no serious actions were pursued.[67] Howell Heflin concluded, as a result of his service on the evidentiary committee, that Congress no longer belonged in the business of impeaching federal judges and promised to introduce a constitutional amendment to change the process.[68]

Harry Claiborne, just nineteen days later, had his first application for parole denied, and ultimately served seventeen months of his two-year sentence.[69] Thereafter, the Nevada supreme court circumvented standard bar disciplinary proceedings and conducted its own investigation of Claiborne's fitness to practice law in the state. In a controversial decision that implied that the bar would not have conducted an impartial and fair investigation, that court refused to deny Claiborne his legal license. It concluded that Claiborne had been a victim of a federal vendetta, had been punished sufficiently, and had always been an upstanding member of the Nevada legal profession, particularly in his willingness to defend pro bono clients. U.S. District Judge Robert C. Broomfield, in 1988, however, ignored the findings of the Nevada court and disbarred Claiborne from federal practice.[70] Claiborne, in his early seventies, associated with the law firm of Richard Wright in Las Vegas and began a casual, semiretirement practice.

Notes

1. *U.S. v. Claiborne*, 727 F.2d 842, at 846 (1984).
2. Ibid., at 848.
3. Ibid., at 849.
4. *Claiborne v. U.S.*, 469 U.S. 829 (1984).
5. *U.S. v. Claiborne*, 781 F.2d 1325, at 1330 (1985).
6. Ibid., at 1333.
7. *U.S. v. Claiborne*, 765 F.2d 784 (1985).
8. *U.S. v. Claiborne*, 781 F.2d 1327, at 1327 (1986).
9. *Claiborne v. U.S.*, 475 U.S. 1120 (1986).
10. As quoted in *Congressional Record*, July 22, 1986, H-4718.
11. *Senate Impeachment Trial Committee*, 1175.
12. "Someone has to stand up to the Government sometime," Claiborne said, "and put a stop to the way they trample on people's rights." Turner, "Jailed U.S. Judge Resists Resigning," A-17.
13. *Hearings before the Subcommittee on Courts*, 3.
14. Ibid., 48.
15. "We are not interested in the substance of the first trial," Kastenmeir reminded his collegues, "that is not before the committee." Ibid., 27.
16. Ibid., 31–32.
17. Ibid.
18. *Markup of House Resolution 461, Impeachment of Judge Harry E. Claiborne.*
19. Ibid., 59.
20. "Impeaching Federal Judges," 363.
21. Senate Resolution 479, 99th Congress, was passed on August 15, 1986 [*Congressional Record*, S-11902] and provided in Section XI of Rules of Procedure and Practice in the Senate When Sitting on Impeachment Trials that "in the trial of any impeachment the Presiding Officer of the Senate, if the Senate so orders, shall appoint a committee to receive

evidence and take testimony at such times and places as the committee may determine. . . . The committee . . . shall report to the Senate in writing a certified copy of the transcript of the proceedings and testimony had and given before such committee . . . and the testimony so taken shall be considered to all intents and purposes . . . as having been received and taken before the Senate."

22. The six Republicans named by Majority Leader Dole were Orrin Hatch of Utah, Charles Mathias of Maryland, Mitch McConnell of Kentucky, Larry Pressler of South Dakota, Warren Rudman of New Hampshire, and John Warner of Virginia. The six Democrats named by Minority Leader Robert Byrd were Jeff Bingaman of New Mexico, Dennis DeConcini of Arizona, Albert Gore of Tennessee, Howell Heflin of Alabama, David Pryor of Arkansas, and Paul Sarbanes of Maryland.

23. Claiborne's counsel had filed a motion *in limine* to expand the scope of the hearings beyond the findings of fact by the jury in his second trial and to include issues of selective prosecution, targeting, and conspiracy. The House managers took the position, one that they would repeatedly assume, that the issue was "Did Judge Claiborne willfully underpay his taxes?" According to the prosecution, all questions of motivation or misconduct on the part of the government amounted to no more than an argument that the judge should not have been caught. *Senate Impeachment Trial Committee*, 464–65.

24. Claiborne submitted an extensive witness list, primarily individuals whose testimony related to subornation of perjured testimony, intimidation of witnesses, and a burglary at the judge's home. The majority of the committee refused to open the hearings to these issues.

25. *Senate Impeachment Trial Committee*, 548.

26. For Alhstrom's testimony, see ibid., 676.

27. Ibid., 584–49.

28. Ibid., 655.

29. Swanson confessed that "I do not know whether this is or is not the person that I saw in Mr. Wright's office." Ibid., 669, 678.

30. Ibid., 700.

31. Ibid., 601.

32. Ibid., 940, 602.

33. The old house was sold for $725,000, with commissions paid of $47,388, making the sale price $677,612. The new residence cost $362,800. The sale price of the old house ($677,612) minus the price of the new house ($362,800) equals the capital gain ($314,812). At that time, an individual over age fifty-five could exercise a one-time exclusion of $100,000 from capital gains for tax purposes. Claiborne, therefore, was liable for taxes on $314,812 minus the $100,000 exclusion, or $213,812. According

to William Wilson, after the 60 percent exclusion, $85,925 of that should have been reported as ordinary income. Ibid., 598–600.

34. Ibid., 603–16.

35. Watson said that on his first meeting with Claiborne he raised the question of taking a loss on the law practice: "I asked him what happened to the business. He told me he closed it, and he told me the circumstances under which he closed it. Based on that, since he didn't sell it or get any money for it, my first reaction was he should have some kind of a loss on that business. And we discussed about that loss." Ibid., 727.

36. Watson testified that Travaglia proposed the $250,000 figure for the law practice as a conservative figure. Watson said that he told her that it made no difference for "the loss that he has on the law practice, if he carries it on that Schedule D, it would take him 100 years to use it up." Ibid., 723.

37. Ibid., 721.

38. Ibid.

39. Ibid., 618.

40. "I had at least a minimal enough knowledge of the law to understand that there are no such things as officers of the grand jury," Watson testified, "and they had no jurisdiction in my office, and they had no right to come and make any demands on my records." Ibid., 712.

41. Ibid., 714.

42. At a later stage of the hearings, Claiborne's attorney would refer to the notion that Watson was his witness as "ludicrous," because "he got my client indicted." Ibid., 755.

43. Ibid., 1085.

44. Ibid., 713–18.

45. Ibid., 751.

46. Donald Skelton of the Internal Revenue Service was questioned primarily about his preparation of Claiborne's first accountant, Jay Wright, for testifying. The twenty-four-year veteran of the IRS had been given a special award for his role in obtaining Claiborne's indictment. Ibid., 886.

47. Ibid., 1042–45.

48. Ibid., 1105.

49. Watson's employee, Charlotte Travaglia, made that statement in the context of a question from Senator Warner (ibid., 806): "Warner: 'Are these just innocent parties, dealing with one another with a total lack of knowledge, in a sort of fumbling way, developed in this situation, or, are these two very skillful, cunning men, contriving a scheme to defraud the people of the United States?' Travaglia: 'Sir, I would like to say this: I don't know Judge Claiborne. I do know Mr. Watson, because I did work with him. I would not call him intelligent. Let it fall where it may.' "

50. Ibid., 1018, 1175.

51. Claiborne said that he rued the choice, but "hindsight is a remarkable thing." Ibid., 1022.

52. Ibid., 961–69.

53. Ibid., 1149. Claiborne also explained his ability as a judge to cope with even complicated tax issues by virtue of pretrial briefs and pretrial motions filed with the magistrate. These two pieces of information cued him to the issues involved and allowed him to familiarize himself with the relevant laws. Ibid., 973.

54. Ibid., 1041. Claiborne referred, in another instance, to being "overly extended," having bought two dwellings and a 25 percent interest in two apartment houses. Ibid., 1126.

55. Ibid., 1172.

56. Ibid., 1174.

57. Ibid., 930–31. In a later response to a question from Senator DeConcini, Claiborne elaborated: "I know from those instances plus one other, when I asked the grand jury to investigate the FBI, that had I never made those remarks, had I never said anything about their activity, and had I not asked the grand jury to investigate the FBI, I would not be in a federal prison today and I would not be sitting here." Ibid., 1153.

58. Ibid., 1132.

59. "Impeaching Federal Judges," 363.

60. Eisler, "Claiborne Gets His Point Across," 13.

61. Ibid., 13.

62. "Claiborne Impeached, Stripped of Judgeship," 80.

63. Congressional Record, October 9, 1986, S-15759–62.

64. Greenhouse, "U.S. Judge Ousted by Impeachment," A-23.

65. Congressional Record, October 9, 1986, S-15752.

66. "Claiborne Impeached, Stripped of Judgeship," 75.

67. Ibid., 80.

68. Greenhouse, "Judge Impeachment Process Assailed," A-24. Heflin, for himself and three others, introduced SJ Res. 113 in April 1987, to amend the Constitution regarding removal of judges. See also, Heflin, "The Impeachment Process, 123–25.

69. "Parole Panel Rejects Bid by Convicted Judge," A-23.

70. Marcus, "Now the Fate of Lawyer Hastings," 4.

4

Hastings under Investigation

Only thirty-two blacks had served on the federal bench before the presidency of Jimmy Carter.[1] They were largely barred from the bench by concentric circles of discrimination in housing, income, and education, and the result was, until quite recently, a bench that was overwhelmingly white and male.[2] Carter altered the complexion of the bench; 14 percent of his 202 district courts appointees were black, among them Alcee Lamar Hastings.[3] Hastings was sworn in as the first black federal judge in Florida in October 1979.[4] He broke with tradition, as he often would, by holding his investiture not at the federal courthouse but at Fort Lauderdale's predominantly black Dillard High School and promised President Carter that "I shall strive to uphold this high office in the manner I am sure you and Senators Stone and Chiles expect of me."[5]

Like fellow Carter appointee Harry Claiborne, Hastings's behavior first came to the attention of federal authorities through the allegations of someone with a long criminal history, William Dredge, who sought a deal for himself on criminal charges. The core accusation levied against Hastings, again the same as initially brought against Claiborne, was bribery. Hastings's defense on the bribery charge, however, led to a number of broader allegations. He, too, accused the prosecution of misconduct and targeting, although mishandling was more likely the correct description. The ineptitude of federal investigators juxtaposed against Hastings's own charismatic personality and unorthodox tactics, however, led to a different outcome than Claiborne's. A jury acquitted Alcee Hastings of all criminal charges.

Hastings's fight in the courts was not limited to his protestations of innocence. He also waged an elaborate constitutional battle in the appellate courts, the results of which entrenched the standards followed in Claiborne's case. What most distinguishes Hastings's prosecution from that of Claiborne's and, indeed from any other in U.S. history, is that the trial jury's verdict of not guilty did not end the matter. The Judicial Conduct Act of 1980 was used for the first time as a preliminary phase of what would become articles of impeachment. Two of Hastings's fellow federal judges in the circuit, after his acquittal, filed a complaint that triggered a judicial ethics investigation. That inquiry began a bit clumsily, for it was a new experience, but eventually proved to be far more thorough than the original prosecution had been. Hastings stood aloof from the process and once again resorted to constitutional arguments to block the investigation.

The case against Alcee Hastings, like that of Harry Claiborne, involved a cast of convicted criminals and sordid plots and revolved around a set of dates, telephone calls, appellate decisions, altered travel plans, yellow legal pages of questionable authenticity, and tape-recorded conversations that were individually mere pieces of a larger mosaic. The case was, by the prosecution's own admission, a circumstantial one; no direct evidence of Hastings's culpability was ever produced. The strategies that secured Hastings's acquittal, nonetheless, proved to be the catalyst for a judicial investigation. His demise as a federal judge was prepared, as his appointment had been, by his friend and fellow attorney William Borders.

Hastings was raised by his grandmother in the central Florida town of Altamonte Springs and was educated at Crooms Academy High School and Fisk University in Nashville. He entered Howard University Law School and was expelled for poor grades, but later completed a law degree at the all black Florida A&M Law School.[6] His entire educational experience had been in segregated environments, which likely spurred him to work for black causes as a student, practicing lawyer, and judge.[7] He hung out his shingle in Fort Lauderdale and began his "you-all come" practice, handling cases "from first degree murder to failure to yield the right of way, domestic relations, civil rights, negligence cases, all sorts of matters."[8] He had, by his own account, borrowed money to start his practice and also to leave it.[9] He was unable, too often, to collect his fees and sought the financial security of a $38,900 annual salary as a Florida circuit court judge, a position to which he was appointed by Governor Ruben Askew in 1977.[10]

Hastings's interest in politics had prompted him to run for public office eight times, all unsuccessfully, and to become involved in the

1976 Carter presidential campaign. When a vacancy was announced on the federal bench for the Southern District of Florida, Hastings aggressively sought it. Among those supporting his candidacy was a Washington, D.C., attorney, William Borders, with whom Hastings worked on the Carter campaign. Borders was well-connected, and Carter had even appointed him to the District of Columbia Judicial Nominations Commission.[11]

Less than two years after Alcee Hastings assumed his place on the federal bench, William Dredge, a convicted felon with long-standing associations in organized crime, walked into the U.S. Attorney's Office in Miami and offered information on a bribery scheme in Hastings's court in return for a deal on drug charges pending against him in Baltimore.[12] Dredge alleged that the organized crime figure Santo Trafficante was going to give a $1 million bribe to Judge Alcee Hastings through attorney William Borders.[13] Within days of that accusation in July 1981, the Public Integrity Section of the Justice Department was involved and anxious to negotiate. Operation Apple Eye was born.

Operation Apple Eye

Dredge had been indicted in Maryland in April 1981, for conspiracy to distribute three thousand methaqualone (Quaalude) tablets interstate.[14] He was operating an antique store in North Miami at the time but had a lengthy criminal record, starting with a conviction for larceny in 1943. Charges against him had ranged from armed robbery and car theft to fraud, forgery, bad checks, and various conspiracies. He approached the U.S. Attorney's Office, rather obviously, to negotiate the dismissal of the Quaalude charges and, he claimed, "because he wished to bring to someone's attention that a United States Federal District Court Judge was corrupt."[15]

Dredge's information related to two alleged bribery schemes, both initiated by William Borders and both, according to Dredge, involving Judge Hastings. The first bribery solicitation involved Santo Trafficante, with whom Borders had held two meetings. The second revolved around *U.S. v. Romano*, a racketeering case already decided in Hastings's court, but in which a final judgment on forfeiture was pending. Dredge told Justice Department attorneys that Borders had asked him to contact defendants Frank and Thomas Romano to convey the message that for $150,000 Borders could fix their case. Dredge made no overtures to the Romanos because he thought, "Well, here's another guy smoking ajax, . . . I have heard for years that people that had federal judges in their pockets."[16] Borders persisted, and Dredge lied in response. Although he never talked to the Romano brothers, he claimed to contact them and said that they did not have the money. This information was sufficient to entice the U.S. Attorney's Office to negotiate for his cooperation.[17]

The Romano brothers had been indicted in November 1978, and their case, a jury trial before Hastings in December 1980, resulted in guilty verdicts. Hastings, however, retained authority over their sentences and over forfeitures under the Racketeering and Corrupt Organizations (RICO) Act that was designed to deprive criminals of their ill-gotten gains. The law provided, in part, that convicted violators must forfeit to the government any interest in an enterprise established through racketeering activities.[18] On May 4, 1981, Judge Hastings entered an order of forfeiture that included the Sea Inn Restaurant in Broward County (valued at $350,000) and $850,000 in cash. Sentencing in the case had been scheduled for May 11 but was postponed by Hastings, and motions for both a new trial and reconsideration of the forfeitures had been filed when Dredge contacted the U.S. Attorney's Office. Borders had told Dredge that the continuance of the sentencing decision on May 11 was a signal that Hastings was indeed a party to the scheme. Then, on July 8, Judge Hastings sentenced both Romanos to three years in prison.

The Romano brothers were never involved in the bribery scheme and, in fact, had reported to their attorney Neal Sonnett that someone other than Borders had made an overture to them.[19] Attorneys with the Justice Department and the FBI decided to employ a retired FBI agent, Paul Rico, to pose as Frank Romano and pursue the bribery investigation, with Dredge's cooperation, in an undercover operation code-named "Apple Eye." Dredge's plea bargain was concluded on September 11, an agreement whereby he pleaded guilty to one count and was guaranteed no more than five years in prison and a $15,000 fine. He was also guaranteed that the government would not call him as a witness in any case. Dredge, in return, called Borders on September 10 to say that the Romanos were ready to deal and arranged for Borders to meet Paul Rico (posing as Frank Romano) at the Miami airport on September 12. Dredge, Rico/Romano, and Borders all met early in the morning, and their exchange, because Rico was wired, was recorded.

Dredge made the introductions and left the two alone. Romano raised the issue of the criminal case, to which Borders responded straightforwardly, "I think we can help you." They finally agreed on the figure of $150,000, and Borders said, "within ten days the order will be signed." He alluded to the return of a "substantial amount" and added that "the other will follow after that."[20] Rico, however, raised the question of verification, "checks and balances." Borders suggested initially that the issuance of the order should be a satisfactory signal, but Rico pressed for another indication that Borders could deliver—a sign by the judge, in this case, a dinner at a time and place previously specified. Borders promised that Judge Hastings would have dinner at the Fontainbleau Hotel's main dining room at 8 the next Wednesday evening, September 16, 1981, and Rico agreed to meet Borders again the following Saturday.[21]

On September 16, William Borders and a girlfriend flew to Las Vegas to see a boxing match; Alcee Hastings and his date, Essie Thompson, had dinner at 8 in the main dining room of the Fontainbleau Hotel, where they were observed by FBI agents. On September 19, Rico and Borders met again, and Rico handed over an envelope with $25,000 in cash. "Um, ah, there'as a um, ah, there's 25, ah, right there," Rico explained, as he pushed for a further signal, "and that's going to be, ah, my indication that, everything is fine, ah, I feel that when the, when the next transaction takes place in ten day, I'll take another 25 and then the remaining hundred on the, ah, on the culmination." Borders objected that Rico's proposal was different from the earlier understanding, but nonetheless instructed Rico to have his attorney withdraw the appeal. The two agreed that a new order on the forfeiture would be issued by October 3.[22]

Borders, following the meeting with Rico, flew from Miami to West Palm Beach, where he attended a family reunion. Hastings had flown to Washington the previous evening, where he met his friend Jesse McCrary for a social weekend before a speaking engagement in Pennsylvania. After going to the reunion, Borders returned to Washington the same night and appeared at Hastings and McCrary's hotel room about 10. He was not, according to Hastings, expected, but Hastings, McCrary, and three others invited Borders to join them for dinner.

Hastings had issued the original forfeiture order on May 4, but two new rulings on RICO statute forfeitures had been decided by the Fifth Circuit Court of Appeals in New Orleans. *U.S. v. Martino*[23] was announced on June 19, 1981, and was followed on August 27, 1981 by *U.S. v. Peacock.*[24] The two opinions substantially altered the interpretation of RICO and, thereby, demanded that the original order in the *Romano* case be reconsidered. The *Martino* case focused on the term *interest* used in the RICO statute and the term's applicability to income or receipts from a racketeering operation as opposed to the enterprise itself. Because the term was not defined in the statute, the question of what could legally be taken by the government was crucial in assessing forfeitures. The Fifth Circuit concluded, as the Ninth Circuit had previously,[25] that forfeitures under the law were limited to the defendant's interest in an enterprise and excluded income or profits from racketeering activity. Monetary forfeitures in the *Martino* case were reversed,[26] and the implication was that the $850,000 ordered forfeited in the *Romano* case would be affected. Judge Hastings's law clerk Jeffrey Miller informed the judge of the *Martino* ruling shortly before the Romanos' sentencing hearing on July 8. Both Neal Sonnett, representing the Romano brothers, and James Deichert, for the government, argued Hastings's earlier judgment of forfeiture in light of the new *Martino* ruling, but the judge did not modify his order. The Romanos filed an appeal. The *Peacock* decision in August reinforced *Martino* and the argument that the $850,000 ordered forfeited by the Romanos should be returned.[27]

October 3, 1981, the day that Borders had promised a new order on the forfeiture, passed uneventfully, and Borders made a number of unsuccessful calls to Hastings. On the morning of October 5, the judge firmly instructed Miller, who was leaving to work for another judge the end of the month, to complete a new order on the Romanos' forfeiture, something the two had discussed when *Martino* was announced and again after the *Peacock* decision. Hastings finally, late that afternoon, returned Borders's call. That taped conversation, together with Hastings's appearance for dinner at the Fontainbleu Hotel, formed the crux of the criminal case:

Borders: Yes, my brother.
Hastings: Hey, my man.
Borders: Um hum.
Hastings: I've drafted all those ah, ah, letters, ah, for Hemp. . . .
Borders: Um hum.
Hastings: . . . and everything's okay. The only thing I was con-

cerned with was, did you hear if, ah, you hear from him after we talked?

Borders: Yea.

Hastings: Oh. Okay.

Borders: Uh huh.

Hastings: All right, then.

Borders: See, I had, I talked to him and he, he wrote some things down for me.

Hastings: I understand.

Borders: And then I was supposed to go back and get some more things.

Hastings: All right. I understand. Well then, there's no great big problem at all. I'll, I'll see to it that, ah, I communicate with him. I'll send the stuff off to Columbia in the morning.[28]

The order restoring approximately $800,000 in cash to the Romanos was signed the next morning.

Borders had served as president of the predominantly black National Bar Association and to honor him a gala boat ride was planned in Washington for October 9. Hastings had long planned to attend and, when he arrived early on the morning of the ninth, Borders met him at the airport. The two then checked into the L'Enfant Plaza Hotel, where they had adjoining rooms. Hastings needed to get some luggage repaired and left with Borders. They stopped at Borders's law office, where Borders returned several calls, one of them to Rico, who was at the Marriott Twin Bridges Hotel in Washington. Hastings left Borders's office on foot and eventually returned to the L'Enfant Plaza.

Borders met Rico shortly after noon at the Marriott Hotel to collect the remainder of the bribe. The two, at Borders's insistence, took a drive. Rico carried a travel case with $125,000 and, unknown to Borders, was recording their conversation. Sirens punctuated the chatter between the two as police vehicles pulled Borders's car to the side. "We're busted," Borders lamented. "I'm afraid so," replied Rico.[29]

Borders was arrested for the bribery attempt and immediately contacted his lawyer, John Shorter, who later that afternoon called the L'Enfant Plaza in an attempt to reach Hastings. He left a message with Borders's and Hastings's good friend Hemphill Pride, saying that the FBI wanted to interview the judge about a bribe in his courtroom. Pride eventually reached Hastings by telephone and asked that Hastings come to his room. Pride relayed the information and advised Hastings to return home to handle the situation. Hastings quickly departed from the hotel and declined Pride's offer of a ride to the airport. He did not take a taxi to nearby Washington National, but rather made a $50 trip to the Baltimore airport. From there he made several calls from pay telephones and caught a flight to Fort Lauderdale (although his car was at the Miami airport), arriving shortly before nine in the evening. He was interviewed by two FBI agents at the home of his lawyer and fiancée Patricia Williams after eleven o'clock that night.[30]

The Criminal Trial

An indictment against both Hastings and Borders was issued on December 29, 1981, accusing them of conspiracy to solicit and accept a bribe and of corruptly influencing and impeding the administration of justice. Borders was also indicted on two counts of interstate travel for unlawful activity. Judge Edward B. Davis, who had presided over the grand jury proceedings, promptly recused himself from the case, as did the other federal judges serving in the district. The chief judge of the circuit petitioned Chief Justice Warren Burger to appoint an out-of-circuit judge to try the case, and Edward T. Gignoux of Maine was named.

Hastings quickly enlisted the highly regarded criminal lawyer Joel Hirschhorn as his chief counsel. He was arraigned on January 13, 1982, and, when asked for his plea, refused to answer; a not guilty plea was entered by the court on his behalf.[31] Hastings unsuccessfully filed a motion to quash the indictment against him for want of jurisdiction, asserting that a sitting federal judge cannot be tried in a criminal case. A pretrial motion hearing was conducted later, and the results of that hearing likely had important ramifications for the outcome of the criminal case. The first item to be considered at the pretrial motion conference was Hirschhorn's request, which Hastings joined, to withdraw from the case. The motion, because it was uncontested, was granted, and Andrew Mavrides assumed the lead role in the Hastings defense. Because of an appeal on jurisdiction, Hastings's defense also requested a stay and, more importantly, a severance of the two cases. The argument for severing the cases rested on the incompatibility of the defenses because the thrust of Borders's defense was that he had committed the acts with which he was charged, but that the government had engaged in entrapment. Borders was not going to testify, whereas

Hastings fully intended to take the stand.[32] Borders's lawyers concurred in the request for a severance, "because we could not endure a battering in the courtroom from the prosecutor and also from Judge Hastings."[33] Borders's trial was set for March and, on a change of venue, was moved to Atlanta, while a stay was granted in the Hastings case pending the outcome of his appeal.[34]

In July, the Eleventh Circuit Court of Appeals rejected Hastings's argument that he was not subject to prosecution for acts involving his exercise of the judicial power.[35] The crux of Hastings's argument, like that of Otto Kerner's, was that Congress alone has the power to try a federal judge through the impeachment process and that separation of powers is breached if the executive department attempts to prosecute a federal judge. Hastings's proposition of total judicial immunity from federal prosecution was rejected because it ran counter to "another treasured value of our constitutional system: no man in this country is so high that he is above the law."[36]

While Hastings fought his case through appeals and pretrial motions, Borders went to trial on March 22, 1982. The trial lasted only a week, and neither Hastings nor Borders testified. The government presented evidence of Borders's travels and his telephone calls, together with the tapes of conversations with Rico, posing as Romano, and their telephone calls. The prime arguments were that Borders could not have known much of the information he passed to Rico without the complicity of Hastings. Borders was found guilty by the jury on all four counts and sentenced to five years in prison for each, with the sentences running concurrently.[37]

Hastings pursued his defense in Miami with a flurry of motions, among them another change of lawyers. Patricia Williams was designated as the new trial lawyer with Hastings as co-counsel, and motions were introduced to allow television coverage of the trial and to compel Dredge to testify.[38] All were denied. The trial began on January 13, 1983, with four days of jury selection; the 313 jurors called were pared to twelve, ten whites and two blacks.

Hastings's original accuser, William Dredge, did not appear, but the interactions between Dredge and the government and those of Dredge and Borders were introduced by Special Agent William Murphy. Paul Rico's testimony about what occurred between him and Borders while he masqueraded as Frank Romano formed the cornerstone of the prosecution's case, supported by a cadre of witnesses who introduced telephone, hotel, and airline records. Several lawyers, those involved in the *Romano* case, testified about the Racketeering and Corrupt Organizations Act forfeitures. The prosecution took all of the pieces of circumstantial evidence of Hastings's involvement in the bribery plot and attempted to demonstrate a pattern—an orderly motif of telephone calls between Borders and Hastings on critical days, altered flight plans to enable an unobserved meeting, or seemingly unplanned encounters between the two. The centerpieces of the prosecution's case were the Fontainbleau Hotel dinner, the cryptic telephone conversation between Hastings and Borders on October 5, 1981, the timing of the order in the *Romano* case, and Hastings's "flight" from Washington after Borders was arrested.

Lead government prosecutor Reid Weingarten summarized the case against Hastings, highlighting the "decisive issue": "was Borders telling the truth when he said Alcee Hastings was involved along with him?"[39] Hastings placed calls to Borders on four crucial days in the *Romano* case: May 4, when the original forfeiture order was issued; May 11, when sentencing was originally scheduled; and the days on either side of July 8, when the forfeiture order was affirmed. The government acknowledged that Hastings was required to return the Romanos' money in light of the *Martino* and *Peacock* decisions but argued that the crucial question was the timing of the order.[40]

Judge Hastings's trip to Washington, D.C., on September 11 was proposed as another critical point in the conspiracy between Hastings and Borders, and its importance increased because of calls between the two the previous day. Although that trip had been planned well in advance, flights were altered, according to the government's version, to allow for a meeting between Borders and Hastings at Washington National Airport. Hastings missed his original departure, which would have gotten him to Washington at six in the evening, and called Borders to say that he was delayed. Borders, however, was supposed to leave Washington for Florida at 7:30 the same evening to attend his family reunion and to meet with Rico/Romano the next morning. Borders, when informed of Hastings's delay, changed his flight for a later one. "Strong evidence," according to prosecutor Weingarten, "that the two met at National Airport for a precise purpose."[41] The next night, while Hastings, McCrary, and their companions were gathered in the hotel room, Borders arrived and joined them all for dinner. He did this, according to Weingarten's version, "to report back on the results of his meeting [with Rico/Romano]."[42]

According to the government, Judge Hastings's dinner at the Fontainbleau at the appointed time clearly demonstrated his complicity in the plot, as did the timing of the final order to return the forfeited funds to the Romanos. Weingarten characterized the October 5, 1981, telephone conversation about "letters for Hemp" as a coded conversation between Borders and Hastings. Borders's statement "I talked to him and . . . I was supposed to go back and get some more things" meant that Rico had given him some money, but he was supposed to go back for more. Hastings's response — "I have drafted those, ah, letters" — was intended, following the logic of a coded conversation, to say that "the order has been drafted." "I will send the stuff off in the morning" meant "it [the order] will be released the following morning." What the two were clearly "talking about in their own coded, cryptic way on October the 5th," according to the government, "was the timing of the issuance of the order." Borders told Rico two days later that the order had been sent "yesterday."[43]

The manner of Hastings's departure was, according to the government, confirmation of his guilt. He left Washington, the prosecution alleged, not because of any news he received through calls to Florida — a defense proposition — but because of his complicity in the bribery scheme. "He took off," Weingarten proposed, "and he was not the least bit interested in what was going on with his friend Bill Borders because he knew precisely what Borders was up to when he got arrested." Hastings avoided the FBI because he wanted time "to collect himself and to put together his story." For that reason, Hastings did not go to the nearby Washington National nor, the government asserted, home, but rather to the home of his fiancée, where the FBI happened to locate him later that night. "Is Alcee Hastings' behavior the behavior of an innocent United States Judge," Weingarten asked, "or the behavior of someone . . . who desperately wanted to avoid an interview until he had time to put his story together?"[44]

Hastings, like Claiborne, argued that he was the victim of a flim-flam man. Borders was, he claimed, a "rainmaker," someone who promised he could make things happen for a price, and sometimes, by coincidence, the promised events occurred. Hastings was merely a victim of his friend's scam. The defense presented witnesses, including the judge's mother, to verify Hastings's presence at various places.

Other witnesses were called to testify about Borders's personality, his secretive way of conducting his affairs, his failure to appear when expected, and his diffident manner on the telephone. Hastings's friend Hemphill Pride testified about Borders and events in Washington when the arrest took place. Hastings, however, called other witnesses, including Pride's wife, to suggest that Hemphill Pride was not always accurate in his recollection of facts. More than fifty exhibits were placed in evidence by the defense, one of which, "the letters for Hemp" mentioned in the critical October 5 telephone conversation, became the focal issue. The star witness and the core of the defense's case was the judge himself, whose performance was so dramatic that even the prosecution referred to him as "the very charming, very attractive man, very bright man that you have seen in court during this trial."[45]

Hastings's defense required that he provide an alternative explanation for the October 5 telephone call, and the judge said the discussion was about "letters for Hemp," his friend Hemphill Pride.[46] Pride had practiced law in South Carolina until 1977, when he was convicted for misappropriating funds in a HUD project and sentenced to three years in prison. He was also, in May 1981, given an indefinite suspension from the South Carolina bar.[47] Unable to practice law, Pride had financial difficulties. The "letters for Hemp," according to Hastings, were letters that he was drafting to solicit both letters and money on behalf of his friend. Hastings claimed that he had been asked to raise money for Pride earlier but was not able to do much because of potential ethical problems.[48] Borders, however, had raised the question of soliciting funds to help Pride again and persisted in pressuring Hastings to act on Pride's behalf despite the potential ethics problem.[49]

Hastings testified that he had finally succumbed to Borders's entreaties and wrote "the letters for Hemp" while trying a case on October 5. Defense Exhibit 29 was a plastic envelope containing three letters, handwritten on yellow legal pages. Like the yellow sheets listing legal fee income offered by Harry Claiborne in his trial, the government disputed the authenticity of the documents and alleged that they had been fabricated at a later time. The first "letter for Hemp" was purported to be a cover letter to Pride, and the other two letters were to "Dear Blank." The first solicited character letters in support of Pride's readmission to the practice of law, and the second asked for financial contributions. None of the letters was ever typed or mailed, because, according to Hastings, on the night of October 5 he "agonized at great length" and "determined that it would be inappropriate for me to send them."[50]

Hastings explained the the crucial October 5 telephone conversation by saying that the comment "and everything's okay" referred "specifically to the call that I received from Mr. Borders either on September 20th or 21st wherein he indicated to me that he expected to see Hemphill again and . . . asking him specifically about his exact financial condition." Pride's financial situation was also, Hastings testified, what Borders meant when he said, "I talked to him and he wrote some things down for me."[51] Hastings explained his reply, "I understand," as simply "an affectation of mine." He said that he assumed Borders's next statement, "and then I was supposed to go back and get some more things," to refer to Pride's financial situation. "That is all that I could have possibly had in my mind at that time."[52]

Weingarten attacked Hastings's testimony strongly on several points. Why did Hastings never mail the "letters" or simply tell Borders "you can't do it; it's unethical"? He seemed less than satisfied with Hastings's counter: "I was going to tell him exactly that." But, Weingarten persisted, "in this call, you say, 'I will send the stuff off to Columbia in the morning.'" Hastings did not, he acknowledged, mail the letters, nor did he take them to Washington on October 9, when he would have seen both Pride and Borders. Hastings "put them in a desk drawer" and said that he did intend to mail the character part but not the financial solicitation. The last element of the government's contention that the letters were forgeries was its notation that the defense had not supplied them until December 1982, more than a year after the initial round of reciprocal discovery. Laboratory tests on the letters, however, were inconclusive in establishing when they were written.[53]

The government scored on the "letters for Hemp" issue when Hemphill Pride testified that, to his knowledge, Hastings was not drafting letters nor soliciting money on his behalf. He said, moreover, that he would not have enlisted the assistance of either Borders or Hastings in securing his legal license because it was "purely a local matter." "The best evidence that those letters are phony," the prosecution argued, "phony evidence to explain away the incriminating 5:12 phone call, comes from the defendant's best friend."[54]

The defense, however, submitted telephone bills showing calls to South Carolina between April and October of 1981 as evidence of Hastings's regular contact with and concern for Pride's situation. Those and other calls were also cited as proof that Hastings had approached mutual friends to seek their cooperation in sending character letters in support of Pride's reinstatement in the South Carolina bar,[55] an assertion that was later disproved when the judicial inquiry began.

The dinner at the Fontainbleau Hotel was explained by Hastings as typical of Borders, who "was cloak and dagger, clandestine and sometimes cryptic."[56] Hastings added that when he was in Washington for the weekend of September 12, Borders told him that he would be in Miami on September 16 at the Fontainbleau. Borders, of course, was not in Miami that day, but in Las Vegas. The judge planned to eat out anyway and agreed to meet Borders, who would be with a friend or friends. "He [Borders] indicated that he would be there at 8:00."[57] Hastings and Essie Thompson arrived at the appointed time, went to the lounge, and later entered the main dining room, where Hastings told the maitre d' that he "was expecting a Mr. William Borders and company." Hastings and Thompson were seated at a table for four, but the other two place settings were removed. Hastings, after ordering, left "for the express purpose of looking for Mr. Borders, and I was unsuccessful in my attempt to find him."[58] The government suggested an alternative motive for Hastings's exit: "to be seen by representatives of the Romanos." But Hastings countered that "I know both of the Romanos very well and I can tell you if I had been involved in such a scheme, I would have been seriously disturbed at not seeing them." And what, the prosecution asked, was Hastings's reaction to Borders's not appearing? "It is not uncustomary for Borders and subsequently when I spoke with him and chided him about it, he chuckled."[59]

The manner of Hastings's departure from his hotel and the Washington area when told of Borders's arrest was another issue. Both Hastings and Pride concurred that the judge seemed totally startled by the news about Borders. Pride testified that he was with Hastings as the judge returned to his room after receiving the information and that Hastings made no telephone calls; nor were any calls recorded by the hotel. Hastings, however, explained his hasty departure by a telephone call that he said he made from his hotel room to his mother and another to Patricia Williams, who told him she had been interviewed by the FBI.[60] He explained that, on reflection, "my best bet was to go home and I did."[61]

Hastings explained his decision to go to the airport in Baltimore rather than the much closer one by his recollection that all planes at that hour from Washington to Miami stopped in Atlanta. The government, however, cited a more logical flight from Washington National to Miami, one Hastings had taken previously and which departed at 5:30. Hastings agreed that the flight was "perfect in retrospect," but he was aiming for, although he missed, the 5:05 Delta flight from Baltimore. Once at the Baltimore airport, Hastings called his mother twice from one pay telephone and then called Patricia Williams from another to ask her to call him back at yet a third. Williams had returned his call from a telephone booth, and the judge went to a fourth booth to call her back at her pay telephone. The judge explained this pay telephone game of tag as a response to his feeling that his "and Ms. Williams' telephones were illegally tapped."[62]

Hastings's car was at the Miami airport, but his flight took him to Fort Lauderdale instead, where he rented a car. Hastings claimed that he went first to his mother's and then to Patricia Williams's house.[63] Later that evening, when the FBI reached the apartment that he shared with his mother, she said that she did not know where he was and had not heard from him.[64] The FBI located the judge at Patricia Williams's home, and, both the defense and prosecution agreed, he willingly submitted to an interview.

The timing of the order to return money forfeited by the Romanos was also critical to Hastings's defense. Jeffrey Miller, the law clerk employed by the judge, testified that he was told to "give the money back" in September after the *Peacock* decision was rendered. The judge on the morning of October 5 told him to get the order out that day but never questioned him about it again, although it was not finished until late the next day. The judge explained the sequence of events in the *Romano* case, beginning with the May 4 forfeiture order that accurately reflected, he believed, the prevailing interpretation of the RICO statute in the Fifth Circuit at the time. Hastings admitted that he had not read the *Martino* case, with its new interpretation, before that hearing but that he had said during the July 8 hearing "that I was familiar with the case." The Romanos' attorney, he said, had not offered anything to convince him that the original order was in error. The judge did not, by his own admission, urge his clerk to complete the *Romano* order until October 5, although he, as Miller corroborated, did ask about the *Romano* case on several occasions. Miller was told to complete the order on October 5 because he would be transferred to another judge on November 1 and Hastings would be out of the office for most of October.[65] Hastings also covered alternative theories for Borders's knowledge of when the order was issued by explaining that law clerks and secretaries often divulge the timing, but not the substance, of an order when asked.

During closing arguments on February 2, 1983, both sides had difficulty bringing the case together. Very few facts were disputed, but the proper twist to place on them was essential. Judge Gignoux's instructions to the jury required almost an hour and a half, after which the jury began its seventeen hours of deliberations. Late in the afternoon of February 4, the jury returned to the courtroom and reported that Alcee Hastings was not guilty. Hastings slipped out of the courtroom and across the hall to the chambers of another judge and called his mother: "It was not guilty, lady." He then marched out of the courthouse and into a throng of supporters on the steps, ironically proclaiming, "I am going to be a judge for life . . . , but I'll beat them wherever I find them."[66]

Questions of ethics began to swim around Hastings, for he had in the trial commented that how he ran his chambers might be unethical "but it's not a crime."[67] The judge noted almost immediately that although he did not regret his comments, some things he said on the stand might result in attempts to sanction him under the Judicial Conduct Act of 1980[68] but, he boasted, "I have no fear of impeachment."[69]

The Constitutional Issues

Less than one month after the trial, Chief Judge John Godbold of the Eleventh Circuit ordered the file of *U.S. v. Hastings* sealed and reported at a meeting of the circuit judicial council in early March that Hastings would presumably be resuming his duties because no complaint had been filed against him. That night over dinner Judge Terrell Hodges of Tampa confided to Anthony Alaimo, his friend and fellow judge on the council, that he would file a grievance against Hastings. Alaimo chose to join in the complaint, despite protests by Hodges that it "was only necessary for one of us to go through this experience."[70] Judge Alaimo persisted, and the next morning the two jurists announced their intention.

Both Hodges and Alaimo admitted that they had no independent knowledge of Hastings's activities or of his trial, for each had met him only casually. They were persuaded to seek a formal inquiry solely because of their reading of an opinion by Circuit Judge Frank Johnson on the appeal of Borders's conviction. Borders had objected to the "uncertain and equivocal" evidence presented in his trial that Hastings had "fled" Washington, as well as to the jury instructions on conspiracy. The core of Borders's argument was, simply put, that he could not be convicted of conspiracy if he acted alone. Judge Johnson, upon reviewing the evidence, concluded that "the government sufficiently established Hastings's activity on October 9 as flight" and that "the jury also had before it other circumstantial evidence tending to show that Hastings was involved."[71] The two judges accepted that Judge Johnson in his December 10, 1982, opinion, not the jury in Miami, had reached the right conclusion about Hastings and the bribery scheme.

The Hodges and Alaimo complaint was filed with the Eleventh Judicial Circuit on March 17, 1983, and was the first of at least three that would be lodged against Hastings before his tenure on the federal bench ended. The Hodges and Alaimo complaint contained six counts of alleged breaches of the Code of Judicial Conduct, all of which related to Hastings's behavior in his criminal trial. Count 1 alleged that Hastings had, contrary to the jury verdict in his criminal case, conspired with Borders to solicit a bribe. Count 2 addressed Hastings's public statements that he was the object of a political and racial vendetta, while count 3 focused on a fund-raising cocktail party that F. Lee Bailey had hosted to raise money for Hastings's legal defense. Counts 4 and 5 involved practices in Hastings's courtroom and office that the judge had revealed in his own testimony in the criminal trial. Count 6 related also to Hastings's testimony that he had used his judicial position to raise funds for Hemphill Pride. All of these charges, the complaint argued, involved "conduct prejudicial to the effective and expeditious administration of the business of the courts."[72]

Judge Godbold, following the requirements of the Judicial Conduct Act of 1980, promptly reviewed the complaint and sent a copy to Hastings. By April 1, he had named a committee of five, including himself, to investigate the allegations. Three district court judges from the circuit were tapped: Gerald Bard Tjoflat of Jacksonville, Sam C. Pointer of Birmingham, and William C. O'Kelly of Atlanta. The fifth member was Judge Frank M. Johnson, author of the appellate decision in *U.S. v. Borders* and a colleague of Judge Godbold's in Montgomery. By April 13, the committee had engaged the services of John Doar, who had gained a national reputation for his investigation of the Watergate scandal, and his associate Stewart Webb to conduct the investigation. Godbold then, on April 15, issued a press release to announce the investigation, the composition of the committee, and the appointment of Doar, although the Judicial Conduct Act specifies that investigations are confidential.[73] Hastings subsequently tried to make the entire investigation public, but only limited parts of the complaint and inquiry were deemed appropriate for release. Hastings, nonetheless, persisted in keeping the subject in the press and in publicly calling for full disclosure, a tactic he had used in his criminal trial when he moved for television coverage.

In March, shortly after its formation, the investigating committee filed a motion for access to records and transcripts of the grand jury that had indicted Hastings and Borders in 1981. The sealed record of the criminal trial was transferred to the Eleventh Circuit Court of Appeals, and the committee's quest for the grand jury materials was transformed into the first of several legal contests on June 3, 1983, when its petition, *In re Petition to Inspect and Copy Grand Jury Material*, was filed in the U.S. District Court in South Florida.[74] Hastings opposed release of the grand jury materials and thereby launched the first of what would be a long list of legal suits to block impeachment.

Oral argument on release of grand jury materials to the investigating committee took place on November 15, 1983, before Judge Eugene Gordon, sitting by designation, and Gordon announced his memorandum order on December 20. He concluded that Rule 6(e) of Federal Rules of Criminal Procedure preserved the confidentiality of grand jury deliberations "except in those rare instances where disclosure is necessary to prevent injustice."[75] Gordon saw that protection, however, as requiring a balance with the investigating committee's congressionally mandated duty to conduct an inquiry into judicial conduct. Granting the committee access, with restrictions to preserve confidentiality, constituted a "minimal trespass upon the traditional values associated with grand jury confidentiality" when compared to the need of the committee for the information.[76] "Public interest in the integrity and independence of the judiciary" was, he decided, more important than Hastings's interest in maintaining the validity of his acquittal.[77]

Hastings again filed suit, this time to enjoin the investigation by arguing that the Judicial Conduct Act of 1980 interferes with judicial independence by delegating impeachment powers to the judiciary and contravening the separation of powers doctrine. The act also, he claimed, violated his right to due process. Judge Gerhardt Gessell of the U.S. Court of Appeals dismissed all of Hastings's allegations, saying that the judge "confuse[s] independence of the judiciary with his desire for unbridled personal independence,"[78] a decision that was upheld on appeal.[79]

John Doar and Stewart Webb, meanwhile, were gathering evidence, locating witnesses, and taking depositions. On April 2, 1985, Judge Godbold, as investigating committee chair, notified Hastings that hearings would commence on May 20, 1985, in Atlanta. Hastings was also apprised of his right to be present, to present evidence, to compel testimony or production of documents, and to cross-examine witnesses. A room in the courthouse, with telephone, typewriter, and locking file as well as photocopying services, was offered. Godbold also reminded the judge that the hearings were administrative in nature and not a trial or an adversarial procedure, and were subject to strict rules of confidentiality. Hastings, nonetheless, declined to participate and, on May 16, 1985, made a special and limited appearance to restate his "constitutional objections to the Investigating Committee's jurisdiction . . . to investigate his role in office" and to confirm that neither he nor his counsel would be present for the hearings.[80]

The committee, in anticipation of the hearings, had issued subpoenas to present and past employees in Hastings's judicial chambers, including the judge's secretary and three of the judge's present or former law clerks. Because of the alleged privilege of confidentiality involved in the conduct of business in a federal judge's office, the arrival of the subpoenas prompted another round of litigation. *In re Matter of Certain Complaints under Investigation by an Investigating Committee* began in the U.S. District Court of South Florida, where the judge and his staff sought injunctive and declaratory relief from the subpoenas, but that claim was dismissed for want of jurisdiction.[81] That case and one initiated by the investigating committee to force compliance with the subpoenas were merged for purposes of appeal. On February 20, 1986, the three out-of-circuit judges sitting by designation decided that the committee was explicitly granted subpoena power by the Judicial Conduct Act and that witnesses could not refuse to testify on the grounds that the law was unconstitutional.[82] The basic investigatory process was upheld as not intruding on judicial independence, partly because of the precedent established in *Chandler* and also because of the number of legitimate outcomes that an investigation might yield.[83] Claims that the Judicial Conduct Act was unconstitutionally overbroad and vague and compromised due process were also unsuccessful. The appeals court did recognize a limited privilege protecting confidential communications among a judge and his or her staff in the performance of judicial duties. That privilege, however, was overcome by the need for information by the investigating committee, and all parties were ordered to testify fully.

Judicial Committee Hearings

The investigating committee had continued its course during these legal skirmishes, hearing testimony in Atlanta and, on one occasion in South Carolina, throughout the summer and fall of 1985. The committee had available to it all of the evidence that had been taken before the juries that convicted William Borders in 1982 and acquitted Hastings in 1983. Its investigation was, however, more far-reaching than those conducted for the criminal trials. It was able to view the whole panorama of Borders's activities, extending to the Trafficante bribe as well as that of the Romano brothers. The initial criminal investigation had been limited to September 10 through October 9, 1981, the dates specified in the indictment, but no similar time frames bound the committee's inquiry. The resources and time available were also greater, as almost $2 million were spent on the services of Doar, Webb, and their investigative team, and the committee was not limited by rules inherent in a jury trial.[84] Although general adherence to Federal Rules of Criminal Procedure was followed, particularly in cases of hearsay testimony, the evidence presented to the committee was more sophisticated and thorough than had been presented to the jury. Much of it was information that the prosecution could have obtained but did not.

William Borders remained the key witness, for only he and Hastings knew absolutely the extent of the judge's involvement in the scheme. He had failed to take the stand in his own defense and had not testified at Hastings's trial. Doar had tried unsuccessfully to interview him in prison and had subpoenaed him, but Borders steadfastly maintained his silence.[85] Hastings's principle accuser, William Dredge, had not, as part of his plea agreement with the government, testified either before the grand jury investigating Hastings and Borders or in either criminal trial. Dredge appeared in the opening days of the investigating committee's hearings, albeit most reluctantly,[86] and chided the committee: "Whatever Hastings did, you guys had a fair shot at him. You took him to trial. He got found not guilty."[87] Dredge's testimony recounted his dealings with Borders, his knowledge of Borders's contacts with mobster Santo Trafficante, and the events to which he was a party when the Public Integrity Section became involved. He could not remember dates or precise figures, suggesting instead hypothetical ones. He said that he assumed Borders was fabricating Hastings's involvement, but "this pipe dream never evaporated," and, indeed, he became convinced that "it in fact was a viable thing."[88] Dredge added little to what was already in the record from his discussions with the Justice Department, but the critical point of his testimony was his conviction that Hastings and Borders were in collusion.[89]

More than 110 witnesses appeared and more than 2,800 exhibits were presented as the committee met sporadically through the summer and fall of 1985 and reconvened again twice in spring and summer of 1986. The committee listened to nineteen tape-recorded conversations during the twenty-seven days of hearings. Much of the terrain covered was merely a revisiting of material presented in the Borders and Hastings trials, but new information emerged in at least five lines of inquiry. Hastings had testified that his decision to leave Washington hurriedly after hearing of Borders's arrest was prompted by two telephone calls he made from his hotel room. The comptroller of the L'Enfant Plaza Hotel had testified at the trial that there were no records of calls from Hastings's room to his mother and to Patricia Williams. Prosecutor Weingarten had emphasized the absence of telephone records in his closing arguments, but he allowed that "sometimes they [hotels] miss bills."[90] The jury apparently accepted the premise that those calls were simply not recorded, but John Doar went further and presented an AT&T expert, who explained in detail how the printing system worked. According to her testimony, the slips printed at the front desk of the L'Enfant Plaza could not possibly miss a long distance call made from the hotel on the afternoon of October 9. "None of the calls Judge Hastings testified he made is to be found."[91]

Hastings's defense in the criminal trial had introduced telephone bills of the judge's to verify that he had been in contact with his friend Hemphill Pride in South Carolina during 1981. These calls were important to the defense argument that, in the crucial October 5, 1981, telephone conversation, the discussion had been straightforwardly about writing "letters for Hemp." Of the four calls cited in the trial as having been made by Borders or Hastings, only one, on July 24, 1981, had actually been to Hemphill Pride. The committee traced the other three calls, and none were connected to Pride.[92]

Judge Hastings had, at his criminal trial, also testified that he was writing letters for Pride as a result of a discussion Pride had with Chief Justice Woodrow Lewis of the South Carolina Supreme Court. Lewis had been subpoenaed by Hastings but never called to testify. The chief justice's testimony was consistent with that of Pride's: he had been visited by Pride, who wanted to apologize for public remarks he had made about the justice, but no mention had been made of Pride's reinstatement. To do so would be premature because Pride would have had to retake the South Carolina bar examination at the conclusion of his two-year suspension. Justice Lewis, moreover, told the committee that Hastings had called him in connection with the criminal case to solicit his testimony. "He wanted me to testify that Hemphill Pride had come to see me about getting reinstated in the bar in South Carolina," Lewis explained, "and I told him I was not going to testify to it."[93] Hastings had also at his trial produced his luggage with a torn strap that he claimed he was trying to have fixed in Washington, the reason he accompanied Borders on the morning of October 9, 1981. The investigating committee, however, heard from an FBI expert that microscopic examination of the break revealed that the strap had obviously been cut, not torn.[94]

The investigating committee also looked at the rationale behind Hastings's many changes of lawyers during the course of his trial preparation. He had initially retained Joel Hirschhorn but then shifted to Andrew Mavrides, and, finally, had relied on Patricia Williams, who had been in practice only four years and had never tried a case in federal court. Hastings had explained all of this to reporters as part of a strategy to keep the defense "a moving target."[95] The committee, however, looked at other possible motives, particularly those that prompted the well-respected Hirschhorn to withdraw. Hirschhorn had invoked attorney-client privilege in a number of areas when questioned about the Hastings's case but told the committee that "Judge Hastings had become like a freight train out of control, a runaway client and impossible to control."[96] The committee, rather than take Hirschhorn's explanation at face value, delved more deeply into the timing of his withdrawal from the case and events that might have precipitated it.

On January 25, 1982, Judge Hastings had gone to South Carolina to interview Hemphill Pride. Hirschhorn had offered to conduct the interview but was dissuaded when Hastings told him that Pride was angry with white people and would not be honest with him. Hirschhorn, therefore, contacted a lawyer in Columbia, Jack Swerling, and asked if an interview between Pride and Hastings could be held in his office and if, to avoid the appearance of impropriety, Swerling would be present. The interview took place in Swerling's presence and related, according to a file memo by Swerling, primarily to what Pride had told the FBI. Swerling noted at the end of his memo that "Pride was going to take the Judge to a taxi[;] the Judge did not want Pride to take him to the airport." Swerling relayed all of this to Hirschhorn by telephone that night.[97] Pride did, however, drive Judge Hastings to the airport and later testified to the committee that Hastings had told him it was important to remember about letters in his behalf.[98] Although Hirschhorn terminated his relationship with the Hastings case in March, in late April Swerling made another memo for the record after a reporter approached him about the case. Swerling noted that Hirschhorn "indicated, as he had several weeks ago, that the Judge may have acted improperly after leaving my office with Pride and that was one of the reasons he was getting out of the case." Further, Hirschhorn had reassured Swerling that "as far as he knew nothing improper was done until after they left my [Swerling's] office pursuant to what Pride has told the prosecutors."[99]

The investigating committee concluded its hearings in July 1986, the same month that the House of Representatives voted to impeach Harry Claiborne. On August 29, the committee resolved that Judge Hastings had "engaged in conduct prejudicial to the effective and expeditious administration of the business of the courts" and, in direct opposition to the jury verdict, found that "the evidence, considered in its totality, clearly and convincingly establishes that Judge Hastings was engaged in a plan designed to obtain a payment of money from defendants" in return for lenient sentencing. The report includes findings that Hastings "did not draft any letters for Hemphill Pride on October 5, 1981" and, moreover, that he intentionally lied in his criminal trial on at least fifteen separate instances. The committee, therefore, unanimously recommended to the next level of inquiry that Hastings had engaged in conduct that "might constitute one or more grounds for impeachment."[100]

Judges Hodges and Alaimo's original complaint had alleged six separate counts of misconduct, but the five that did not involve bribery
were, without dissent, dismissed. The findings and recommendations
were forwarded to the United States Judicial Conference while Hastings
once more took his defense to the press, where he described the judicial
inquiry as a "witch hunt."[101] The Judicial Conference met within days
of receiving certification from the investigating committee of the Eleventh Circuit but took no action.[102] A special meeting was possible, but
none was called. Justice Warren Burger announced his retirement, and
Associate Justice William Rehnquist replaced him. The Judicial Conference's next regular meeting was in March 1987, and the conference,
with the new chief justice at the helm, certified the case to the House
of Representatives. Minutes of that meeting state only that "no additional . . . investigation [is] appropriate."[103] Justice Rehnquist's certification warranted no more than a brief insert in the *Congressional
Record* under the title "Executive Communications, Etc." in paragraph
917: "A letter from the Chief Justice of the United States, Judicial
Conference of the United States, transmitting a certification that consideration of impeachment against a Federal judge may be warranted,
pursuant to 28 U.S.C. 37(c)(8); to the Committee on the Judiciary."

Additional Complaints

The complaint filed by Judges Hodges and Alaimo was only
the first to be filed against Hastings for misconduct. On September 26,
1984, a second was filed by Thomas M. Tucker, a St. Petersburg lawyer,
that focused on a speech in which Hastings allegedly urged people to
vote for Democratic presidential candidate Walter Mondale. The committee considered that complaint separately but reported no specific
action.[104]

William F. Weld, a former assistant attorney general, filed another
complaint on September 26, 1986, that carried a much more serious
accusation. Weld alleged that Hastings had leaked information about
a confidential electronic wiretap investigation for which Hastings was
the supervising judge.[105] A month earlier, on August 28, 1986, attorneys
for the Public Integrity Section of the Justice Department had served
notice that, after a complete investigation that included grand jury
proceedings, the government declined to prosecute Hastings because
"our proof simply is not firm enough." The assistant U.S. attorneys

investigating the case, however, volunteered to prepare the necessary documentation for a judicial inquiry under the Judicial Conduct Act.[106]

The wiretap leak allegation involved a FBI undercover investigation of corrupt practices in the International Longshoreman's Association that controlled the Port of Miami. That probe was expanded over the next few months to include related corruption schemes in Hialeah and in the tiny municipality of North Bay Village. The inquiry was dependent primarily on the activities and information provided by an undercover agent known as Johnny Rivero, who had ingratiated himself with Kevin "Waxy" Gordon, a former employee of the City of Miami and, at that time, a zoning enforcer in the City of Surfside, also in Dade County. Rivero's findings were sufficiently fruitful that additional undercover agents were introduced into the probe, and federal surveillance centered on several figures.

To build a viable case, the U.S. Attorney's Office decided in July to seek the required court order to intercept telephone conversations of Gordon and other figures. Assistant U.S. Attorneys Roberto Martinez and Mack Schnapp, along with FBI agent Geoffrey Santini, met with Judge Hastings on July 15, 1985, to secure his approval of an order to institute wiretapping. They alleged that probable cause existed to believe that Gordon and others were engaged in racketeering activities, extortion, narcotics distribution, and illegal union activities. Hastings signed the order permitting the wiretaps and sealing the allegations.[107]

The first two progress reports were, at the appropriate times, submitted to Judge Hastings for his concurrence that the investigation was progressing toward the objectives stated in the authorizing order. Roberto Martinez delivered the second progress report on August 29, 1985, and recalled that, between sentencings, Hastings read part of the material and then asked Martinez to join him in his chambers. There, Martinez said, Hastings commented, "pretty heavy stuff," to which Martinez responded, "do you mean Mayor Clark?" At one point Hastings, according to Martinez's recollections, commented, "Clark better be careful because he can get in trouble hanging around Waxy."[108] The remarks about Dade County Mayor Steve Clark were prompted by a footnote in the progress report for August 22, 1985, saying that Waxy Gordon told undercover agent Johnny Rivero that "Steve [Clark] is going to take care of this Hialeah thing for us."[109] Within days, the electronic surveillance process turned up a surprising piece of information in a conversation between Waxy Gordon and his attorney.

Gordon said, "Ah . . . Steve called me over there to tell me that he had heard from Alcee Hastings . . . you know a Federal Judge. There's some rumor that I was involved with . . . ah . . . Clark, Ferguson and a councilman from Hialeah on some deal."[110]

U.S. Attorney Leon Kellner was promptly advised of the apparent leak, and shortly afterward Judge Peter Fay of the Eleventh Judicial Circuit was consulted. Fay talked with Judge Godbold, who recommended that the U.S. attorneys involved discuss the situation with the chief judge of the district, Lawrence King. King met with Kellner and the various assistant U.S. attorneys involved and agreed that redacted progress reports should be given to Judge Hastings in which all references to Mayor Clark's information from Hastings were deleted. The complete progress reports were, thereafter, to be reviewed by Judge King personally. Two of the three major investigations were terminated as a result of the leak.[111]

The FBI confronted Gordon about his involvement in the sale and distribution of cocaine, and he readily agreed to cooperate with the government in return for a plea agreement. He agreed to wear a recording device in a meeting with Steve Clark to pursue the mayor's knowledge of the investigation from Hastings. In the recording of that encounter, Gordon asked Clark how Hastings would know about any investigation:

> Clark: Here, here's what happened. We're down at the Hyatt Regency and he [Hastings] is the guest speaker. He rips the hair on all the fuckin judges' ass, but he's my friend though. . . . I remember saying "hello judge," and he comes to me saying Stevie I want to tell you something . . . don't get near Kevin [long pause] christ almighty, your last name. . . . I don't know how the fuck that he, but Kevin Gordon is involved in some zoning in Hialeah and don't, I'm just telling you, don't, don't just walk away from it. Don't get near it, because he's got problems and that's ah, I came back and told you immediately.[112]

Clark, when interviewed by FBI agents, claimed that he had been at a meeting of the Metro Miami Action Plan (MMAP) at the Regency Hyatt in early September, where Judge Hastings was the guest speaker. Clark recounted that after Hastings's speech, the judge "walked down from the podium and moved directly towards him," shook his hand, and steered him away from anyone else. The judge allegedly said, "stay away from Kevin Gordon; he's hot; he's been using your name in

Hialeah." Clark told the FBI agents that Hastings might have mentioned zoning, but he was not certain.[113]

Waxy Gordon had died, but Clark and Special Agent Christopher Mazzella both testified before the federal grand jury in Miami. An indictment was not forthcoming, and in August 1986, Public Integrity Section attorneys drafted a memo to explain their disinclination to prosecute that listed a number of problems, not the least of which was the impact Hastings's first trial would have on a second one. The prosecutors, however, noted some other significant flaws in their case. They could not, they admitted, isolate any motive, as neither friendship nor politics were implicated and bribery was not a possibility. They were unable even to find a statute that was applicable. Lack of a corrupt motive or an ongoing proceeding foreclosed use of obstruction of justice provisions. They could, they noted, charge Hastings with contempt, which would raise interesting issues, because they would have to prove that "Hastings should be held in contempt of his own order."[114] Shifting the burden to the machinery of the Judicial Conduct Act seemed to be the most viable course.

Chief Judge Paul Roney of the Eleventh Circuit Court of Appeals formed a special investigating committee of only three judges: Circuit Court of Appeals Judge James Hill, U.S. District Court Judge Truman Hobbs, and himself. The services of two Atlanta lawyers were engaged to tackle the matter. Hearings began in April 1988, and Hastings, this time, participated fully. Only seven witnesses were presented, although the investigation had cast a much wider net, and only three of these had a direct impact on the committee's work.

The investigating committee was in a particularly awkward situation, as hearings in the House of Representatives were scheduled to begin on Hastings's impeachment on the other charges in just one month's time. Protecting the confidentiality of grand jury hearings and the testimony of some witnesses called before the judges were obstacles, but the three-judge committee, nonetheless, launched its inquiry on April 12, 1988, by hearing first from Judge Hastings. The judge, on direct examination by his lawyer Terrence Anderson, explained that he did not convey any Title III wiretap information to Mayor Clark after his speech because he did not speak to the mayor at that time. Hastings explained that the meeting started late and that he was in a hurry because a jury trial was on hold at the courthouse pending his arrival. He had asked that his car be retrieved from valet parking early, and he exited to the rear of the stage. The judge offered that in advance of his speech he had spoken to Mayor Clark in the presence of Monsignor Bryan Walsh. Only general greetings, he explained, had been exchanged. Mayor Clark testified consistently with his earlier statements, both those given to FBI agents and the recorded conversation with Waxy Gordon. Thus Clark and Hastings directly contradicted each other. Clark explained that he had called his campaign manager, Pete Ferguson, and asked him to contact Gordon and "have him meet me at the Miami Outboard Club at 11:30."[115] At that meeting, according to Clark, he confronted Gordon and directed him to stop using his name. When Gordon asked his source, Clark claimed to have told him that it was Alcee Hastings.

MAAP employee Joy Royals worked at the Hyatt on the day of Hastings's alleged disclosure to Clark, and her version of events supported Hastings's. She had retrieved the judge from his room before his speech and escorted him to the meeting. Among other things, she brought photographs that were taken at the meeting of both the audience and of the judge making his presentation. More important, she testified that when he finished speaking at about 10:15, she accompanied the judge through a service area, then to the elevators, upstairs to the lobby, and out to his car.[116]

The investigating committee, in concluding its hearings, noted a major discrepancy, one that the investigators had recognized but were unable to reconcile. The call that Clark made to Ferguson that morning was at 8:58, but Hastings, by all accounts, did not finish his speech until around ten. "Even if he [Steve Clark] was Jesse Owens," Judge Hobbes mused, "he would have had difficulty having this conversation with the judge, as I understand it, [and] communicating with Mr. Ferguson." The committee agreed to conclude their report and forward their recommendations to the circuit judicial council within the next two months. Before the judges could finalize their recommendations, the supposedly confidential allegations found their way to the House of Representatives.

Notes

1. Blacks did reach state court benches from time to time. Robert Morris, who served as a magistrate in Boston in 1852, was the first. Their numbers, however, remained small. Jones and King-Robinson, "Choices," 20.

2. One explanation for the predominance on the bench of whites was offered by Judge Edward F. Bell, a black judge in Wayne County, Michigan: "Whenever the white man surrenders to you one of his benches, he has given up one of his most precious tools." As quoted in Ware, "A Sense of History," 36. Blacks fared slightly better on state benches, where, in 1977, eighty were serving. Most of these were concentrated in a few non-southern metropolitan areas. The state courts, like the national ones, were overwhelmingly white (96 percent) and male (98 percent). Ryan et al., *American Trial Judges*, 128.

3. Goldman, "Carter's Judicial Appointments," 348.

4. The memo recommending Hastings was forwarded to President Carter by Harley Frankel, deputy director of the Presidential Personnel Office, on August 17, 1979. Carter Presidential Library, Document No. FG53/ST9/A.

5. Ibid.

6. *Directory of Florida Judges, 1985*, 584.

7. Friend, "Peer Pressure," 82.

8. *U.S. v. Hastings*, Case No. 81–00596–ETG, 1769–70.

9. Ibid., 1771–72.

10. Friend, "Peer Pressure," 83.

11. *Borders v. Reagan*, 518 F. Supp 250 (1981).

12. Dredge had earlier approached Alcohol, Tobacco, and Firearms agent Jimmy Harmon, asking, "what would it be worth to turn up a federal judge?" Harmon knew that the judge must be black, as Dredge had prefaced his question with disparaging comments about blacks and Hispanics, saying that "he wasn't going to let them put him in a position where they were going to run the country." Harmon told Dredge that he was not interested. *In the Matter of the Impeachment Inquiry Concerning U.S. District Judge Alcee L. Hastings*, 24. [Hereafter cited as *House Hearings*.]

13. Dredge said that Borders had already met twice with Trafficante in Miami and was scheduled to meet with him again the next day. Because the two were already in direct contact, Dredge could be of little assistance. U.S. attorneys decided to focus on another case, the Romanos, that appeared to have more potential for building a case.

14. *U.S. v Dredge and Nodolski, et al.*, Case No. K-81–0209 (Baltimore, Maryland).

15. *Report of the Senate Impeachment Trial Committee on the Articles Against Judge Alcee L. Hastings, Hearings*, Part IIIB, 2394. [Hereafter cited as *Senate Hearings*.]

16. Ibid., IIIB, 2025.

17. Ibid., IIIB, 2396–97.

18. 18 U.S.C.A. 1961–63.

19. Sonnett wrote a memo for his own files, dated April 16, 1981, noting that defendant Tom Romano had received a call from Phillip Moscatto about a solicitation for a bribe in the case. *Senate Hearings,* IIIA, 251.

20. The figure of $150,000 was never spoken. "You know what the number is, right?" Borders inquired of Rico, who responded, "Ah, I, I've heard it second hand. I haven't heard it first hand." Borders then wrote the number. Ibid., IIIA, 308–18.

21. Ibid.

22. Ibid., IIIA, 327.

23. 648 F.2d 367 (5th Cir. 1981).

24. 654 F.2d 339 (5th Cir. 1981).

25. See *U.S. v Marubeni America Corp.,* 611 F.2d 763 (9th Cir. 1980).

26. 648 F.2d 367, at 417 (5th Cir. 1981).

27. The forfeiture involved in *Peacock* was reversed, because, relying on *Martino,* only the enterprise and not the income generated by it was affected by the RICO statute. *U.S. v. Peacock,* 654 F.2d 339, at 351 (5th Cir. 1981).

28. Ibid., IIIA, 364–65.

29. Ibid., IIIA, 388.

30. *U.S. v. Hastings,* 1936–37.

31. Hastings was released on a $1,000 personal recognizance bond, while Borders was required to present a $25,000 surety bond. Borders was arraigned separately on January 6, 1982. Docket Sheet, *U.S. v. Borders and Hastings,* Case No. 81–00596–CR–ETG.

32. Shorter, representing Borders, objected strenuously to Hastings's motion, which he explained resulted from conferences between himself and Hirschhorn that he had assumed were confidential. "I certainly did not expect to see spread out in a motion that would fully alert the Government as to what strategy was being formulated at that time." *U.S. v. Borders and Hastings,* Pretrial Motion Hearing, 38.

33. Ibid., 39.

34. Ibid., 63–64.

35. The Fifth Circuit that included Florida was divided into two circuits subsequent to Hastings's consideration of the *Romano* case. Florida was placed in the newly created Eleventh Circuit, sitting in Atlanta.

36. *U.S. v. Hastings,* 681 F.2d 706 (11th Cir. 1982), at 711. Hastings requested a rehearing and rehearing *en banc* by the Eleventh Circuit, both of which were denied on September 22, 1982 (689 F.2d 706 [11th Cir. 1982]). The U.S. Supreme Court denied a request for a stay the next January (459 U.S. 1094 [1983]) and *certiorari* the following month (459 U.S. 1203 [1983]).

37. Border's appeals were all unsuccessful. See *U.S. v. Borders,* 693 F.2d
1318 (11th Cir. 1982); *Borders v. U.S.,* 461 U.S. 905 (1983), *certiorari* denied.

38. Television coverage had been strictly prohibited in federal courts
since *Estes v. U.S.* in 1965. The motion denied by Judge Gignoux on
November 30 was also appealed by intervenors in the case (Post-News-
week Stations) to the Eleventh Circuit Court of Appeals. The three-judge
appellate panel rejected the claims: "Just because television coverage is
not constitutionally prohibited does not mean that television coverage is
constitutionally mandated." *U.S. v. Hastings,* 695 F.2d 1278 (11th Cir. 1983),
at 1280. The court's interests in maintaining proper decorum and in as-
suring a fair trial, moreover, were held to take priority over any claim of
access by the press. Cited at ibid., 1284. A petition for rehearing *en banc*
was likewise denied in May 1983. *U.S. v. Hastings,* 704 F.2d 559 (11th Cir.
1983).

39. *U.S. v. Hastings,* Case No. 81–00596–CR-ETG, 2503.

40. Ibid., 2506–7.

41. Ibid., 2511.

42. Ibid., 2515.

43. Ibid., 2525–27.

44. Ibid., 2541–48.

45. Ibid., 2549.

46. Hastings and Pride had been friends since their days at Florida
A&M Law School, a friendship that Hastings described as "very, very
close"; the men are godfathers to each other's children. Ibid., 1782–83.

47. *Senate Hearings,* IIIB, 2843–45.

48. A letter from Pride to Hastings, dated July 18, 1980, in which
Hemphill asked Hastings to "raise some money to help keep me going
and pay Julius [Pride's lawyer]," was Defense Exhibit 27.

49. Hastings testified that "he [Borders] asked again about the financial
consideration for Hemphill, as he did in just about every conversation
that I had with him, either by phone or in person." *U.S. v. Hastings,* 1825.

50. Ibid., 1855.

51. Pride, as Hastings himself noted, testified that he had not written
anything down for Borders. Hastings explained, however, that "this is a
conversation with Mr. Borders and I and this is what I thought Mr. Borders
meant." Ibid., 2182.

52. Hastings described Borders's telephone manner as "different as any
that I have ever known, and I have heard countless witnesses describe
that manner and I concur in large part with everything that they have
said. . . . A lot of times when you talk with Bill on the telephone, you
know what you're saying but you may not always know what he is saying."
Ibid., 1778.

53. Ibid., 2187–99.

54. Ibid., 2540.

55. Ibid., 2047–52.

56. Ibid., 2064.

57. Ibid., 1844.

58. Ibid., 2011.

59. Ibid., 2115–20.

60. Ibid., 1914–15.

61. Ibid., 1919.

62. Ibid., 2219–32.

63. Ibid., 2233.

64. Ibid., 2548. Hastings's mother, Mildred Hastings, testified that her son had called to tell her to allow the FBI to wait for him and to search the apartment if they had a warrant. She substantiated Hastings's claim that he had come home before going to Williams's house. When asked if she had told the FBI agent who called later that she did not know where Hastings was, Mrs. Hastings answered, "I probably did." Ibid., 797–807.

65. Ibid., 1967–68.

66. Slevin, "Judge Vows to Return to Federal Bench," A-6.

67. Skene, "Alcee Hastings Faces His Next 'Trial,' " A-14.

68. Stuart, "Judge Expects New Attacks after Acquittal in Bribe Plot," Y-15.

69. Liff, "Hastings Trial Stirs Nest of Ethical Legal Questions," 1.

70. House Hearings, 288.

71. U.S. v. Borders, 693 F.2d 1318 (1982), at 1327.

72. Hearings before the Subcommittee on Criminal Justice , 435–43. [Hereafter cited as Judicial Inquiry.]

73. See News Release, 735 F.2d. 1276 (1983).

74. Edward Gignoux, who had presided over the trial, remained in charge of the case through June 24, when he issued an oral decision in preliminary issues of the investigation. In August, all judges in the district recused and disqualified themselves from participating in the case. Eugene A. Gordon, senior judge for the Middle District of North Carolina, assumed responsibility for it on September 23, 1983.

75. In re Petition to Inspect and Copy Grand Jury Materials, 576 F. Supp. 1275 (1983), at 1280.

76. Ibid., at 1281.

77. Ibid., at 1282. That ruling was affirmed (735 F.2d 1261 [11th Cir. 1984]).

78. Hastings v. Judicial Conference of the United States, 593 F. Supp. 1371 (1984), at 1383.

79. Hastings v. Judicial Conference, 770 F.2d 1093 (D.C., 1985), at 1110.

80. *Judicial Inquiry,* 493.

81. *In re Certain Complaints under Investigation by an Investigating Committee of the Judicial Council of the Eleventh Circuit,* 610 F. Supp. 169 (1985).

82. The court, reasoning from the ruling in *Blair v. U.S.* that challenged the Federal Corrupt Practices Act, concluded that allegations of unconstitutionality did not bar witnesses from testifying before a grand jury. *In re Matter of Certain Complaints Under Investigation,* 783 F.2d 1488 (11th Cir. 1986), at 1501.

83. Ibid., at 1510.

84. Doar's fees, at the bargain basement price of only $90 per hour, came to $560,000. The billable hours of his associate Stewart Webb (also at a discounted fee), his paralegal, and their expenses totaled between $800,000 and $1 million. *House Hearings,* 285.

85. Ibid., 127.

86. Dredge did not want to be sworn when he appeared before the committee because, "I really don't believe that I should be here. I entered into an agreement with the United States Government. I say that because it's, they have been making or attempting to make a distinction with me about three different parts of the government. . . . When I entered into this agreement . . . [it was] with the entire United States government." He also objected that his testiony could jeopardize his life: "You keep putting me in jeopardy. You guys don't walk down the street and wonder if somebody is going to blow your brains out. I do and did and have." *Report of the Senate Impeachment Trial Committee, . . . Exhibits Admitted into Evidence,* IIIB, 1999–2003. [Hereafter cited as *Senate Exhibits.*]

87. Ibid., 2001.

88. Ibid., 2029.

89. Dredge was asked: "Did you conclude that . . . Mr. Borders did have an arrangement with Judge Hastings with respect to —" Dredge interrupted with, "Absolutely. No question in my mind." The reason for this conclusion was that Borders accurately predicted the actions that Hastings would take in the *Romano* case. Ibid., 2032.

90. *U.S. v. Hastings,* Case No. 81–00596–CR-ETG, 2542.

91. *Judicial Inquiry,* 292.

92. Ibid., 261–69.

93. Ibid., 271.

94. Ibid., 286.

95. Slevin, "Justice Vows to Return to Federal Bench," 16A.

96. *Judicial Inquiry,* 167.

97. Ibid., 763.

98. Ibid., 167–68.

99. Ibid., 764–65.

100. Ibid., 341–58.

101. Shenon, "Judge Acquitted in 1983 Says Panel Wants Him Impeached," Y-14.

102. The Judicial Conference is a group of twenty-seven federal judges, including the chief justice of the Supreme Court and judges from each of the eleven circuits and the District of Columbia. Under the Judicial Conduct Act of 1980, the conference is the body that refers investigations to the House of Representatives for impeachment proceedings.

103. *Report of the Proceedings of the Judicial Conference of the United States*, 303.

104. *Judicial Inquiry*, 5.

105. *Hearings before the Subcommittee on Criminal Justice, . . . , Materials Relating to Wiretap Disclosure*, 89–91.

106. Ibid., 84–85.

107. When a Title III wiretap is authorized, the supervising judge must not only agree that there exists probable cause for the interceptions to begin, but must also monitor the results of the taps at periodic intervals, all of which were duly specified in the initial order. Ibid., 676–85.

108. Ibid., 315–16.

109. The footnote in the report referred to a meeting at the Miami Outboard Club on August 22, 1985, at which Rivero reported that Gordon had told him about Clark. Ibid., 925–26.

110. Ibid., 952.

111. Ibid., 337–44.

112. The conversation would present problems for Clark later when it became public as a result of hearings before the Senate: "Clark: 'How in the hell would he know that?' Gordon: 'I have no idea.' Clark: 'Did you deal with any spooks on that thing?' " Ibid., 124–25.

113. Ibid., 1172.

114. Ibid., 82–83.

115. Ibid., 415.

116. Royals testified that at about 9:40 she had checked the judge out of his room and sent for his car from valet parking. She then went behind the speaker's platform in the main ballroom, where she crouched, waiting for Hastings to complete his speech. Ibid., 520–27.

5

Hastings before Congress

Alcee Hastings's impeachment proceedings in Congress were markedly different from those of Harry Claiborne's. Whereas Claiborne's conviction made his impeachment and conviction a foregone conclusion, Hastings's acquittal made his case a particularly sticky one. It could not be treated in the almost pro forma manner with which the House had acted on Claiborne's case. The Hastings proceedings, both in the press and before Congress, were further complicated by his claims of persecution, first by federal agents and then by other judges. His crime, he claimed, was being a black, outspoken, liberal activist, far more serious allegations than Claiborne's charges of selective prosecution and targeting. His acquittal, moreover, allowed the introduction of a new variable into the equation, Would congressional action constitute double jeopardy? The flamboyant judge managed to capture national media attention with his protestations, whereas most of the coverage of Claiborne's case was in the Nevada press.

The House and Senate had dispatched their obligations in the Claiborne case rather quickly, but Hastings used every possible delaying tactic, with long bouts of legal and political sparring and a mountain of motions. The mood of the times, however, was against him. During the more than two and a half years that his case was before Congress, public officials of all political stripes and all levels of government were under attack for abusing their offices. All of Hastings's constitutional and partisan maneuvers could not save him from removal. His only victory was his unanimous vindication by the Senate on the wiretap leak charge. The Hastings case is a landmark, for the judge was not just the sixth judge to be removed from office; he was the first to be found guilty by the Senate after an acquittal by a jury.

Preliminary Rounds

Alcee Hastings and his defense team took the offensive by filing a 169–page report and petition to the House calling for special hearings. The document likened the judicial inquiry to "the Star Chamber or a Moscow political trial." Hastings's counsel, Terrence Anderson, claimed to be particularly irritated by the judiciary's refusal to release its 381–page report, although both he and Hastings had been allowed to review the document.The defense's strategy was to attribute racial motives to the judges who had investigated the case, and Anderson predicted that "the judge [will] have very substantial support on Capitol Hill."[1] The Judicial Conference's certification that impeachment might be warranted moved onto the agenda of the House of Representatives on March 23, 1987, when Representatives James Sensenbrenner and Henry Hyde filed House Resolution 128, "impeaching Alcee L. Hastings, judge of the United States District Court for the Southern District of Florida, of high crimes and misdemeanors."[2]

Representative Peter Rodino, chair of the House Judiciary Committee, in July 1987, requested access to the grand jury materials in the indictments of Hastings and Borders, which Chief Judge Lawrence King granted. Hastings, however, promptly moved for a stay, and an out-of-circuit judge, John Butzner, was assigned to the case. Butzner affirmed the earlier order, citing the House's power to impeach, Federal Rules of Criminal Procedure, and the inherent power of the district court to disclose grand jury proceedings.[3] Hastings was also granted access to the record, but, contrary to his request, the materials were not made public immediately. He appealed but was unsuccessful in each of his attempts to thwart Judiciary Committee access to the documents or, later, to grand jury materials related to the wiretap allegations.[4]

The report of the judicial investigation was finally made public in October 1987, an event Hastings heralded with dramatic fanfare. He was in his element when he held an "impromptu" press conference following his collection of the report. He kidded with reporters, decrying the $392 airplane ticket and the line in which he had stood to receive his copies of the report. Before he departed, he quipped, "when I determine I no longer want to be a judge, then I'll no longer be one" and added, perhaps more prophetically, "I wasn't born a judge, and I don't have to die one."[5]

Hastings exploited the racist angle while adding the double jeopardy twist to the case. The racism argument played well on his home turf of Miami, where one of his supporters urged that "no white judge would be put through this."[6] He also found a wider audience for his allegations, with his case featured on national broadcasts. Proving racism in the investigation was elusive, however, and the allegation was eventually totally defused.

The double jeopardy defense proved more fruitful. "It walks like double jeopardy, it talks like double jeopardy, it sounds like double jeopardy," and, Hastings asserted, "it feels like double jeopardy."[7] Even the conservative columnist James Kilpatrick wrote that impeachment should be barred, "not because he is innocent—I suspect that the fellow is as guilty as Cain—but because the ancient principle of double jeopardy ought to be jealously guarded."[8] The judicial investigating committee, however, concluded that impeachment did not constitute double jeopardy, for "no one would seriously argue that double jeopardy would apply if Judge Hastings had been convicted."[9]

Hastings's impeachment was referred to the House Judiciary Committee, but there was no enthusiasm for the task. Tackling Harry Claiborne's case had been difficult and time-consuming enough—and he had already been convicted by a jury. Hastings's charges of racism made members of the House, all of whom faced reelections in the fall, less than comfortable. "It's a lose-lose situation," a congressional insider was quoted as lamenting, "not only politically for the members, but it is a disaster for the system."[10] Most in Congress wished that Hastings would, like others before him, simply resign. Rodino had difficulty persuading a subcommittee of the larger House Judiciary Committee to assume the job, and at least two chairs, Barney Frank and Robert Kastenmeier, declined. The third subcommittee chair whom Rodino approached, John Conyers, accepted[11] and, as a liberal black democrat from Michigan, was the perfect choice.[12] Any apprehensions that Conyers might coddle a "brother" were quickly dispelled when the subcommittee began its deliberations.[13]

House Action

The subcommittee, flanked by a legal staff of ten lawyers and three clerks, began hearings on the morning of May 18, 1988. After procedural formalities were out of the way, the committee moved to the central event, the ten-minute opening statement by Alcee Hastings. Two hundred years earlier, Warren Hastings had offered his defense before the British House of Commons with great formality and dignity,[14] and Alcee Hastings's was almost eerie in its similarity: "I come here with no trepidation." He then recounted the injustices of the criminal trial, the jury verdict, the duplication of evidence at the trial, and the judicial investigation. "I am," he declared, "not guilty, but not free."[15]

Hastings's assertions of innocence were countered by John Doar, who dryly but thoroughly tied all of the pieces of evidence together and wove a convincing tale of complicity between Borders and Hastings and of attempts by Hastings to hide his involvement. He testified, moreover, that neither racial motives nor racial feelings had tainted the original prosecution. His testimony was broken to introduce various taped conversations between Hastings and Borders and to explain the inferences that might be drawn from them. Committee members, despite Doar's exhaustive presentation, questioned him closely on a number of points.

Twelve witnesses appeared before the committee, several of whom had been quizzed earlier by the Judicial Investigating Committee, and there was little, if any, variation in their recollections of events. The only really new angle on the bribery scheme was the testimony of Professor Roger W. Shuy, a linguist at Georgetown University, who analyzed the crucial October 5 conversation between Borders and Hastings and verified that, using discourse analysis of twelve taped conversations involving Borders and transcripts of Hastings's testimony, the two were indeed speaking in code on the telephone that day.[16]

William Borders, who had not testified in his own defense or at Hastings's trial or for any investigation, was called but only made a statement: "I was convicted . . . , held in contempt after refusing to testify in the grand jury. I served 30 days in prison. After serving 30 months at Allenwood and being on parole, paying a $35,000 fine and returning $25,000, I believe my legal debt to society expired May 22, 1988, after release from parole. . . . I respectfully refuse to answer any and all questions under the 1st, 4th, 5th, and 8th Amendments to the U.S. Constitution."[17] The committee took no action to coerce Borders because of the additional delay that would be caused, the limited range of remedies available, and a suspicion that his testimony would not be credible anyway.

The judicial inquiry into the complaint that Judge Hastings had illegally disclosed wiretap information had not been concluded, but the allegation, nonetheless, reached the House committee. Assistant U.S. Attorney Roberto Martinez, Mayor Steve Clark, Agent Geoffrey Santini, and Special Agent Christopher Mazzella were each examined about Hastings's role in the leak, while Joy Royals and Monsignor Bryan Walsh testified that Mayor Clark's version of events could not be accurate. The most damaging inroads to Clark's explanation of how he knew of the FBI investigation were made, however, when Hastings's lawyer questioned the mayor about his many contacts with FBI personnel. Clark admitted that he played golf with two agents and knew another. He was even acquainted with Paul Rico, who had posed as Frank Romano in the sting operation that caught Borders. Clark, however, insisted that none of them had told him about an investigation of Waxy Gordon. Hastings's lawyer even questioned the validity of a lie detector test that Clark had taken to verify his veracity in the Hastings allegation, a polygraph examination that had also been conducted by an FBI agent.[18]

Judge Hastings was invited by the subcommittee, after all other witnesses had been questioned, to testify in his own behalf. Citing instructions from counsel, however, he declined the invitation.[19] That decision drew mixed reactions. Representative Patrick Swindall said, "I have to draw the inference that he has something to hide," while George Gekas took the position that "you could also draw the conclusion that he has nothing to add."[20] Terry Anderson, Hastings's attorney, summarized the testimony and argued that the bribery charge evidence was merely hearsay because "the witnesses weren't there." His most direct attack on the bribery allegations, however, was "when the jury speaks, it is over." He also discredited the wiretap charge with the testimony of Monsignor Walsh and Joy Royals, both of whom contradicted Mayor Clark. "He [Hastings] has been called to account," Anderson concluded, "his accusers never have."[21] After only seven days of testimony, the subcommittee closed its hearings on June 9, 1988.

The committee reconvened the next month to consider seventeen articles of impeachment against Alcee Hastings. Article 1 addressed Hastings's conspiracy with Borders to solicit a bribe from the Romano brothers, and Articles 2 through 15 alleged that Hastings had lied or fabricated evidence in his criminal trial. Article 16 charged that Hastings had leaked confidential Title III wiretap information, and Article 17

was a catchall article that summarized the preceding sixteen and alleged
that Hastings had, through commission of all of those corrupt activities,
brought "disrepute on the Federal courts." Representative Conyers,
before the vote, stated that his decision to vote for impeachment was
the most difficult he had made in his twenty-four years in Congress
but that "we must demand that all persons live up to the same high
standards that we demand of everyone else."[22] The committee unanimously voted to forward all seventeen articles to the full committee
that also voted favorably on all articles.[23]

Peter Rodino, on August 3, rose to call a privileged resolution before
the House, Resolution 499 impeaching Judge Alcee Hastings of high
crimes and misdemeanors. The clerk of the House read the full text of
the seventeen articles, after which Rodino addressed the novel circum-
stance of impeaching a judge who had been acquitted previously in a
jury trial. The processes, he explained, "are two separate and distinct
proceedings"; the critical difference was that "we are not here to punish
Judge Hastings."[24] John Conyers summarized the evidence and emphasized Hastings's failure to testify. That "left uncontroverted these
numerous damning allegations." He also raised the subplot of racism:
"When I first heard of this matter, I and other Members of Congress . . . were skeptical. A charismatic and outspoken black judge, whose
progressive views I share, was involved. I then paid close attention to
the possibility that racism, not misconduct, was involved."[25]

That, however, he concluded was not the case. "Judge Hastings'
conduct, evaluated by the standard applicable to all Federal judges,
has not measured up to what it should be."[26] Conyers's speech was
followed by others from the subcommittee, all of whom were persuaded
that Hastings should be impeached. Only Representative Joseph Early
of Massachusetts offered a counter argument, the politicization of the
system.[27] The vote of the House was, not unexpectedly, overwhelmingly
against Judge Hastings: 413 for impeachment and a mere three against.[28]
A committee of House managers—Rodino and Conyers, along with
Don Edwards, John Bryant, Hamilton Fish, and George Gekas—was
appointed to prosecute the case before the Senate, and necessary fund-
ing authority was granted to them.[29]

Senate Action

Early in the following year, Senate Resolution 38 was introduced to try Hastings, but the judge pursued alternative routes to solve

his dilemma. He announced, on January 6, 1989, that he had blocked arteries and had been ordered by his doctors to avoid stress. The staff counsel for the House managers, however, said that he had not been contacted about a possible delay in the trial.[30] Hastings's attorneys apparently also explored briefly the possibility of negotiating a conclusion to the case whereby Hastings might retire and forego the Senate trial, but those discussions were not fruitful.[31] Hastings and his lawyers were granted a hearing before the full Senate on March 16 to ask that all of the articles of impeachment that related to the bribery charge on which he had previously been acquitted be quashed; the wiretap disclosure was not included. Once again, Hastings took his case to the public. Speaking on a Washington radio talk program that had a primarily black audience, he invited listeners to pack the galleries and "witness this charade," while the talk show's host hammered on the racist angle of the prosecution.[32]

Seventy senators listened to Hastings's plea that he had "not committed a crime" and, moreover, that to try him on the bribery articles constituted double jeopardy. "Common sense and human instinct" argued against a second trial, he said, because "in America, the government only gets one shot." Representative Bryant, for the House managers, countered that impeachment and trial did not constitute double jeopardy, that the case "involves the most egregious misconduct by a federal official" because Hastings "conspired to sell his public office for personal gain."[33] Hastings's position failed, and Senate Resolution 38 passed.

A bipartisan evidentiary committee to hear testimony and receive evidence, a device first used in the Claiborne trial, was appointed and named Jeff Bingaman of New Mexico as chair and Arlen Specter of Pennsylvania as vice chair.[34] The two sides in the case, thereafter, began their legal sparring over discovery, evidence, and witnesses. The committee acted on various pretrial issues, among them Hastings's witness list of sixty-six names ranging from retired Chief Justice Warren Burger, all judges on the investigating committee, all judges who had served with Hastings, and Rudolph Giuliani from the Justice Department to a long list of government attorneys and FBI agents. The list "is about as broad a net as you can cast of everybody in the world," Senator Rudman observed.[35] Hastings's defense team also raised its persistent request for funds to cover the defense.[36] The committee met sporadically throughout April, May, and June to dispose of a witness list for the defense (pared to only thirty) and various stipulations, motions, and statements.

On July 10, 1989, the Evidentiary Committee began its hearings, which would continue through the summer, with the District's steamy weather accentuated by the television lights. The senators, who would arrive in their business suits, soon adopted the habit of shedding their jackets and rolling up their shirt sleeves. The hearings opened with a statement by lead House Manager Jack Bryant, a statement that ran parallel to the closing argument of Reid Weingarten in Hastings's criminal trial. Anderson, speaking for Hastings, introduced the circumstances that suggested political motivations for the proceedings against his client, placing particular emphasis on a decision by Judge Hastings that concerned Haitian boat people.[37] He attacked the competence and motivation of the FBI, William Dredge, and others who had a part in accusing Hastings in 1981.

The committee hearings extended from July 10 to August 3, with eighteen full days devoted to the case. They were divided into two discrete inquiries, one dealing with the bribery charges and a second with the wiretap disclosures. The committee had difficulty maintaining a quorum, and, aside from a few minor events, the proceedings were largely monotonous. Most evidence on the bribery and cover-up charges was a replay of that first presented in the criminal trial in Miami and later in the judiciary hearings in Atlanta. Characters in the drama, who had been only disembodied voices in other hearings, in particular Dredge and Borders, were produced but offered little, if any, new insights into the guilt or innocence of Alcee Hastings.

The lead witness was James Deichert, who had prosecuted the *Romano* case before Hastings in 1980 and 1981; he set the stage for introduction and authentication of all of the orders and documentation in that case. He was followed by William Dredge, who testified in closed session for his own protection.[38] Those who might have corroborated or contradicted his accounts of the bribery scheme were no longer available. Many of the organized crime figures involved in the original case—Willie Dara, the Romano brothers, Phillip Moscatto, and Santo Trafficante—were dead; Joseph Nesline was ill and mentally incompetent to testify. Dredge's recollection of dates, times, and specific events was greatly improved since his testimony before the judicial panel in Atlanta, although he assured the committee that he had always testified truthfully and had no intent to mislead.[39] Anderson, on Hastings's behalf, hammered at Dredge's credibility and even charged that Dredge was merely acting as underworld figure Nesline's bagman in the bribery scheme.[40]

Roger Shuy, the Georgetown University linguist, presented essentially the same analysis of the "coded" October 5, 1981, conversation between Borders and Hastings, but this time Hastings's team vigorously protested admission of his testimony. "Whether it is witchcraft or science," argued Anderson, "is open to question." The meaning of an ordinary conversation, he continued, has been committed "throughout history, civil and criminal, to juries."[41] The committee, however, heard Shuy's assessment that the crucial conversation had all of the characteristics of a code—repeated words, pause fillers, false starts near significant words, and logical inconsistency.[42]

A long list of people was offered by the House to testify about airline tickets, about Borders's "unexpected" arrival at the Sheraton Hotel in Washington on September 11, 1981, and about Hastings's dinner at the Fontainbleau on September 16. Hemphill Pride was again presented to explain both what had happened when he told Hastings that Borders had been arrested and about his conversation with Hastings in South Carolina after leaving Jack Swerling's office. Prior testimony of others was admitted into the record, and FBI agents and government attorneys involved in the investigation were paraded before the committee. One of the few interesting developments was the notation by the Romano brothers' appellate lawyer, Neal Sonnett, that the conviction of the brothers was eventually overturned by a higher court and that his clients, the defendants in the case, had "very high regard for Judge Hastings" and for his integrity.[43] William Borders appeared under a grant of immunity from a U.S. District Court but again refused to answer questions although he faced civil contempt charges for his refusal.[44]

A new angle was provided by committee response to FBI tactics in deciding to arrest Borders when they did. Agent William Murphy explained that the Bureau "did not feel that we could successfully follow the money for more than a very, very short period of time." Senator Patrick Leahy, noting the millions of dollars that had subsequently been spent investigating Hastings, responded sarcastically, "do you base the substance of your case on whether you have got $25,000 or $100,000 in buy money out there?"[45] Martin Raskin, a former assistant U.S. attorney in Miami, also testified that the decision to arrest Borders and the attempt to persuade him to "flip" (cooperate) "was a terrible idea." Both he and former U.S. Attorney Atlee Wampler had even tried to persuade the Public Integrity Section to change its strategy.[46]

The defense's presentations included few witnesses who could offer information on the bribery scheme. Only two new twists were introduced into the scenario: testimony by FBI agent Kendall Shull about conversations he had with Joseph Nesline and evidence by Kenneth Robinson, a lawyer who had been approached to represent Dredge. Shull, who in an undercover capacity had become close to Nesline, reported two separate conversations in which Nesline said that "he did not believe that Borders had any control or influence over Judge Hastings . . . and that Mr. Borders was scamming his friend."[47] Robinson, a lawyer whom Nesline introduced to Dredge, testified that Dredge, when he wanted to retain Robinson, had tried to elicit guarantees that a judge or a district attorney could be reached to fix his case. Robinson never represented Dredge but reported that after Borders's and Hastings's criminal trials were over he ran into Nesline. He told Robinson that "Borders was puffing, and he got out-conned by a con man, and that Hastings wasn't involved."[48]

The article alleging that Hastings had leaked confidential wiretap information to Mayor Steve Clark drew a more lively round of testimony. The House managers presented Assistant U.S. Attorney Roberto Martinez and two FBI agents who had handled the zoning corruption case, all of whom testified much as they had before the judicial investigating committee about the leak and their response to it. Mayor Clark also related how Hastings had approached him after speaking at the Metro Miami Action Plan (MMAP) meeting to warn him away from Waxy Gordon. Hastings himself conducted the cross-examination of Martinez and forcefully persisted in demonstrating the narrowness of the FBI's inquiry into the leak. "So then it was automatic," Hastings challenged, "if Clark said it, it was true?" When Martinez answered in the negative, Hastings followed with the question, "Who in your office was interviewed?"[49] At least six people in the U.S. Attorney's office, in addition to typists and secretaries, knew of the investigation and of the wiretap, Martinez admitted, but none was questioned. Hastings, through his cross-examination, raised at least two other alternative theories for the wiretap information.[50] Senator Rudman also asked Martinez about the investigation of other possible sources of the leak, but there had been none.[51] To rebut the House managers' argument, Hastings's defense team introduced four people who were involved in the MMAP conference the morning that Hastings allegedly shared the information with Clark. All testified consistently that Hastings left the speaker's platform to the rear and could not have talked with Mayor Clark after his speech.[52]

The defense also presented a number of FBI agents who were golfing partners of Clark's in the summer of 1985. Agent Tom Dowd and his wife, who was employed by Paul Rico at Miami Jai Alai, had been married by Mayor Clark. Dowd testified that he had, in July 1985, received a call from Glenn Whittle, an insurance agent and part of the golf foursome with Mayor Clark, asking if there was an investigation underway that involved Clark and his campaign manager Pete Ferguson. Dowd prepared a memo about the call for the record, in which he noted that Whittle said he was asking because of something said by "your wife's boss [Paul Rico]." Rico, when questioned, absolutely denied any knowledge of the investigation. Senator Leahy raised a significant question about Rico's veracity, because the supreme court of Rhode Island had recently upheld an allegation that Rico had directed a witness to testify falsely.[53] Whittle failed to recall anything about the call but suggested that if he did make it, his information was from the newspaper.[54] Anthony Amoroso, an FBI agent involved in the original bribery investigation of Hastings, and FBI agent Jerry Forrester, moreover, were golf partners who played regularly with Clark and Whittle.[55] The defense had, in short, developed at least a substantial alternative theory for how Clark came to know about the investigation.

Alcee Hastings's testimony on his own behalf was the main event, but his explanation of the Borders' bribery scheme was much the same as in his trial. However, he went article by article through the list of impeachable offenses with which he was charged and attempted to explain each. Cross examination by Alan Baron for the House was virtually identical on the bribery charges to Reid Weingarten's in the 1983 criminal trial. When Baron moved to the allegations of falsifying testimony in the criminal trial, Hastings was both contrite and sincere, saying that any discrepancies in his trial testimony were the result of honest mistakes.[56]

On the first round of questioning by the senators, the October 5, 1981, telephone call and Hastings's lack of animosity toward Borders were the primary areas probed. Senator Specter captured the problem when he commented that Hastings appeared to be angry when he talked about the FBI, about the judges who investigated him, and about others whom he thought persecuted him, but, when he discussed Borders, "there isn't the passion in your voice . . . , there isn't the outrage."[57] Warren Rudman pushed the judge for an explanation of the coincidence of events that formed the circumstantial case. Hastings replied that the incidents seemed to form a pattern only when "telescoped," for many other things were occurring simultaneously and accounted for some of the "coincidences."[58]

In closing arguments, Jack Bryant, speaking for the House managers, and Terry Anderson, representing the judge, each offered droll summations that rivaled one another for dryness. Their comments were tied to the facts and their presentations were straightforward, although each tried to conjure some drama to retain the interest of the weary committee. Anderson softened his professorial discourse near the end as he turned to his client and said, "there is a man who, in my view, is touched with greatness."[59] The hearings that had consumed most of the summer concluded unceremoniously with several procedural matters. The committee, thereafter, distilled their findings into a 172-page document and transmited that neutral report to the Senate.[60]

The Senate Trial

The report of the committee, along with volumes of committee transcripts and more volumes reproducing all of the evidence, were provided to the full Senate along with video tapes of the entire hearing. The final act in the trial commenced on October 18, 1989, when the sergeant-at-arms rose and pronounced again the words "Hear ye, hear ye, hear ye," calling the Senate into session as a high court of impeachment. The well of the Senate had again been converted into a quasi-courtroom, with the House managers and the defense team facing the senators.

Closing arguments of two hours for each side began with three presentations by the House managers. Representative Jack Bryant of Texas addressed the issue of overturning a jury verdict and shunted it aside by noting that the case encompassed the conclusions of two juries; one had convicted Borders of conspiracy and one had acquitted Hastings. The House, he asserted, was moved to impeach by facts that were "overwhelming,"[61] and dismissed the "rainmaking" defense by arguing that Borders would not be so foolish as to try to trick organized crime boss Santo Trafficante. There was more "than a cloud of suspicion," Bryant concluded: "it is a mountain of evidence pointing to his certain guilt."[62] He then deferred to George Gekas, who summarized the case against Hastings on Article 16, the wiretap disclosure.

The most moving presentation by the House managers was that of John Conyers, who expressed his sadness at urging "the removal of one of the handful of black judges who presently occupy the federal bench." Hastings, he argued, had forfeited his right to hold that position because "we did not wage the civil rights struggle in order to substitute one form of judicial corruption for another."[63] The mass of evidence required that Hastings be impeached, he urged, and nothing "is wrong with circumstantial evidence."[64]

Hastings finally rose to answer the charges and submitted that he did not believe that "outstanding oratory or word wizardry" would convince the assembled senators. He then launched into the best of his own ringing rhetoric to set aside racism as his defense and to explain how time had soothed some of his anger at Borders. "I am not guilty of having committed any crime," he proclaimed, "and that is my defense, was my defense in 1983, and has been and is and will remain until I die, my defense."[65] His final plea for fairness was met with applause in the gallery. Patricia Williams then stood to address the wiretap disclosure and highlight how Mayor Clark's version of the events "makes no sense."[66] The final words to be spoken on behalf of Judge Hastings were those of Terry Anderson, who, after reviewing the evidence, allowed that Hastings was unable to dispel suspicions, but "they [the House managers] could not prove guilt."[67] His plea was one directed at history, at the record of the Senate that had twice failed to convict in contested impeachment cases.

The Senate reconvened the next day in a closed session to deliberate Hastings's removal from office, and their discussions extended almost seven and a half hours, until 9:30 at night. The hearings, although not part of the public record, were revealed in part by the statements for the record that various senators offered after the vote. Both Jeff Bingaman, who had chaired the evidentiary committee, and Arlen Specter, who served as vice chair, declared their belief that an acquittal vote was appropriate. Bingaman based his decision on the ambiguity of the proof,[68] while Specter was persuaded by the significant gaps in the evidence, the absence of a "smoking gun," and the persuasiveness of Hastings's own testimony.[69] They were joined by Senator Joseph Lieberman and, on three counts, by Slade Gorton, both of whom had served on the committee.[70] Of those senators who heard all of the testimony, only David Durenberger spoke on the record to explain his decision to vote guilty on some counts.[71] Those who rose to explain their vote for conviction emphasized the October 5, 1981, "coded" conversation between Hastings and Borders as decisive.

The final verdict on Alcee Hastings's fitness to serve as a U.S. district judge was made by a vote of the full Senate on October 20, 1989. Although the vote was, in some ways, mixed, Hastings was found guilty by the requisite two-thirds majority of conspiring with Borders to solicit a bribe (Article 1), lying in his trial about his complicity (Articles 2 and 4), lying about the dinner at the Fontainbleau Hotel (Article 5), lying about his instructions to his law clerk (Article 7), lying about the "letters for Hemp" (Article 8), and fabricating the three documents that purported to be the "letters for Hemp" (Article 9). By prior agreement, no votes were taken on Articles 10 through 15, the outcomes of which were predetermined by votes on earlier articles. Hastings was acquitted by a vote of 48 to 47 on Article 6, which charged that he had lied about not expecting Borders to appear at the Sheraton Hotel in Washington. Article 16, the charge of wiretap disclosure, brought unanimous vindication, a vote of zero guilty and 95 not guilty. The summary article, Article 17, also failed to achieve a two-thirds majority (60 guilty to 35 not guilty), probably because it included in its particulars the wiretap disclosure charge.[72] Alcee Hastings was then the sixth U.S. judge to be convicted by the Senate and removed from office.

Hastings won the affection of some of the senators who came to know him through the hearings, but his case was considered at a time when the issue of the ethics of public officials was capturing the headlines. Earlier in the year, former Senator John Tower had been rejected by the Senate for the post of secretary of defense because of his alleged drinking problems; the House Ethics Committee charged Speaker Jim Wright with sixty-nine violations, and his resignation followed shortly; and Wright's expected successor, Democratic Whip Tony Coehlo, resigned in advance of an investigation in May. The Senate Evidentiary Committee began considering the Hastings case in July, while congressional hearings commenced into political corruption involving billions of dollars in HUD funds. Even Patrick Swindall, who had served on the House subcommittee that recommended impeaching Hastings, was convicted that summer on nine counts of perjury for lying to a grand jury about a money laundering scheme. The shifting line on public ethics and the intensity of press attention produced a climate conducive to Alcee Hastings's conviction.

Hastings, whose desk at the federal courthouse had always borne the sign "Living Well Is the Best Revenge," within days after his conviction went to the Florida state capitol in Tallahassee, filed papers, and declared his candidacy for the Democratic nomination for governor, an action generally regarded as more amusing than serious.[73] Actions, if any, by the state bar association to disbar Hastings were shrouded in confidentiality,[74] and his initial attempts to capitalize on his "negative celebrity" failed. The former judge, still in his early fifties, did not slip into obscurity, but rather won the run-off election in the fall of 1992 in a bid for the Democratic nomination for Florida's Twenty-third Congressional District.

Notes

1. Shenon, "Judge Suggests Racism Is Motivating Inquiry," Y-13.
2. H. Res. 128, 100th Cong., 1st ses. (March 23, 1987).
3. *In re Grand Jury Proceedings*, 669 F. Supp. 1072 (1987), at 1075–76.
4. *In re Request for Access to Grand Jury Materials*, 833 F. 2d 1438 (1987); *In re Grand Jury Proceedings*, 841 F. 2d 1948 (1988).
5. Hedges, "Judge Calls Report 'Slopped-Up Ink,' " A-1.
6. Friend, "Peer Pressure," 86.
7. Ibid., 82.
8. Kilpatrick, "Impeachable Character or Not, It's Double Jeopardy," A-31.
9. *In the Matter of the Impeachment Inquiry Concerning U.S. District Judge Alcee L. Hastings*, 330.
10. Marcus, "Congress Reluctantly Takes up Hastings's Ouster," 1.
11. Ibid., 1.
12. Conyers, who had served in the House since 1964, had helped to organize the Black Congressional Caucus and had served on the committee that had voted to impeach President Richard Nixon. His politics paralleled those of Hastings, even in their assessment of the Reagan administration. "Never have we known an administration," Conyers was quoted as saying, "that has so politicized the administration of law." Zaldivar and Hedges, "Lawyer," A-13.
13. The eight-member committee included Hamilton Fish of New York, John Bryant of Texas, Don Edwards of California, Mike Synar of Oklahoma,

Rick Boucher of Virginia, George Gekas of Pennsylvania, and Patrick Swindall of Georgia.

14. The records of Warren Hastings's presentation do not reflect whether he answered charges under oath. Alcee Hastings, however, when asked to be sworn, questioned the implications of the oath: "Does it mean . . . I [am] then a witness forever during the subcommittee's undertaking?"

15. *Hearings Before the Subcommittee on Criminal Justice of the Committee on the Judiciary, House of Representatives*, 15. [Hereafter cited as *House Hearings*.]

16. Ibid., 188.

17. Ibid., 225.

18. Ibid., 367–38.

19. Ibid., 481.

20. Zaldivar, "Impeachment Saga Nears Finish," A-6.

21. *House Hearings*, 482–83.

22. Ibid., 495.

23. The vote of the full committee was 32 to 1 in favor of impeachment.

24. *Congressional Record*, August 3, 1988, H-6183.

25. Ibid., H-6186.

26. Ibid.

27. Early argued that "Ethics is not supposed to be a political thing. . . . Now what are we going to do with every other judge, Federal judge that is accused, just accused, whether a Democrat or a Republican? It is going to be politicized." When a vote was finally taken, however, Early registered only a "present," casting neither a "yea" nor a "nay" vote. Ibid., H-6192.

28. Representatives Mervyn Dymally, Edward Roybal, and Gus Savage voted against the resolution.

29. H. Res. 512, empowering the committee of House managers, was passed by a voice vote. *Congressional Record*, August 3, 1988, H-6195.

30. "Hastings: Heart Ailment May Delay Senate Trial," D-1.

31. Fiedler, "Hastings Briefly Explored Deal to Avoid Senate Trial," B-3.

32. The talk show host said sarcastically that "in order to get black folks back in line, we've got to get rid of black judges, particularly militant black judges like Alcee Hastings. That's the long and short of it." Zaldivar, "Hastings Asks D.C. Radio Listeners to Pack Galleries," A-9.

33. Zaldivar, "Hastings' Senate Fight Begins," A-1.

34. The committee, named jointly by the majority and minority leaders of the Senate, also consisted of Patrick Leahy, David Pryor, Richard Bryan, Robert Kerrey, Joseph Lieberman, Dave Durenberger, Warren Rudman, Christopher Bond, Slade Gordon, and Conrad Burns.

35. *Report of the Senate Impeachment Trial Committee on the Articles Against Judge Alcee L. Hastings,* 1:264.

36. Hastings reported that he was $50,000 in debt at the conclusion of his first trial. His defense team frequently argued that they were severely limited by a shortage of funds and that they were receiving no compensation.

37. *Hearings Before the Senate Impeachment Trial Committee, U.S. Senate,* 2A:13–14. [Hereafter cited as *Senate Hearings.*]

38. Harmon, who also testified in closed hearings and whose testimony was redacted because of its content, confirmed that word on the street was that "there was a contract on his [Dredge's] head," placed there by Santo Trafficante's organization. Ibid., 1872.

39. Ibid., 98.

40. Ibid., 139.

41. Ibid., 519.

42. A coded conversation, according to Shuy, is one that "has in it meanings which are not necessarily apparent to other people, and if the conversation is in code, it is necessary that both parties understand it, and since it is partial code, the burden is even heavier on the participants to make sure that each knows what the other is talking about." Ibid., 543.

43. Ibid., 199.

44. Ibid., 2526–44.

45. Ibid., 406.

46. "That way you would either know that Judge Hastings was guilty," Raskin explained, "or you know that Judge Hastings was innocent." Ibid., 1894.

47. Ibid., 1822.

48. Ibid., 1837.

49. Ibid., 1063–64.

50. Alberto San Pedro, known locally as the "great corrupter," had allegedly been involved in a number of schemes in Miami and Hialeah, including one to get access to FBI records in 1985 and 1986. An employee of the telephone company, who installed wiretaps in 1985, had also pled guilty to accepting bribes from San Pedro to reveal information obtained through wiretaps. Ibid., 1071–72.

51. Ibid., 1082.

52. Patricia Thomas, Joy Royals Vickers, Lanny Sumpter, and Robert Ruiz were all involved in the MMAP conference and testified about it.

53. In July 1988, the supreme court of Rhode Island, in the case of *Lerner v. Moran,* had overturned an eighteen-year-old murder conviction because it found that Paul Rico had suborned perjury and had testified falsely at the defendant's trial. *Senate Hearings,* 1330.

54. Ibid., 1334–37.

55. Amoroso said that he was directed in the summer of 1985 to quit playing golf with Clark because "his name had surfaced in an investigation," and the golf arrangement was not good for "the image of the Bureau." Ibid., 1355.

56. Ibid., 2391.

57. Ibid., 2401–2.

58. Ibid., 2423.

59. Ibid., 2531.

60. *Report of the Senate Impeachment Trial Committee on the Articles Against Judge Alcee L. Hastings.*

61. *Congressional Record*, October 18, 1989, S-13618.

62. Ibid., S-13623.

63. Ibid., S-13625.

64. Ibid., S-13626.

65. Ibid., S-13627.

66. Ibid., S-13630.

67. Ibid., S-13636.

68. *Congressional Record*, October 20, 1989, S-13790.

69. Ibid., S-13796.

70. *Congressional Record*, October 27, 1989, S-14358–64; *Congressional Record*, October 24, 1989, S-14006–9.

71. Durenberger, in 1990, was sanctioned by the full Senate for ethics violations.

72. Senator Patrick Leahy, in advance of the vote on Article 17, had asked, "would a Senator be within his or her rights to interpret this as saying that a guilty or not guilty verdict would have to be based on a finding on each one of the four items as either guilty or not guilty?" The president pro tempore had responded that such an interpretation was possible. *Congressional Record*, October 20, 1989, S-13787. For the text of all of the votes, see S-13783–88.

73. Anderson, "Hastings Opens Campaign for Governor," A-16. The move was met with dry sarcasm in his hometown press, as seen in an editorial by Carl Hiaasen, "Hastings' Race Will Be Fun, but Not Real," B-1. Hastings later, after former Senator Lawton Chiles declared in the race, shifted to the race for secretary of state. McGarrahan, "Hastings Quits Governor's Race," B-4. He finished so poorly in that contest as not to merit a percentage tally.

74. Marcus, "Now, the Fate of Lawyer Hastings," 1.

6

Trying Walter Nixon

Walter L. Nixon's prosecution made any flaw in those of Harry Claiborne's and Alcee Hastings's pale. The pivotal point in each was the accusation of abuse of office for money, but Judge Nixon was investigated for the more tame and elusive crime of accepting an illegal gratuity. Like Harry Claiborne, he was never convicted of that, but rather of peripheral perjury counts. His is the story of a jurist with a long career behind him and a promising one in the future. The prosecution of Nixon matches, in many ways, both those of Claiborne and Hastings—instigated by an informer with his own agenda, decided by an attempt to reconcile competing recollections, and complicated by a maze of financial details and dates. Nixon's antagonist, Reid Weingarten, had unsuccessfully prosecuted Alcee Hastings less than a year before entering the Nixon case.

The inception of Walter Nixon's unenviable distinction as the seventh U.S. judge to be removed from office was his decision to enter into a completely ethical business investment that entangled him in a bizarre intrigue involving family animosities and jealousies. Wiley Fairchild, with whom Nixon entered into a business transaction, had a son charged in a marijuana smuggling scheme, a case with which the judge had no official involvement. That case, as it was bounced about in local Mississippi legal politics, was the snare in which Nixon was, by all accounts, unwittingly caught. Alcee Hastings and Harry Claiborne fought their prosecutions with numerous constitutional and pretrial appeals, but Nixon offered no challenges and sought no delays. Yet he was finally convicted of the felony of lying before a grand jury.

Nixon was, at least in Mississippi terms, to the manner born. His entire life, save for his education, was spent in his native Biloxi, where his father had been a local politician and where even a bridge bore the family's name. The circumstances of Nixon's life were completely opposite those of Alcee Hastings's, for he was part of the southern white establishment. Nixon was thirty-nine when he assumed the federal bench in 1968 and became the youngest U.S. judge in the nation. He had only been a candidate for public office once, an unsuccessful bid for the board of supervisors in Harrison County, the same seat his father held from 1923 to 1939. His activities, however, in other political campaigns had brought him into the graces of both U.S. senators from Mississippi.

When a new position on the federal bench for southern Mississippi was created in 1966, Nixon was nominated by President Lyndon Johnson, with the support of Senators James Eastland and John Stennis. Eastland, chair of the Senate Judiciary Committee, personally introduced Nixon at the confirmation hearing, noting that he had known the young Nixon for most of his life; the nomination was seconded by Stennis. Nixon had received a "qualified" rating from the American Bar Association and the hearty approval of both the Mississippi State Bar and the local Jones County Bar Association. The hearing, in June 1968, lasted a mere five minutes,[1] and confirmation by the full Senate followed quickly. Judge Nixon became the third federal judge in the Southern District of Mississippi, based in Biloxi but also holding court in Jackson, Hattiesburg, Vicksburg, and Meridian.

Nixon had been admitted to the Mississippi bar in 1952,[2] and, because he served in the Air Force during the Korean conflict, did not enter the legal profession until 1955. He soon had a thriving and lucrative civil practice, largely handling personal injury cases. He earned more than $200,000 during his last year in practice and thus took a substantial pay cut to assume a judgeship. That diminution of income took no toll on his life-style until after he married for the second time.[3] By 1979, he realized that college educations for five daughters were facing him and that his judicial salary of $54,000 was hardly adequate. He sought wholly ethical outside investments, one of which was a trio of oil and gas interests purchased from Wiley Fairchild.

The Drew Fairchild Case

The web into which Nixon was drawn through the business transaction with Fairchild is a tale of family discord, power, and wealth that bared the tradition of legal politics and good old boy networking in southern Mississippi. Sometime in 1979 or 1980—recollections varied—Judge Nixon asked his friend Carroll Ingram to approach the aging patriarch of the Fairchild family about the prospect of entering into an oil or gas investment. That such an investment was entirely within the bounds of judicial ethics was never in doubt, and that Nixon was motivated by his concerns about educating his children was not disputed. The timing of the investment, however, and the rationale behind Wiley Fairchild's willingness to include the judge in his commercial dealings became central.

Wiley Fairchild was, at the time, almost seventy; although he had little formal education, he successfully headed a multimillion-dollar empire.[4] To grow up in Hattiesburg was to know the Fairchilds. Wiley Fairchild was not only wealthy, but also interested in politics and known for making large contributions to political candidates[5] because he liked to be "close to people like governors."[6] His control of the Fairchild financial empire reflected his forceful personality; "he rule[d] things with an iron hand."[7] He was known, in particular, for his business acumen in the oil and gas business. When Judge Nixon, in early 1979 by his account, began seeking means of supplementing his income, he mentioned to Ingram, one of Fairchild's attorneys and a second cousin, that he was looking for investments. Nixon claimed that he was only vaguely aware of Fairchild Construction and of Fairchild's reputation. Discovering that Fairchild was highly successful in the oil and gas business, Judge Nixon then asked Ingram "if he would have the opportunity to mention to Mr. Fairchild that I would like to invest with him if possible." He testified that Ingram had said that "he would be happy to do that, would get back in touch."[8] Ingram, however, according to Nixon, did not immediately respond with additional information, and the judge to prodded him several times.[9]

Ingram corroborated Nixon's recollection that the overtures about investing with Wiley Fairchild began in 1979, but he remembered the conversation as occurring nearer the end of the year. He added, however, that he procrastinated in conveying the request because he "felt on the spot about it" but "didn't see anything improper about talking to Mr. Fairchild about it."[10] Some time passed, but in late 1979 or early 1980, according to both Ingram and Nixon, Ingram approached Fairchild, who readily agreed to do business with Nixon.[11] Fairchild later, still according to both in late 1979 or early 1980, identified three mineral properties that he would sell to the judge for $9,500. Nixon claimed that Ingram called him early in 1980 to arrange a meeting with Fairchild, after which Nixon believed they had "a gentlemen's agreement" about the sale. Ingram, however, testified that no meeting occurred until sometime in 1981, and Fairchild dated the first encounter in 1982.[12]

No paperwork was forthcoming, which was worrisome to Nixon, who needed to arrange a loan for the $9,500. On February 25, 1981, Robert "Skip" Jarvis, Fairchild's administrative assistant, was told to draft three blank overriding royalty conveyances covering one oil well in Mobile County, Alabama, and others in Marion and Covington counties, Mississippi.[13] The deeds giving Nixon a royalty interest were delivered to Ingram later that month or early in March, but finalizing them was delayed because of an error in the acreage. The corrected deeds were back dated to February 25, 1980. This back dating, which became a crucial element in the case against Nixon, was, according to Ingram, probably because "Mr. Fairchild was attempting to approximate the date and the time when this transaction took place."[14] Ingram also, when delivering the deeds, told Nixon that Fairchild was willing to hold the paper on the deal at a fair rate of interest and drew up three promissory notes at 10 percent.

The timing of the transactions became an important detail, as did the value of the royalty interests that Nixon purchased. Was this a "sweetheart deal," as the prosecution would later argue, or, as Nixon claimed, an "arm's length transaction"?[15] The three wells were not producing, and, therefore, returning no income when they were conveyed. Evaluating a well in advance of its going on line is difficult, but Nixon testified that he believed he was paying fair market price. One well, indeed, was not particularly good, but the other two amply compensated.

Wiley Fairchild and his first wife had divorced shortly after the birth of a son, Reddit Andrew "Drew" Fairchild. Although their relationship was always strained, when Drew was twelve he came to live with his father.[16] The younger Fairchild finished only the eighth grade and, as a result, worked largely for the family business. Sometime in early 1979, his father sent word for him to leave the business and the two, thereafter, did not speak. Drew Fairchild co-owned an oil company with Bob Royals, with offices at the Hattiesburg Airport. He, Royals, and several others conspired to fly a load of marijuana from Colombia into the airport for refueling. On August 4, 1980, the plane carrying the marijuana landed as planned but was pursued by a chase plane.

The pilot, Robert Watkins, escaped, but two others in the plane were arrested, and a third conspirator was detained that night.[17]

Drew Fairchild, although not immediately apprehended, knew that he was directly implicated and retained a criminal lawyer, William Porter. A plea agreement was negotiated with George Phillips, the U.S. attorney in Jackson, and signed on November 19, 1980. In return for Drew's cooperation in prosecuting the case against the others, he would plead guilty and be sentenced to five years of probation and incur a $15,000 fine.[18] The plea was placed in abeyance and sentencing deferred to ensure his cooperation until the other defendants were tried.

Porter, a close friend of the Forrest County District Attorney Paul H. "Bud" Holmes and of Drew's business partner Bob Royals, was not, however, able to secure payment for his services on Drew's behalf and filed suit for unpaid legal fees. Porter mentioned the debt to Royals and insisted that Wiley Fairchild could cover it. Royals, although responding "that won't do Drew no good," nonetheless approached the elder Fairchild.[19] Drew told his father that he owed Porter for twenty-five hours of work, and Wiley Fairchild sent a check to the lawyer for $2,669.19.[20] Unsatisfied, Porter complained to his friend Bud Holmes, who called George Phillips at the federal office. He was told that because Drew had never been indicted and the case involved concurrent state and federal jurisdiction, he had no objection to Holmes's pursuing the case at the state level. Holmes presented the case to the Forrest County grand jury and obtained a Mississippi indictment against Drew Fairchild in August. He later admitted that "the triggering mechanism was the fact Bill [Porter] was up there fussing Drew never had paid him."[21]

The tactic was effective. Porter was paid the remainder of the $10,000 fee the following month,[22] and Fairchild was arraigned in state court the same day. Holmes, in January of the next year, reached another plea agreement with Drew Fairchild. For his cooperation in the extradition from Texas of Robert Watkins, the pilot who had escaped, the agreement provided for probation and a $5,000 fine but was contingent upon Drew's testimony. The pilot skipped out on the $5,000 fugitive bond holding him in Texas, and the case dragged until October 1982, when Watkins was captured again in Florida, but the extradition process extended into the next year.[23] At no time during this elaborate set of proceedings was Judge Nixon involved in the case in any official capacity; he had no jurisdiction for either the federal or the state charges against Drew Fairchild.

After Watkins's apprehension in Florida, the event occurred on which the entire case against Judge Nixon hinged. The case against Drew Fairchild was passed to the files, that is, placed on inactive status, on December 23, 1982. Generally, a case that has passed to the files is not reactivated, although there is no prohibition on retrieving it. Holmes initiated the order, had it approved by a Mississippi state judge, and gave the papers to Ingram, who delivered copies to Wiley Fairchild as "a Christmas present."[24] District Attorney Holmes made the decision to pass the case to the files, but it was generally agreed that his decision came after a conversation with Judge Nixon, and that Wiley Fairchild was informed of the settlement in a late-evening telephone call. When the decision was made, the motivation behind it and the timing of the understanding were all contested and central to the case against Judge Nixon. In sorting the events and the conflicting recollections of Holmes, Ingram, Wiley Fairchild, and Walter Nixon, the government and defense were both forced to agree that "somebody is flat out wrong."[25]

The irony of the fact that Drew Fairchild's case passed to the files rests in the unusual fate of that action. The case was reactivated almost immediately, when, on January 26, 1983, Robert Watkins was finally extradited from Florida. Bond of $100,000 was placed on Watkins, who, even so, skipped again. And, Drew Fairchild's case "just remained . . . ; he was not to be sentenced until after his testimony [against Watkins]." Drew's attorney, Porter, was killed in a plane crash that November; Holmes left the office of district attorney on January 1, 1984; and still Drew Fairchild's case remained "on active docket, waiting to be sentenced."[26]

Investigation of Nixon

Robert L. Jarvis was married to the granddaughter of Wiley Fairchild's eldest sister and employed as Fairchild's administrative assistant in the oil and gas side of the business from August 1979 until May 1983. Fairchild not only paid him a salary, but also covered his tuition for law school. Jarvis was involved in drafting the initial deeds for the transfer of the royalty interests in the oil wells from Fairchild to Nixon and claimed to have become suspicious about the arrangement when he first drafted the deeds without the purchaser's name. His concerns were heightened, he explained, when he was later asked to redo the deeds in the first week of March 1981 and to back date them. When he realized that Judge Nixon was the recipient of the properties, Jarvis said that he suggested having the royalties paid directly by the oil companies rather than through Fairchild Construction because Fairchild was "too obvious in what you have done." Jarvis assumed that the transfer of properties to the judge was related to Drew Fairchild's criminal case, but Wiley Fairchild "became extremely irritated and upset" at the suggestion.[27] Jarvis, nonetheless, remained convinced that Fairchild and Judge Nixon were involved in an illegal transaction to buy an end to Drew's legal difficulties.

Jarvis was fired by Fairchild in May 1983, when he refused to take a polygraph examination, but his salary and tuition payments continued. He was, even so, later asked to take care of a matter for the company in Jackson and offered a company car for the journey. On that trip his brakes failed because hydraulic fluid had been used instead of brake fluid, and Jarvis was convinced that Wiley Fairchild was trying to murder him because "the car had been sabotaged."[28] Jarvis, certain that Fairchild was involved in illegal activities with the judge—and apparently fearful for his own life—made an anonymous call to the FBI. He pretended that he had simply stumbled onto the deal[29] and fed information to the FBI in three calls in November and more in the next year, all of which were recorded. As he identified possible sources and other avenues for the investigation, Jarvis at one point exclaimed to the FBI agent, "I feel like Dick Tracy, you know."[30] After much cajoling, he finally came forward in February 1984. The prosecution eventually concluded that "he [Jarvis] offers no evidence of misconduct against Judge Nixon."[31] In fact, "a lot of what he said was wrong."[32] The government nevertheless launched an investigation that would ultimately result in indictments against Wiley Fairchild, Bud Holmes, and Judge Nixon.

On April 19, 1984, Agent Ken White-Spunner of the FBI and Reid Weingarten of the Public Integrity Section of the Justice Department arranged an interview, which was tape recorded, with Judge Nixon. The subject of the interview was explained to Nixon as involving the Drew Fairchild case and the judge's investments with Wiley Fairchild. Nixon, even in that preliminary interview, said to Weingarten, "if you can detect or know of anything at all where I ever had any connection [with] his [Wiley's] son's case or the disposition or handling of it or anything to do with it, I sure wish you'd tell me." Weingarten assured him that "we have no information to that effect"[33] but also asked if Carroll Ingram, Bud Holmes, or Wiley Fairchild had ever asked the judge to do anything about the case.

Nixon later testified that when Weingarten and White-Spunner left his office, he "was puzzled, confused, and very mad, angry"[34] and called Ingram, Holmes, George Phillips, and Weldon Kennedy, the Mississippi head of the FBI. Kennedy told Nixon that he was not really involved in the investigation but thought it was just perfunctory. A few days later, Bud Holmes was also visited by the FBI; Carroll Ingram was interviewed in May 1984; and both Ingram and Holmes first appeared before the grand jury that July. Wiley Fairchild was also approached and interviewed four times that April by the FBI and representatives of the Justice Department.

Nixon was on vacation with his family in Florida when, on July 18, 1984, he was invited to appear before the grand jury and deliver certain documents. He cut his vacation short to testify before the grand jury, and the following questions and his answers in that forum became the basis of a four-count indictment against him. The italicized portions were alleged in Nixon's trial to have been false.

Q: Did Wiley Fairchild ever discuss the case with you?
A: *No, not to the best of my recollection.* I think I would recall that if he had, believe me, *but I don't recall that he ever did.*
Q: Did Wiley Fairchild ever ask you to do anything vis-à-vis his son's case?
A. *Absolutely not.*

The next interchange for which Nixon was charged was:

Q: Did he [Bud Holmes] ever discuss the Drew Fairchild case with you?
A: *No, not to the best of my recollection.* I think I would recall if he had.

The final perjury charge resulted from comments that Judge Nixon chose to make at the conclusion of his interrogation.

A: Now *I have had nothing whatsoever officially or unofficially to do with the Drew Fairchild criminal case in federal court or state court.* I don't need to reconstruct anything with reference to that. I've told you that from the beginning. I have never talked to anyone about the case, any federal judge or state judge, federal prosecutor or state prosecutor, and I never handled any aspect of this case in federal court. As you know where—someone told me maybe Judge Russell handled one of the other defendants also and—but *I never handled any part of it, never had a thing to do with it at all, and never talked to anyone, state or federal, prosecutor or judge, in any way influence anybody with respect to this case.* Didn't know anything about it until I read that account in the newspaper. Didn't even know Mr. Fairchild had a son when I was dealing with him in the business transaction.[35]

Wiley Fairchild's initial interview with the FBI had been unexpected, and he responded to investigators' questions about his son's case by telling them about a blackmail plot involving Drew's lawyer and District Attorney Holmes. Four days after that first encounter, Jarvis, still playing his Dick Tracy role, contacted Fairchild and arranged a meeting, surreptitiously taped, in which he tried to elicit information about the oil lease transaction with Nixon. Fairchild, however, insisted that the arrangement with Nixon was concluded solely because Ingram had requested it, and "everything is legal." As Jarvis pressed about the back dating of the deeds, Fairchild explained that "we just dated it back to when it was made." When asked about a connection with Drew's criminal case, Fairchild sternly claimed, "that didn't have a damn thing to do with Drew."[36]

Only in the third interview did the federal agents introduce the issue of Wiley Fairchild's connection with Judge Nixon, and the FBI report on the interview noted that "he became visibly upset" when the subject was broached. Fairchild, however, provided the interviewers with documentation of his transaction with Nixon. The fourth interview, on May 4, 1984, the last before Wiley Fairchild's grand jury appearance, focused solely on his relationship with Nixon. He explained that the transaction occurred long in advance of his son's criminal problems and that it was a normal business arrangement, similar to ones he had with other Mississippi political figures. His only motivation for including Nixon was Carroll Ingram's request that he do so.[37] Fairchild subsequently appeared before the grand jury, where he repeated essentially the same version and was, in September, indicted on one count of perjury and one count of making an illegal gratuity to Judge Nixon (the mineral royalty leases).

Fairchild, on the advice of his attorneys, sought a plea agreement and made his first proffer to the government, what Reid Weingarten called his first "salvo in potential plea negotiations," on November 1, 1984.[38] He began by outlining a tale of payoffs to Holmes and Judge Nixon by a friend of his, Preacher Shows. By this time, Fairchild claimed that he responded to Ingram's request to include Nixon in some investments "because I was scared not to." He admitted his confusion in trying to date events, blamed "them three damn crooks" — Ingram, Holmes, and the judge — for the whole problem, and claimed that he told Ingram to bring the judge to his office. When Ingram arrived with Nixon, Fairchild told him how angry he was at the handling of his son's case. Later that evening, Wiley Fairchild said that he got a telephone call from the judge, who said, "I've talked to him and things are going to be all right." Bud Holmes, according to Fairchild, then got on the telephone and said, "when this man asks me to do something . . . I don't ask no questions, I just do it."

When Weingarten asked the elderly Fairchild why he had summoned Judge Nixon to discuss his son's case, he replied, "he owed me a favor; that's the way I looked at it."[39] A plea agreement was quickly concluded, providing that no incarceration would be recommended if Fairchild cooperated.[40] He later testified that he pled guilty because of his attorneys' advice but "had no idea that I was committing a crime."[41] His crime, as he understood it, was selling too cheaply,[42] and he believed that if he gave information against Judge Nixon an arrangement was possible.[43] His cooperation led to the indictment of Bud Holmes on March 29, 1985, and, on August 29, 1985, a four-count indictment against Nixon.[44] Fairchild, having fulfilled his obligation, was sentenced in September to two months in a halfway house in Jackson, a $10,000 fine, and three years of unsupervised probation.[45]

Holmes was the other important witness in building a case against Judge Nixon,[46] although he was, even by the prosecution's account, "a flawed man."[47] Holmes was first interviewed by the FBI on April 25, 1984, and subsequently appeared before the grand jury three times. His role in passing the Drew Fairchild case to the files and in the telephone call to Wiley Fairchild was crucial to any wrongdoing by Judge Nixon. Holmes admitted that he covered up the telephone call, which he later described as just "two drunks call somebody up." When he discovered from Carroll Ingram that the federal authorities were aware of the call, he contacted Nixon to discuss a strategy and tried "to encourage him, let's go ahead and tell about the thing, because I didn't see there was anything to hide on it." Nixon, he said, responded that "he didn't know what I was talking about, he didn't know about the phone call and then chastised me."[48] Holmes also attempted, according to one of his employees in the district attorney's office, Katie Smith Matison, to cover up his involvement in the Fairchild case by trying to convince her that she had handled the whole case. He even said, "it was your case, do you know anything wrong with the case?"[49] She claimed that later she even received an indirect threat from Holmes.[50]

Holmes testified that Weingarten called him in March 1985 to say that he was authorized to ask the grand jury for an indictment against him, but that could be avoided if Holmes acted fast. When he met with Weingarten shortly thereafter, he was given the impression that he "wouldn't be indicted if you give them Judge Nixon."[51] Holmes did not produce and was indicted on five counts of perjury. His case promptly went to trial, but, after a jury had been selected, the government offered to reduce the charges to misdemeanor contempt. Holmes accepted and in June entered an agreement with the government that pledged his cooperation.[52] Although he had faced up to twenty-five years in prison if convicted (five years on each count of perjury), Holmes was sentenced in December 1985 to one year in prison and a $10,000 fine.[53] Weingarten had by then lined up the witnesses needed to seek the indictment of Judge Nixon that was forthcoming on August 29, 1985. He was charged with receiving an unlawful gratuity from Wiley Fairchild and three counts of perjury to conceal that act before the grand jury.

Nixon before the Jury

Nixon employed criminal attorney Michael S. Fawer of New Orleans to represent him, and Fawer proved to be a vigorous and zealous rival in verbal duels with lead prosecutor Weingarten. Four days were needed to select twelve jurors, largely because of the considerable publicity that the case had generated, and, for that reason, the jury was sequestered for the trial. Weingarten characterized the case against Nixon appropriately as involving two parallel tracks: the Drew Fairchild case and the transaction between Nixon and the elder Fairchild. The two issues for the jury to decide were whether the business arrangement was "an arm's length transaction" or an illegal gratuity[54] and whether or not Judge Nixon was involved in the Drew Fairchild case.[55]

Volumes of exhibits and sixteen witnesses were presented, from the foreman of the grand jury before which Nixon appeared to experts on mineral leases. Nixon's leases had been purchased for $9,500 and, including the interest payments, cost him approximately $11,000, but by 1986 had produced income of approximately $62,000. Nixon had repaid all of the promissory notes and interest with income directly from the wells. The questions in deciding whether the leases were an illegal gratuity were their timing, the motives of Fairchild and Nixon when the arrangement was made, and the fair market value of the leases when Fairchild sold them.

The central feature of the charges of perjury before the grand jury was a discussion that Judge Nixon admittedly had with Wiley Fairchild and a telephone call from Holmes and the judge to Fairchild. The dates of these two events, as well as the substance of both the face-to-face and telephone conversations between Fairchild and the judge, were essential in deciding whether the judge had knowingly given false testimony to the grand jury when he said three times that he had nothing to do with Drew Fairchild's case.

Only four witnesses, Fairchild, Holmes, Ingram, and Nixon, were central to the resolution of both issues, and their testimonies did not mesh. The jury was left with the task of sorting and balancing the credibility of each. Wiley Fairchild, by then seventy-three, was fuzzy in his recollections of dates, and his plea bargain clouded his version of events. When Weingarten led him through his testimony, he explained that Nixon had at one time "thanked me for putting him a good oil deal and he said if I can ever help you, I will; and if I can't, I'll tell you."[56] Based on that statement and his knowledge of Nixon's friendship with Holmes, Fairchild said that when he was angered about his son's case, he either got in touch with the judge or asked Ingram to do so. When Nixon, he said, came to his office, Fairchild "wanted him [Nixon] to get Bud Holmes to do what he had promised to do." What was promised apparently had to do with blackmail and with prosecution of Drew Fairchild's business partner Bob Royals. Fairchild testified, however, that Nixon said little if anything while in the office, but he called at about seven that evening to say, "Wiley, you know that man we was talking to this evening . . . ? Well, I'm in his home, and everything's going to be taken care of to your satisfaction." Bud Holmes then got on the telephone to confirm, and Fairchild thanked them both. Although he was at a loss about when the meeting and telephone call occurred, he was certain it was before the case was passed to the files in December 1982.[57]

Fawer's cross-examination of Fairchild was masterful as he, too, tried to make Fairchild date the telephone call.[58] If it followed the passing of the case to the files—after December 1982—the judge could not have used any influence. If, as the prosecution argued, the call preceded the action, Nixon was guilty of improper interference. Wiley Fairchild could not remember but did acknowledge that he never discussed his son's case with the judge nor asked Nixon to do anything. He added that although Nixon said nothing, "I knew he got the message."[59] Fairchild did not budge on his testimony about the substance of the telephone conversation or about his insistence that Nixon spoke to him first.[60] Fawer, however, suggested that Fairchild's memory was clouded by his drinking. Fairchild readily admitted that he started drinking about 5:30 in the afternoon but insisted that he was totally cognizant during the telephone call.[61]

Weingarten also raised the issue of the oil leases for Nixon, and Fairchild testified that the agreement was struck in 1980 after his son's case was pending in federal court, a contention that conflicted with both Nixon's and Ingram's recollections. The back dating of deeds, he said, was Ingram's suggestion because "it would look better if it was back dated."[62] The damning aspect of Fairchild's testimony, however, was his assertion that "when I sell something, I want to get something, of course, for it, and something, something where it won't look like a hundred per cent gift."[63] He added, moreover, that he could not recall having ever before taken a note back when selling a mineral royalty interest.[64] However, he concurred that in comparison to the $250 per acre that he had originally paid for the leases sold to Nixon, he made a tidy profit[65] and that the leases had been corrected because of an error in the acreage.[66]

Carroll Ingram, the only one of the principals who was not indicted, was quite explicit about the separability of Drew Fairchild's case and Judge Nixon's oil lease purchase from Wiley Fairchild.[67] Because he had initiated the original contact between Nixon and Fairchild, Ingram was equally convinced that the transaction "certainly occurred before August of 1980 in my mind."[68] It, in short, had definitely preceded Drew Fairchild's legal difficulties. Ingram, although he had no direct knowledge of the fateful telephone call, served as a pivot point among Holmes, Fairchild, and Nixon, each of whom had mentioned the event to him. His testimony on that point was less favorable to Nixon. "Sometime in the late fall of 1982," Ingram explained on direct examination, "Mr. Fairchild told me that he had asked Judge Nixon to talk to Mr. Holmes about Drew Fairchild's case." Fairchild, according to Ingram, said that "Drew Fairchild's case was going to be okay," and both Nixon and Fairchild, according to Ingram, confirmed that conversation. Ingram, who had carried copies of the order passing the case to the files between Holmes and Fairchild, was certain that the discussion between Fairchild and Nixon had preceded the passing of the case to the files.[69]

Holmes, from the witness stand, was quite elaborate about the circumstances of the call, explaining that Nixon first mentioned the Drew Fairchild case to him when the judge and Ingram came by his office one Friday afternoon to collect some turkeys from an earlier hunting trip. After they had a drink or two, according to Holmes, Nixon left his car at the district attorney's office and rode with Holmes to his farm. On the ride to the farm, Holmes explained, the following conversation occurred: "Judge Nixon told me, he said, 'Bud . . . , I was out at Mr. Fairchild's and he asked me to put in a good word for his boy, or would I say something to you about Drew.' He said 'I'm not asking you to do anything, I'm just saying that Mr. Fairchild asked me to put in a good word.' Well, I knew Mr. Fairchild and the judge were kind of getting to be buddy-buddies there."[70]

Holmes said that he then offered to pass the case to the files, but Nixon objected, saying that he was not asking Holmes to do anything. When they arrived at the farm, Holmes said, they had probably two drinks, when Nixon asked, "Do you mind if I call and tell Wiley?" He then called Fairchild. Holmes got on the telephone and claimed to have told Fairchild, "I want to let you know that I want Judge Nixon to have credit for helping the boy" and said that he would pass the case to the files.[71]

Holmes said that the call was made on May 14, 1982, which directly contradicted Nixon's version and placed the call well in advance of passing the case to the files. Holmes, on cross by Fawer, said that he dated the call from a wedding he attended, an altercation at a bar that night, and notations on his secretary's calendar.[72] When Fawer persisted that the call was made in 1983, Holmes responded, "it was prior to when I passed it to the file."[73] Fawer argued, however, that Nixon was holding a trial in Biloxi on May 14, 1982. "If Judge Nixon says he wasn't here," Holmes allowed, "I'll take his word he wasn't here."[74]

Fawer's more convincing attack on Holmes's version of the call, however, came from a surreptitious tape of a conversation, an "ugly . . . very foul" exchange Holmes had with Paul McMullan in July 1985, in which Holmes said, "Goddamn, two drunks call somebody, all they got to do is see to the agreement had been worked out a year earlier takes place." Holmes concurred that a year earlier would mean that the call was made in 1983, but then pleaded, "that phone call, Mr. Fawer, was the most insignificant thing that we made that night." "Nobody intended anything," he continued, "they have taken and blown this thing into where we are right now."[75] Weingarten, however, noted the contradiction that if the call had been made in 1983, Holmes was lying about passing it to the files.[76]

Nixon, who had been selected chief judge of his district in 1982 and offered by both Senator Thad Cochran and Congressman Trent Lott the nomination to the Fifth Circuit Court of Appeals, was the last to take the stand. He did not deny the fateful telephone call to Wiley Fairchild, but his version of the events varied considerably from the accounts of Fairchild and Holmes, and the timing differed from Ingram's understanding. Nixon recalled that he had been presiding over a bank robbery trial on March 10 and 11, 1983, and the case went to the jury in the late morning. Deliberations lasted only forty-five minutes, and thus the judge was free for the rest of the day. From his chambers, Nixon called Holmes and Fairchild and made arrangements to see both. He had, he explained, only recently made his final payments on the notes to Fairchild and wanted to talk to him about the wells. He went to Fairchild's office alone in the early afternoon, and Fairchild launched into a harangue about his son's legal woes and the plea bargain he thought had been struck. "He said," Nixon continued, "I believe Bud Holmes is blackmailing me and he said I think Carroll Ingram might be in it too." He was, according to the judge, angry but did not ask him to do anything, although "I got the impression," Nixon said, "that he wanted me to mention something about that to Bud Holmes."[77] Nixon claimed he left almost immediately and returned to his chambers, where he spent most of the afternoon with his law clerk.

Nixon had already, he explained, made plans to meet Holmes at the farm that night to borrow some records. The two, according to Nixon, had a drink, listened to some music, and talked, but Fairchild's accusations bothered him. Nixon said he finally broached the subject of Holmes's blackmailing Fairchild by "dragging the good Fairchild name through the mud in the news media." Holmes, he said, responded that Fairchild was paranoid, thought "everybody is after his money," but offered to tell him about the case. Nixon stopped him because "I'd have been there all night." Holmes said simply that it was all worked out anyway; the two changed the conversation and had another drink. When Nixon resumed browsing through records, Holmes made a telephone call and later called to Nixon, "Here, talk to Wiley Fairchild." Fairchild then thanked him for interceding with Holmes, and Nixon handed the telephone back. He claimed to have questioned Holmes about the motive behind the call, to which Holmes replied, "I just wanted to get the damn thing straightened out."[78] The judge explained that Holmes's version of the event could not have been accurate because he was in Biloxi trying a case on March 14, 1982, although no one could verify absolutely that he was in his chambers that entire afternoon.[79]

Weingarten summarized the contested issues in the case. Was the oil and gas transaction a legitimate business deal or an illegal gratuity? On the perjury charges, was Nixon involved in the Drew Fairchild case?[80] Weingarten also tried to reconcile the various versions of events, explaining that "Carroll Ingram, Bud Holmes, and Wiley Fairchild are different people, but in terms of these questions, they fit nicely." All three, he contended, agreed that the call to Wiley Fairchild occurred before the case was passed to the files and was intended to convey good news to Fairchild. Only Ingram, he argued, sustained the judge's version of the oil and gas transaction, but Weingarten persisted in arguing that it was a "sweetheart deal."[81]

Fawer, on the other hand, attacked the government's zealous prosecution of Nixon and focused on the credibility of the government's witnesses. Why would Wiley Fairchild lie? He was, according to Fawer, an "old man selling whatever he could to the government at whatever cost."[82] He characterized Holmes as "a disgrace to the legal profession, and a disgrace to himself as a human being."[83] Jarvis he referred to as "this looney-tunes character . . . trying to create a paper trail."[84] Fawer dismissed the perjury charges as involving no more than the government's attempts "to make a case against the judge, that all of this is twisted and distorted and perverted for your listening pleasure," for no one was asked to do anything and no one discussed the case.[85] The illegal gratuity was a failed charge, he argued, based on the consistent testimony of Ingram, Fairchild, and Nixon.[86]

On February 8, the jury was charged and carefully instructed about how to weigh the testimony given by Wiley Fairchild and Holmes because of their plea bargains and grants of immunity. The verdict, after eighteen hours of deliberation, was a compromise—acquittal on the illegal gratuity and one count of perjury and guilty of the remaining two perjury counts (discussing Drew Fairchild's case with Holmes and with any official involved in its prosecution). On March 31, 1986, Nixon was sentenced to two concurrent five-year prison terms.

Notes

1. *Nomination of Walter L. Nixon, Jr.*, 1968.
2. He had attended Louisiana State University for one year, after attending the Marion Military Institute in Alabama his first year, and then received his law degree from Tulane University.
3. Nixon had two children by his first wife, but when he married Barbara Castello in 1976, he assumed responsibility for her four small children and then the couple had a child of their own.
4. *U.S. v. Nixon*, H85–00012 (1986), 1157.
5. Ibid., 723.
6. Ibid., 727. Wiley Fairchild explained his penchant for making large political contributions—for example, $300,000 to the gubernatorial campaign of Evelyn Gandy—by saying, "I like to have a friend in the Governor's mansion." He also contributed to campaigns for senator, attorney general, and secretary of state. Ibid., 467.
7. Ibid., 312. Skip Jarvis, who was a former employee of Fairchild Construction and married to a grandniece of Fairchild's, added that Wiley Fairchild also had a fluid and volatile personality. Ibid., 320–21.
8. Ibid., 1482.
9. Ibid., 726.
10. Ibid., 1028.
11. Ingram testified that Fairchild responded that "he would be delighted to have an opportunity to make an investment with Judge Nixon when and if an appropriate time came for him to do that." Ibid., 1036. Nixon's version is virtually identical. See Ibid., 1484.
12. Ibid., 1486.
13. Ibid., 281–83.
14. Ibid., 1048.
15. A royalty interest, which Nixon bought, in an oil well or any mineral property is distinguished from a working interest. The latter pays for the

cost of production, whereas a royalty interest strictly receives income. No money is made by either type of investment until a well is producing.

16. *U.S. v. Nixon*, 462.

17. Ibid., 108–13.

18. Ibid., 114. Porter had talked about the Drew Fairchild case with Holmes, who recommended seeking a plea bargain with the federal agents and even called U.S. attorney Phillips on Porter's behalf to set up the appointment. Ibid., 730–31.

19. Ibid., 152–53.

20. Ibid., 155. Wiley Fairchild read about Porter's lawsuit in the paper and, when approached by Royals, paid Porter $2,500 plus some expenses. He did not, however, tell Drew Fairchild that he had done so. His motivation was to make Porter drop the lawsuit and to get the affair out of the newspapers. Ibid., 475–76.

21. Ibid., 734.

22. Holmes explained that when "you live in a small community down here, these kind of things go on." He then elaborated his perception of the typical practice of defense attorneys' asking for continuances pending the payment of their fees. "Most common thing in the world, is a standing joke, whenever, they say have you been employed? No, I haven't been fully employed yet, meaning I haven't been paid. They will continue cases, these things happen all the time in the practice of law." Ibid., 840.

23. Ibid., 856–67.

24. Ibid., 753–54.

25. Ibid., 1861.

26. Ibid., 756.

27. Ibid., 298.

28. Ibid., 311.

29. Jarvis, as UM (unidentified male) in the transcripts, explained to his contact, Special Agent Ken White-Spunner: "It's ah—I tripped and fell over this stuff, and I've been sittin' on it and going holy shit, and didn't know what to do with it. . . . So I—one thing led to another, and curiosity got the best of me, and I started asking questions." *Report of the Senate Impeachment Trial Committee on the Articles Against Judge Walter L. Nixon, Jr.*, 2:757. [Hereafter cited as *Senate Exhibits*.]

30. Ibid., 827.

31. *U.S. v. Nixon*, 1837.

32. Ibid., 1962.

33. *Senate Exhibits*, 240–41.

34. *U.S. v. Nixon*, 1571.

35. *Senate Exhibits*, 472–76.

36. Ibid., 182–92.

37. Ibid., 857–72.

38. Ibid., 903.

39. Ibid., 903–11.

40. Ibid., 411–12.

41. *U.S. v. Nixon*, 673.

42. Ibid., 705.

43. Ibid., 704, 692.

44. The indictment of Holmes and Wiley Fairchild's guilty plea prompted Jarvis, who had first contacted the FBI, to write to White-Spunner: "By the way, four down (Wiley, Drew, Royals, and Holmes). I'm eager to go after the big prize." *Senate Exhibits*, 915. He later testified that Judge Nixon was "the big prize" to whom he referred. *U.S. v. Nixon*, 426.

45. *Senate Exhibits*, 923–35.

46. *U.S. v. Nixon*, 1839.

47. Holmes was a lawyer, educated at Southern Mississippi and "Ol' Miss" Law School, who had a general practice in Forrest County, except for his four-year stint as district attorney from 1980 to 1984. He had found financial success as an agent for professional football players, including Walter Payton and Ray Guy. Ibid., 1851.

48. Ibid., 764.

49. Ibid., 1358–59.

50. Ibid., 1364–67.

51. Ibid., 814.

52. *Senate Exhibits*, 451–54.

53. Holmes challenged the sentence subsequently, arguing that the statute under which he pled guilty provided for *either* a fine *or* one year in prison; both sentences could not be imposed. *U.S. v. Nixon*, 772.

54. Weingarten explained that bribery was not in question, because a bribe is payment to a public official to perform a specific act. "He [Nixon] is not charged with receiving the oil interests in return for a promise to fix Drew's case. Rather, he's charged with receiving something of value with knowledge that it was given to him because of his official position." *U.S. v. Nixon*, 23.

55. Ibid.

56. Ibid., 482.

57. Ibid., 481–86.

58. In his closing arguments, Weingarten even conceded, "Mr. Fawer is a brilliant lawyer. He's an incomparably skilled cross-examiner; from a purely technical point of view it was fun, frankly, to watch him." Ibid., 1850.

59. Ibid., 641–44.

60. Ibid., 650.

61. Fairchild explained that "I got a little old brown bottle, with a funnel; I fill that bottle, I drink, watch the NBC news, eat, and go to bed. . . . [I]t's about six high balls." When Fawer asked if that much alcohol gave him a little buzz, he answered, "that's what I drink it for." Ibid., 636–37.

62. Ibid., 499.

63. Ibid., 506.

64. Ibid., 516.

65. Fawer proposed that if the eleven acres involved were multiplied by $250 an acre, Fairchild's profit was 300 percent. Wiley responded, "if you want to compare it to what I'd paid." Ibid., 566.

66. Ibid., 588.

67. Ibid., 1082.

68. Ibid., 1117.

69. Ibid., 1068–69.

70. Ibid., 736–37.

71. Ibid., 738–40.

72. The wedding of a friend was in Jackson on the fifteenth of that month. More vivid in Holmes's mind, however, was a bar fight, a hair-pulling argument, between Holmes's girlfriend and his secretary. The judge, he explained, had already left when the fracas began. Ibid., 882–83.

73. Ibid., 901.

74. Ibid., 908.

75. Ibid., 912–14.

76. Ibid., 934.

77. Ibid., 1535–36.

78. Ibid., 1539–42.

79. See the testimony of U.S. Magistrate John M. Roper (ibid., 1436) and the testimony of Mark Carlson, a law clerk (ibid., 1417–18).

80. Ibid., 1834.

81. Ibid., 1869–70.

82. Ibid., 1882.

83. Ibid., 1908.

84. Ibid., 1916.

85. Ibid., 1933.

86. Ibid., 1962.

7

Nixon before Congress

Events following Walter Nixon's criminal trial bore witness to the impact of the Hastings and Claiborne cases in the courts, in the judicial investigation process, and in Congress. The system had been vastly clarified but had not yet evolved into a routine. Nixon filed the standard postconviction appeal, but his petition focused on the trial and, unlike those of Claiborne and Hastings, raised no constitutional points and argued no abstract issues of separation of powers. He, instead, moved for a judgment of acquittal or a new trial. While all available avenues in the appellate system were pursued, Nixon remained a free man, and prison was postponed.

The judicial council, as appeals faltered, dutifully certified that Nixon's conviction might constitute grounds for impeachment but did not hold lengthy hearings as had been done in Hastings's case, nor ignore the situation as had happened after Claiborne's conviction. Targeting and selective prosecution had been alleged by Claiborne and Hastings but were only a muted theme in Nixon's criminal trial. In hearings before Congress, however, a similar assertion and a clear connection were offered between one decision Nixon made against the government and his subsequent criminal investigation. The evidence of prosecutorial misconduct was less tangential in Nixon's case than in the other ones.

Nixon's impeachment by the House and conviction by the Senate were, like Harry Claiborne's, foregone conclusions. A convicted felon could not be returned to the bench, and the absence of alternatives to impeachment seemed to imbue House deliberations with lethargy. Although the senators were livelier in their participation and engaged in six hours of debate on the case, there was, in fact, no viable course, in light of the jury's verdict, but to convict.

Nixon's initial motion for a new trial was promptly denied, and the record established by Claiborne and Hastings on the constitutional arguments was assumed, most likely, to be fixed precedent. Nixon argued only the legal technicalities of the trial: the materiality of the so-called perjured testimony to the grand jury investigation, insufficiency of evidence, taint of the trial by inclusion of the illegal gratuity charge, juror bias, the inclusion of perjured testimony by Bud Holmes, and prosecutorial misconduct in withholding evidence from the defense. When Nixon's conviction was affirmed by a panel of out-of-circuit jurists,[1] he appealed for a rehearing of his motions and a rehearing *en banc*, a request denied by the same three-judge panel.[2] *Certiorari* was denied by the Supreme Court in January 1988, leaving Nixon with only the slimmest chance of relief through habeas corpus or the similar Section 2255 petition. Nixon, nonetheless, held a press conference the next day and vowed not to resign. "I have committed no crime," he asserted, "and I will continue to seek justice."[3] When impeachment was mentioned, his proud nature showed, and he responded, "there I should at least get a jury of my peers."[4] With all appeals exhausted, Nixon entered Eglin Air Force Base Prison Camp on March 23, 1988.

House Action

The Judicial Council of the Fifth Circuit determined that, based on the trial and appeals, Nixon had engaged in conduct that might warrant impeachment and certified that conclusion to the Judicial Conference. That certification was ratified by the national judicial body and forwarded, together with the record, to the House of Representatives on March 15, 1988. Within two days, that certification was transformed into House Resolution 407, impeaching Judge Nixon for high crimes and misdemeanors. The resolution was referred to the Subcommittee on Civil and Constitutional Rights of the Judiciary Committee, many of whose members had been involved in either the Claiborne or the Hastings impeachments. The whole process of impeachment in the House, so novel and tentative when Claiborne's arose in 1986, was now orderly and systematic. Ground rules were set by letters and telephone calls without involving the representatives.

Nixon asked to present only four witnesses, including Reid Weingarten and two reporters, but written proffers, in lieu of appearances by the journalists, were preferred by the committee.[5] Nixon asked to make a statement, but, at least at the outset, requested not to testify or be questioned. His opening address was a brief assertion of his innocence, and he argued that his prosecution was "begun on false premises and . . . pursued for the wrong reasons." He added, however, that he still believed that "in the end justice will prevail, and my innocence will be understood and recognized."[6]

Throughout the criminal trial there was a subplot, "Petit Bois," that repeatedly recurred at sidebar conferences but always beyond the earshot of the jury. Petit Bois was finally identified as a six-mile-long barrier island in the Gulf of Mexico that the United States had sought to condemn in a case decided by Judge Nixon in 1982. The government had wanted the land for $330,000, on the assumption that it was only usable as undeveloped parkland, but the owner of the property, John Stocks, and his general counsel, Eugene Lewis, contested that evaluation. Judge Nixon ruled that the fair market value of the land was $6.2 million, and the government found no basis for an appeal.

A grand jury, subsequently, was empaneled in Tallahassee to investigate any wrongdoing in the trial, in particular any connection between Judge Nixon and either Stocks or Lewis. One allegation, offered in plea negotiations in another case, was that Nixon had been paid a $300,000 bribe by Stocks and Lewis. Both were indicted but never tried. The grand jury empaneled in Hattiesburg in 1984 investigated the Petit Bois case, as well as the relationship between Nixon and Wiley Fairchild. Nixon's defense urged that the Public Integrity Section of the Justice Department had targeted Judge Nixon and, because they were unable to locate any corruption in the context of Petit Bois, manufactured indictable offenses in the Wiley Fairchild affair.[7]

Reid Weingarten, by then in private practice with a prestigious Washington firm, was called to probe the issue of prosecutorial misconduct and his earlier unsuccessful criminal prosecution of Alcee Hastings. Weingarten was the vehicle for introducing the chronology of events that led to Nixon's conviction, and his testimony was punctuated by requests that the committee don headsets to hear recordings of various taped interviews and Nixon's testimony before the grand jury. Under questioning by Nixon's attorney, David Stewart of Washington, the Petit Bois Island case surfaced. Weingarten disavowed any involvement in that investigation and claimed that his introduction into the Nixon matter was triggered by Skip Jarvis's calls and knowledge that "there was something screwy going on with the Drew Fairchild case."[8] He admitted, however, under close questioning, that the grand jury that ultimately indicted Nixon had originally been formed to investigate Nixon and Petit Bois. Although insisting that he had not been a participant in the Petit Bois probe, Weingarten demonstrated familiarity with the case, acknowledged that the Public Integrity Section had discussed the mishandling of the condemnation case at trial, and eventually conceded that the two investigations had, at some point, dovetailed. The allegation that Nixon and Holmes received a $300,000 bribe brought him into Petit Bois discussions[9] but, Weingarten persisted, "the Petit Bois case had nothing to do with the investigation that I conducted."[10]

Weingarten was also asked about the credibility of the government's witnesses in the Nixon trial. All of the other principals in the case received lesser punishments than did the judge. Holmes, who ultimately won an appeal, served no prison time and paid only a $10,000 fine; Wiley Fairchild served thirty days in a halfway house; and Drew Fairchild, in the end, had only a six-month sentence. "These three defendants really didn't do badly," commented Representative Don Edwards, although "they were accused of pretty serious crimes."[11]

The believability of two of Weingarten's star witnesses was attacked as another aspect of prosecutorial misconduct, and Weingarten himself allowed that testimony by Holmes and Wiley Fairchild was problematic. Weingarten even conceded that he was always skeptical of Holmes, who had lied in three separate grand jury appearances and told even a fourth version of events in his initial FBI interview.[12] Weingarten, however, reconciled the conflicting testimony offered by his two most crucial witnesses by explaining that "simply because two witnesses testify inconsistently doesn't make one a liar."[13] Fairchild's veracity also questioned, with the implication that Weingarten had intimidated the old man into tailoring his testimony to avoid prison. Fairchild's attorney for plea discussions with Weingarten had filed an affidavit saying that Weingarten had held out the prospect of a dismissal of the charges against the elder Fairchild, or a recommendation of no prison time, or, at least, help in securing a pardon if Fairchild cooperated. Weingarten, however, contended that he always made disclaimers of what he might be able to do for Fairchild and that none of these issues were part of the plea bargain. "Once Wiley Fairchild started cooperating, I believe Wiley Fairchild was being as cooperative with the Government as he could." Even so, Weingarten allowed that he was dubious about the testimony that Fairchild offered.[14] He also acknowledged that he intervened in a limited way to protect Drew Fairchild from unfair retaliation in the state court system, but argued that all he did was to secure a federal indictment against Drew, arrange for his plea the same day, and recommend "fair treatment," a six-month sentence.[15]

Semantics were also debated. What constitutes a "false statement," and what is the meaning of "discuss"? Part of Nixon's defense was that he never "discussed" Drew Fairchild's case with anyone, that he merely relayed an allegation of blackmail from Wiley Fairchild to Bud Holmes. Weingarten did not budge in his contention that a discussion could be short, no more than two seconds, because "it depends on the import of what is being said," any "give and take." The only exception was if one person simply received information. With that understanding of "discuss," Weingarten had no difficulty in attributing false statements to Nixon before the grand jury.[16]

The committee met for only two days in June, hearing, in addition to Reid Weingarten, only Barbara Nixon. The judge's wife was called to explain how and why the Nixons had neglected to realize that the judge had been in Hattiesburg on May 14, 1982, having dental work done. The judge had flatly denied his presence in Hattiesburg that day more than once in his trial as an explanation for why Holmes was mistaken about the timing of the call to Fairchild. Mrs. Nixon said that she was informed that the FBI had taken the family's dental records and, because the government did not produce the records in the trial, the Nixons assumed they were not relevant.[17]

The committee reconvened the next month to hear the testimony of the principle government witnesses from the criminal trial, and Fairchild, Holmes, and Ingram each related much the same story about the oil leases, the telephone call, and the grand jury investigation that the jury had heard the first time. What was essentially new was what Fairchild and Holmes said about their dealings with the Public Integrity Section and Reid Weingarten. Wiley Fairchild, now seventy-five, admitted that his memory was blurred, and "I just get confused every time it's brought up."[18] He confirmed, however, that he believed that his testimony at Nixon's trial must please Weingarten if he expected help but added that he tried, nonetheless, to tell the truth. In his zeal to please the prosecutors, in fact, one of his representatives and Weingarten discussed all of the questions that might be asked at the trial. Weingarten posed the questions and John Baltar, for Fairchild, proposed possible answers, which were typed for Fairchild to memorize.[19] Weingarten had even provided the statement to be read at Fairchild's sentencing hearing, a statement that included his admission to offering the oil leases to Nixon in order to help his son. In fact, Fairchild said, "I never asked the judge to help Drew out."[20]

Holmes's testimony was parallel to what he had said at the trial until questions about his dealings with Weingarten were broached. Weingarten, for example, according to Holmes, brought the Petit Bois case before the grand jury twice. It was clear both to Holmes and to his attorney that Weingarten's main interest was getting Nixon off the bench, and he was convinced that he could avoid indictment if he could provide some damning evidence on Nixon. Holmes, whose story was substantiated by an affidavit from his lawyer, said that at one point they proposed to persuade Nixon to resign if that would satisfy the prosecutor. Weingarten, however, rejected their offer. Holmes, in fact, quoted the prosecutor as saying, "you can convict a Congressman any time, but getting a Federal judge convicted is tough."[21]

Carroll Ingram, like the other two, varied his testimony little until the issue of Petit Bois was raised. "I knew," he said, "that the Petit Bois case was under the purview of this grand jury."[22] Moreover, he had retained the elder statesman of trial lawyers, Joel Blass, when the FBI approached him. The night before Ingram's grand jury testimony, Blass had insisted that Ingram be informed about any documents, information, or anything relevant of which Ingram might not be aware. "I appeared in the grand jury under the impression that—almost that I was in the care of the Government." When he was confronted, nonetheless, with the oil leases that had not been back dated, which he did not know existed, Blass was upset about the "treatment I had received."[23] By the end of Ingram's testimony, Weingarten's behavior was an issue equal to that of Nixon's fitness for office.

Nixon's original request that he only make an opening statement was explained by his inability to prepare adequately while incarcerated. When a second invitation was issued, however, Nixon agreed to testify about the events between 1979 and 1985. He apologized to the committee for his erroneous testimony that he had not been in Hattiesburg on May 14, 1982, when, in fact, he had seen a dentist there.[24] Several members of the subcommittee asked Nixon about the propriety and the ethics of his behavior in the Drew Fairchild case. What was the distinction, if any, between what might be legal and what might be ethical?[25] Representative James Sensenbrenner raised a more telling question, one that likely remained paramount in the subcommittee's collective thoughts throughout: "What do you think the public respect for the Federal judiciary is when a Federal judge is incarcerated?"[26] In the same vein, John Conyers added, "you would be the only jurist in American history convicted of an impeachable offense, serves time, paid during that period, and then return to the bench."[27] That comment probably underscored why the House would, despite any evidence of a possible miscarriage of justice, see no alternative to impeaching Judge Nixon.

The subcommittee ended its hearings on July 12, 1988, and subsequently voted unanimously to impeach, a recommendation that was also unanimously confirmed by the full Judiciary Committee. The case did not surface for further action until May 10, 1989, when what had originally been House Resolution 407 in the previous Congress emerged as House Resolution 87, impeaching Walter L. Nixon, Jr., on three articles. Articles 1 and 2 covered the two charges of perjury on which Nixon had originally been convicted; the third was a summary alleging that Nixon had "brought disrepute on the Federal courts and the administration of justice."[28] That count then listed fourteen allegations of false or misleading statements, seven in Nixon's initial interview with federal agents and seven in his grand jury testimony.

Representative Jack Brooks of the House Judiciary Committee introduced the impeachment resolution, and subcommittee chair Don Edwards provided the particulars. Edwards contended that "at the outset we determined not to rubber stamp the jury's verdict,"[29] but concluded that Nixon had been involved in a "pattern of lies, concealment and deceit" and ought to be impeached.[30] The House voted, 417 to 0, in favor of the resolution,[31] and the normal resolutions naming managers and empowering them to act on behalf of the House were made.[32]

Before the Senate

Nixon continued to seek relief in the courts and filed for a Section 2255 hearing, akin to a habeas corpus petition, for a new trial, and two days of hearings were held in August that focused largely on allegations of false testimony by the Fairchilds, induced by the prosecution, at Nixon's trial. He also argued that the prosecution had withheld information (the dental records) from the defense. The motion for a new trial was denied,[33] and Nixon appealed to the Fifth Circuit Court of Appeals, where his plea that Wiley Fairchild had recanted his earlier testimony was equally unsuccessful.[34]

Senate Resolution 128, establishing an evidentiary committee to receive testimony and other information, was approved on May 11, 1989,[35] and, with far more speed than in either the Claiborne or the Hastings cases, a committee was organized. Alcee Hastings's case was, in fact, still in the pretrial stages, which complicated consideration of the Nixon matter because Jack Brooks was designated as lead House manager in both. To avoid unnecessary delay, Don Edwards eventually assumed the primary prosecutorial role against Nixon. The special committee, composed as was now the established norm of an equal number of Democrats and Republicans,[36] held its first organizational meeting on May 16 to name Wyche Fowler chair. Two members of the committee, Howell Heflin and Orrin Hatch, were veterans of the Claiborne impeachment committee.

Nixon's defense team filed a raft of pretrial motions requesting a trial before the full Senate, immunity for Robert Royals (Drew Fairchild's partner at the airport at the time of the drug smuggling episode), dismissal of the third article of impeachment as redundant, and appropriation of defense funds.[37] The pretrial filings on both sides relied heavily on both the Claiborne and Hastings cases as precedents, although even British practices were cited. The Senate evidentiary committee heard arguments on the motions and rejected all. Nixon's defense before the Senate relied heavily on the assertion that Wiley Fairchild had recanted his testimony at the criminal trial. Fairchild was almost seventy-seven by the time the senators heard his version of the oil leases, the telephone call, and his allegations of blackmail.[38] He undercut the judge's assertions of false testimony almost from the beginning by stating that he never intended to testify falsely, but that "I was awfully confused" when testifying in the House and also at the hearing for a new trial. "It didn't come out like I intended to because what I said was based on what my brother Rodney had said," he admitted, "and that's just not the way it was, the best that I can recollect."[39] He denied that any earlier recantation was accurate,[40] but his memory was obviously fuzzy and muddled about the crucial events of eight or nine years earlier. Chairman Fowler, however, tried to capture the essence of what Fairchild intended to say. First, he wanted both Royals and his son prosecuted or neither and, second, Nixon had told him on the telephone that things were arranged to his satisfaction, although what constituted that arrangement was not clear.[41]

Holmes assumed a less abrasive style and tone than in his earlier presentations but embroidered his version of the drive to the farm and telephone call to Fairchild from there. Porter's unpaid legal fees receded into the background in Holmes's explanation of his decision to indict Drew Fairchild in state court; the call to Wiley Fairchild, this time, might have been instigated by Holmes;[42] and his explanation for not telling the grand jury about the call was altered. "Well, quite frankly, I just didn't want to counter or contradict what Judge Nixon had already said in the public statement," Holmes claimed, "and I guess he was just trying to protect his public image."[43] His most damning testimony was his description of the disputed "discussion" as clearly a "two to three minute conversation."[44] He even said that Nixon had attempted to influence him but added that "I was the aggressor in the thing, I went forward and said, well, shoot, let's pick you up some brownie points; it's no skin off my teeth."[45]

Carroll Ingram did not vary his testimony but, when questioned by Senator Herbert Kohl, touched the base of the whole case against Nixon. The senator noted, "And I seem to hear you say that in and around Hattiesburg, he having done what he did, if in fact he did it, would not have been so unusual, not illegal, not immoral, not necessarily unethical, but that his problem is that he just never told the grand jury that he did it when in fact he had done it."[46] "I think that's the essence," Ingram replied coolly, "of why we are here."[47] Senator Harry Reid subsequently commented that "I can think of very few instances where I have seen a bigger waste of taxpayers' money than this whole proceeding here" and bemoaned that the Justice Department, considering the savings and loan scandal and drug enforcement problems, was "wasting their time on this kind of stuff."[48]

Nixon's defense introduced prior testimony or affidavits of several people, as well as character witnesses, in lieu of their physical appearance before the committee. The primary defense witness, however, was Judge Nixon, who began his testimony on the afternoon of September 12 and continued the following day. Nixon testified that he had failed to mention the conversations relating to blackmail to federal agents in the April 1984 interview because "it didn't, simply did not come to my mind."[49] He pleaded that he had tried to tell the truth in that interview, but "it caught me—I was just hit cold on matters that

had happened, apparently, from one to five years before."[50] He used
the same logic to explain his failure to tell the grand jury about the
Holmes conversation.[51] The crux of his testimony was his repeated
claim that any discrepancies between his grand jury testimony and
reality were either the result of interpretation — for example, the meaning of "discuss" or "influence" — or simple lack of recall. Senator after
senator questioned Nixon about his not remembering the discussion
between the April interview and his grand jury testimony in July. Why
did he fail to return to the grand jury to clarify his error when he did
recognize it?

House manager Edwards briefly summarized the case: "Judge Nixon
is not the kind of a defendant who has shredded documents or left
the scene of a crime, laundered money. He is a Federal judge for 20
years of excellent reputation." But, Edwards continued, the House was
"firmly convinced" that Nixon had committed serious crimes when he
lied to federal investigators and to the grand jury.[52] At the close of
committee hearings both sides were instructed to be prepared for presentations to the Senate by October 17, but, ironically, Alcee Hastings's
case was the one the full Senate heard that week. Twelve days after
Hastings's conviction, on Wednesday, November 1, Nixon's final arguments were presented on the floor of the Senate.

Each side addressed three issues in its presentation: motions for a
trial before the full Senate, dismissal of the third omnibus article, and
the guilt or innocence of Judge Nixon. Representative Edwards described the elements of the case against Nixon and the specifics of the
three articles of impeachment. Then James Sensenbrenner carefully
dissected the arguments offered by Nixon to the evidentiary committee
and argued that, even if all of his version of events was accurate, a
discussion of the Drew Fairchild case clearly occurred. The defense
that Nixon simply forgot about the conversation with Holmes and the
subsequent call to Wiley Fairchild, moreover, Sensenbrenner asserted,
"defies the imagination."[53] Benjamin Cardin concluded the case by
claiming that the "evidence is overwhelming," that "Judge Nixon helped
a drug smuggler . . . [and] lied about his involvement."[54]

Judge Nixon then rose to address the senators with his plea of
innocence. "I am paying a debt that is not owed," he said, "I have
committed no crime"[55] and am "convicted of perjury on the basis of
admittedly perjured testimony."[56] His attorney followed with a detailed
answer to each charge, referring to the instances of alleged perjury as

"misstatements" and arguing that none were material or intentional and, further, that the charges rested on the testimony of Holmes and Fairchild, "witnesses without credibility."[57]

Senators were permitted in the Nixon case to submit written questions addressed to either the House managers or to the defense, and many chose to exercise that option. Questions of entrapment, prosecutorial misconduct, and Jarvis's role as a confidential informant were raised, as were queries about the intent of the third article and the evidence of targeting. Judge Nixon was asked to reconcile his various statements and to explain if concealment was tantamount to perjury. Explanations for back dating the deeds on the oil leases and Nixon's failure to correct his testimony before the grand jury were sought as the senators directed questions equally to the House managers and to Nixon's defense.

The Senate recessed as a court of impeachment until the next afternoon, when six hours of closed-door deliberations began. All that is known of the discussions that occurred on the afternoon of November 2 is what can be gleaned from the statements later entered into the record by senators explaining their votes. Howard Levin justified his vote for conviction on the first two articles on his belief that the original jury reached the right verdict,[58] whereas Terry Sanford lamented that "it is more than regrettable that the Justice Department made a criminal of this judge."[59] Howard Grassley argued that Nixon's version simply failed to equal the facts but, more importantly, upon his release from federal custody, "the Senate would be sending a convicted felon . . . to sit in judgment of others."[60] Senator Kohl, who had served on the evidentiary committee, voted for removal but added that he had a fundamental objection to the "shotgun or blunderbuss" tactics of the Justice Department in its prosecution of the case.[61] Jeffords, who also served on the evidentiary committee, stated for the record that Nixon's failure to correct his testimony before the grand jury was unfathomable. Nixon's explanations on that score, he argued, were unsatisfactory and implied that he was trying to hide aspects of his transactions with Wiley Fairchild.[62]

The Senate gathered on November 3, 1989, with only three members absent, to repeat a task that was becoming all too familiar. Formal voting on Nixon's fate began with a poll on the two motions. The first, for a full Senate trial, failed overwhelmingly, 90 to 7, although three of the seven voting for a full trial had been involved directly in hearings on either Nixon's case or that of Hastings. The motion to dismiss the third article of impeachment, that which alleged fourteen separate instances of lying, required only a simple majority and failed, with 34 voting in favor and 63 against. Again, seven of the senators who served on the evidentiary committee voted to dismiss.

The Senate, having settled the final motions, voted on each article of impeachment in turn. Article 1, alleging that Nixon had made a false statement to the grand jury when he did not acknowledge that District Attorney Holmes had discussed the Drew Fairchild case with him, was a replication of the first charge on which Nixon had been convicted in the criminal trial. The guilty vote on the first article was overwhelming, 89 to 8, although three of the senators who had heard testimony and received evidence in the Senate committee were among those voting not guilty. Article 2 was the charge that in his closing statements to the grand jury Nixon had lied when he said he had never influenced anyone in the case; the vote again was guilty, although the margin was somewhat smaller, 78 to 19. Among those voting to acquit were, again, five members of the evidentiary committee. Article 3, the omnibus allegation of fourteen separate instances of lying, however, was rejected in a vote of 57 to 40, short of the required two-thirds majority to convict. Walter L. Nixon, Jr., was convicted by the Senate and removed from the office of federal judge.

Reid Weingarten, no longer with the Justice Department, continued in the private practice of law and likely took pride in seeing his prosecution of Nixon confirmed. He, moreover, probably felt that his efforts to prosecute Alcee Hastings were vindicated by the Senate's actions only two weeks earlier. By the conclusion of the congressional process, Wiley Fairchild had completed his thirty days in a halfway facility in Jackson, and Drew Fairchild had finished the six-month sentence he received for his part in the drug smuggling scheme. Bud Holmes, having won his appeal, was free from any prison time and, although disbarred, maintained a substantial ownership in a restaurant and lounge chain. Walter Nixon returned to Eglin Air Force Base Prison Camp to complete his term of incarceration, although soon he would be eligible for parole.

Notes

1. *U.S. v. Nixon*, 816 F.2d 1022 (1987).
2. The appellate court held that a rehearing *en banc* could be held only if voted by a majority of the judges who had not recused themselves. No

en banc poll, however, had been requested. The circuit followed its normal practice of not granting an *en banc* hearing except in cases involving "precedent setting error of exceptional public importance or an opinion that directly conflicts with prior Supreme Court or Fifth Circuit precedent." *U.S. v. Nixon*, 827 F.2d 1019 (1987).

3. Solov, "Judge Nixon Refuses to Resign," 1.

4. Strasser, "A Judge's Fall from Grace," 24.

5. Tom Brennan, a former Mississippi newspaper reporter, and Fred Strasser, author of an article in the *National Law Journal*, were requested by Nixon because of their coverage of his trial. Both had been privy to discussions with prosecutor Reid Weingarten and others. Another witness who had been convicted of bank fraud was also on Nixon's list. Personal appearances by all three were denied by the House subcommittee.

6. Nixon told the subcommittee that "if I believed for a moment that I had committed a crime, I would have resigned as a judge and this hearing would not be necessary." *Hearings before the Subcommittee on Civil and Constitutional Rights, Judge Walter L. Nixon, Jr.,* 5. [Hereafter cited as *House Hearings.*]

7. *Report of the Senate Impeachment Trial Committee on the Articles Against Judge Walter L. Nixon, Jr.,: Exhibit 2,* 2:1849–58. [Hereafter cited as *Senate Exhibits.*]

8. *House Hearings,* 16–17.

9. Ibid., 61–63.

10. Ibid., 98.

11. Ibid., 31.

12. Weingarten said that Holmes had been subjected to a polygraph, but only on Petit Bois questions. Ibid., 32.

13. Ibid., 35.

14. Ibid., 51.

15. Ibid., 55–61.

16. Confusion over the meaning of "discuss" was not apparently simply a defense maneuver. Weingarten affirmed that the jury had, at one point in its deliberations, asked the judge for a definition. Its request was denied. Even Weingarten, when pushed about the possible interpretations that Judge Nixon might have put on the word when he answered questions before the grand jury, responded, "Is it technically false? Is it legally false? I mean, you're asking me an almost impossible question." Ibid., 44.

17. Ibid., 103.

18. Ibid., 155.

19. Ibid., 216–19.

20. Ibid., 223.

21. Ibid., 292.

22. Ibid., 390.
23. Ibid., 395.
24. Ibid., 456.
25. Nixon's lawyer had sought an opinion from Yale Law Professor Geoffrey Hazard regarding any possible violation of the Canons of Judicial Conduct. Hazard had found none, whether accepting Nixon's version or that of Holmes. That memorandum of opinion was submitted to the subcommittee. *Senate Exhibits,* 1263–70.
26. *House Hearings,* 463.
27. Ibid., 496.
28. *Congressional Record,* May 10, 1989, H-1802.
29. Ibid., H-1803.
30. Ibid., H-1805.
31. Ibid.
32. The House managers named were Jack Brooks, Don Edwards, Benjamin Cardin, James Sensenbrenner, and William Dannemeyer. Ibid.
33. *U.S. v. Nixon,* 703 F.Supp. 538 (1988).
34. 881 F.2d 1305 (1989).
35. *Congressional Record,* May 11, 1989, S-5133–34.
36. The committee consisted of Democrats Wyche Fowler, Howell Heflin, Timothy Wirth, Harry Reid, Charles Robb, and Herbert Kohl, as well as Republicans Orrin Hatch, John Chaffee, Frank Murkowski, James Jeffords, Connie Mack, and Steve Symms.
37. Nixon, in his motion filed on June 23, 1989, said that his legal fees for the initial criminal trial had exceeded $400,000 and that his costs thus far in congressional proceedings had passed $100,000. He projected that another five hundred to a thousand hours of attorney time (at $75 an hour) and other expenses would be incurred by the conclusion of the Senate trial. *Report of the Senate Impeachment Trial Committee on the Articles Against Judge Walter L. Nixon, Jr., Pretrial,* 1:117. The House managers responded that defense funds had been requested by Charles Swayne in 1905 and by Alcee Hastings in 1989, but that none had ever been granted. Ibid., 241.
38. *Hearings Before the Senate Impeachment Trial Committee, United States Senate,* 2:47.
39. He stated that the prosecutors at the original trial might have tried to influence him to testify falsely, but quickly tempered that answer: "I mean, they could have, but I just—there's so much negotiation going on, but just intentionally try to get me to lie, no, I don't think they did." Ibid., 55.
40. Ibid., 85.
41. Ibid.

42. "My memory on the thing was the question said, 'Do you mind if I tell him?'" Holmes, unlike in previous testimony, added, "And I could have been the one who said, 'Let's call him,' or 'I'll call him.'" Ibid., 101.

43. Ibid., 107.

44. Ibid., 114.

45. Ibid., 146.

46. Ibid., 189.

47. Ibid.

48. Ibid., 196.

49. Ibid., 241.

50. Ibid., 263.

51. Ibid., 241.

52. Ibid., 320.

53. *Congressional Record*, November 1, 1989, S-14498.

54. Ibid., S-14502.

55. Ibid.

56. Ibid.

57. Ibid., S-14506.

58. *Congressional Record*, November 3, 1989, 14636–37.

59. Ibid., S-14637.

60. Ibid., S-14368.

61. *Congressional Record*, November 7, 1989, S-15191.

62. *Congressional Record*, November 9, 1989, S-15394–95.

8

As Thou Urgest Justice

"If men were angels," James Madison wrote, "no government would be necessary." Because that is not the case, he noted, "experience has taught . . . the necessity of auxiliary precautions."[1] The tendencies of human nature toward despotism and greed prompted those who framed governments in Anglo-American history to seek means of dividing power and placing checks on authority. Judicial independence, as a bulwark against tyranny, was recognized by the British under William III, and by 1776 the maxim was well established that judges, in order to maintain their dignity and independence, should serve as long as they do well.[2] That concept was embodied in the American Constitution and justified by Alexander Hamilton as "the best expedient which can be devised in any government, to secure a steady, upright, and impartial administration of the laws."[3] The difficulty lies, unfortunately, in balancing that maxim with the equally important precept that no one is above the law.

The scheme of impeachment by the lower chamber and trial by the upper house was devised more than seven hundred years ago to check the unbridled independence, not just of judges, but more importantly, of ministers of the executive branch. The initially crude design begun in 1376 evolved in Britain over centuries, although judges were exempted from the process as part of the Settlement of 1701, and fifteen years in advance of the American Revolution, in 1761, were granted complete independence.[4] The concept of impeachment was transposed and adapted to the United States and began its own two-hundred-year-long evolution. Only two of the sixteen impeachments voted by the House of Representatives did not involve judges, and even that use lay dormant for fifty years after the Senate trial of Halsted Ritter.

Impeachment entered a new phase in the 1980s and ceased to be a novelty, more potent in its threat than in its practice.

The New Era

What has prompted the resurrection of impeachment as a tool to protect against the whim or caprice of life-tenured judges? Coincidence of events would suggest that the Judicial Conduct Act of 1980 played a role in ferreting out misbehaving or felonious judges. On closer examination, however, one sees that the new law for policing the judicial ranks played a significant role only in the impeachment of Alcee Hastings. After his acquittal in a jury trial, in fact, Hastings would have escaped all censure without the procedures of the Judicial Conduct Act. In the Claiborne case, that process was not invoked at all because of the assumption of the Ninth Circuit judges that the new law was to be used in cases of minor complaints and only Congress was constitutionally empowered to act in cases involving a felony conviction. The Eleventh Circuit, which had actively pursued the Hastings allegations, did no more than certify the record of conviction in the later Nixon case.

Impeachment has changed, according to some, by virtue of the sheer number of federal judges. The federal bench swelled to almost nine hundred judges during the seventies and eighties and, so the argument goes, as there are more judges, there is a greater likelihood that more will abuse their offices. That proposition falls flat if it implies that fewer than a thousand honest and qualified members of the legal profession can be attracted to the federal bench. The more likely problem was probably touched by Representative Henry Hyde in the House arguments on the impeachment of Walter Nixon. The upper house, he suggested, should, in the confirmation process, "spend more time on the character of the nominees rather than their ideology."[5] Executive agendas for the judiciary have truly assumed greater influence in judicial nominations in this century than in past ones. Beginning with the presidency of Theodore Roosevelt, emphasis shifted toward the policy orientation of nominees and away from patronage.[6] Franklin Roosevelt sought appointees sympathetic to his vision of government, and Richard Nixon chose only those who he thought were "strict constructionists."[7] All administrations rewarded party faithful with judicial posts, but both Jimmy Carter's and Ronald Reagan's clearly subordinated all other criteria to their own policy goals. Carter tried to bring greater ethnic and gender diversity to the bench, while Reagan tried to pack the bench with judicial conservatives.[8] The Senate's role in the appointment process is limited only to advice and consent; it can reject, but it cannot choose.

In the Justice Department, the executive branch has a tool that might be used to keep undesirable judges in check, and Claiborne, Hastings, and Nixon argued that they were the victims of such selective prosecution. Hastings and Claiborne were liberal Democrats and vocal critics of the Reagan administration, facts that they claimed prompted partisan vendettas against them. Nixon, however, suggested no partisan political basis for the investigations that focused on him. He had been nominated by Democratic President Lyndon Johnson, but he was also asked to accept a nomination by Republican President Ronald Reagan to the Fifth Circuit Court of Appeals, apparently because he was among the many southern Democrats who changed party loyalties. Local-level politics may have played a role in the prosecution of Harry Claiborne and possibly even that of Alcee Hastings, but, again, are not evident in Walter Nixon's case.

Alexander Hamilton labeled impeachment as political in nature, and some, such as Jacobus Ten Broek, have argued that most earlier judicial impeachments were inspired by partisan aims. In the new era of impeachment, however, politics seem to have been relevant only in the broadest sense of the term, and partisan politics, if involved at all, were muted. That conclusion seems particularly apparent in the treatment that each of the three judges received in Congress. Votes in neither house split along partisan or ideological lines. Whereas Hamilton had predicted in the *Federalist Papers* that "the comparative strength of parties" would be more decisive than the innocence or guilt of the accused,[9] impeachments in the 1980s were not overtly partisan.

Theme and Variations in the 1980s

Representative Robert Kastenmeier, in his comments on the Nixon impeachment, noted that the House had considered impeachments of three judges in fewer than three years and that "these three cases are very much alike."[10] The similarities that he noted were that all three men had been given criminal trials and all refused to resign. Kastenmeier's comments were, of course, correct but touch only on the most superficial similarities among the three cases. The three individuals were totally different in their backgrounds and their records on the bench. Claiborne and Hastings were self-made men who had achieved their ambitions through their own initiatives. Nixon, although he liked to note his early paper routes and other menial jobs, was born into a political family with a place in the southern Mississippi establishment. Claiborne was noted as an outstanding defense attorney, whereas Nixon was acclaimed as a brilliant jurist; Hastings was described as hard-working and courteous. Both Claiborne and Nixon had successful and lucrative law practices that they abandoned for a place on the bench, but Alcee Hastings found that the judiciary offered the financial stability that had eluded him in private practice. Nixon assumed his judgeship at the relatively early age of thirty-nine, whereas Hastings and Claiborne came to the bench at more advanced ages. The three, moreover, represented distinctly different parts of the country, geographically and culturally.

Bribery was the core charge against each judge, at least at the inception of investigations. Hastings was accused of soliciting a bribe, as was Claiborne in his first criminal trial; Nixon was accused of the more minor offense of accepting an illegal gratuity. Bribery of judges has traditionally been viewed as a particularly heinous offense, for "this sordid vice" contaminates the process of impartial justice. Blackstone, writing in 1778, had noted that bribery of any official was criminal, "but in judges, particularly the superior ones, it hath been always looked upon as so heinous an offense that the chief justice Thorpe was hanged for it."[11] English judges convicted of the crime were fined three times the bribe, punished, and discharged from public service forever.

The seriousness of bribery allegations against sitting federal judges undoubtedly warrants intensive Justice Department scrutiny, but even though that charge eventually evaporated in both the Claiborne and Nixon cases, the Public Integrity Section was tenacious in pursuing convictions on any grounds. Conversely, in the Hastings case, the gravity of the allegation was discounted by concern for a mere $125,000 that the authorities were unwilling to "let run." The only means of solidly linking Hastings to the bribery attempt by Borders was to see if the money would find its way to the judge. The Justice Department was unwilling to take that gamble, and millions were later spent to prosecute Hastings in a criminal case before the judiciary and in Congress. The jury verdict in the Hastings case will always cloud the Senate action.

Priests and parsons are rarely government informants, but those who accused these judges were a particularly unsavory lot. Joseph Conforte, facing multiple federal and state charges and substantial income tax liabilities, fingered Claiborne, and William Dredge, a small-time crook, accused Hastings. Conforte and Dredge had no motive in mind when they approached federal authorities other than cutting beneficial deals for themselves, and each negotiated quite a bargain. Conforte's five-year sentence for tax evasion was reduced to fifteen months, and, on a Nevada bribery charge that carried a ten-year maximum penalty, he managed a mere eighteen-month sentence that ran concurrently with the federal one. Federal charges of bail-jumping and flight and a Nevada prosecution under the habitual criminal statute were dismissed. His tax liability was reduced from some $19 million to $7.3 million, and he was granted immunity for his testimony about offering two bribes. Dredge was not an equally skilled negotiator but, even so, managed to win a guarantee of no more than five years in prison and a $15,000 fine for his part in a conspiracy to distribute Quaaludes.

Conforte's testimony, judged by the decision to dismiss all bribery charges against Claiborne, did not prove credible. Dredge never appeared in the criminal case against Hastings, and his information about a bribery plot between mobster Santo Trafficante and Borders was not pursued. The motives and reliability of either informant do not inspire great confidence, but the Public Integrity Section staked their cases against Claiborne and Hastings on them.

Skip Jarvis, described by Nixon's defense lawyer as a "looney tunes character," was not a convicted felon trying to cut a deal for himself. Instead, he was a lawyer with a personal feud, not with Nixon but rather with Wiley Fairchild. His self-described "Dick Tracy" antics were ultimately fruitless, for even the prosecution concluded that much of the information he offered was wrong and the jury rejected the allegation of any wrongdoing in the oil leases. The Justice Department, when the allegations offered by Jarvis and Conforte dissolved, pursued lesser charges. Claiborne's tax returns would normally have been the subjects of an audit and possible civil penalties. The zeal of the prosecution, once the bribery charges were set aside, however, made the tax questions matters of criminality. Nixon's testimony, voluntarily offered before the grand jury, became the focus of the Public Integrity

Section. Nixon dug a hole for himself, but the Justice Department, according to Senator Terry Sanford, "made a criminal of this judge."[12]

All three judges were subject to criminal trials that led to different outcomes. Claiborne and Nixon were convicted, but Hastings was exonerated. The Constitution, in Article I, section 2, clearly does not preclude criminal liability in addition to impeachment, but, as Hamilton noted in the ratification debates, "the strong bias of one decision would be apt to overrule the influence of any new lights which might be brought to vary the complexion of the other decision."[13] The jury verdicts in the Nixon and Claiborne cases clearly determined the outcomes of their cases before the Senate. The comment that a convicted felon simply cannot serve as a federal judge was repeatedly echoed in one form or another; the contradiction is both obvious and unavoidable.

Hastings posed the opposite dilemma, for he returned to the bench after his acquittal, but the very fact of his accusation and trial cast a shadow on his judicial actions. The potential problem of an assumption of bias in all cases in which the government was a party was noted in appeals by both Claiborne and Hastings. Must a judge who has been the object of a Justice Department prosecution be recused in every criminal case that comes before him? The Hastings case answered that question in the negative. It raised, however, another problem that is perhaps more troublesome, for there apparently remained among federal agents an assumption of criminality, as demonstrated in the investigation of the wiretap disclosure. When evidence surfaced that a wiretap leak occurred, the Justice Department immediately assumed Hastings's culpability and accepted Miami Mayor Steve Clark's version of events without question. Federal investigators failed to explore even the most obvious possibilities for alternative sources of Clark's information, whereas Hastings's defense had little difficulty in providing several other plausible explanations. The impeachment article against Hastings on the wiretap disclosure was rejected unanimously by the Senate. However, the taint of the charges, even after his criminal trial, tracked Hastings, and his reputation and standing in the legal community suffered.[14] The additional difficulty that arises from a judge's defending a criminal prosecution, regardless of the verdict, is the cost of mounting a legal battle. Fighting a criminal charge is an expensive burden, a form of punishment that falls equally on both the innocent and the guilty.

The role that the 1980 Judicial Conduct Act played in each case is also instructive. That law was the subject of considerable criticism and of appeals by Alcee Hastings. Even in its earlier incarnation, Senator Sam Ervin had characterized the proposal for judges supervising one another as a "hazing commission."[15] Justice William Douglas, in his dissent in *Chandler v. Judicial Council,* had expressed a similar concern. "But I search the Constitution in vain for any power of surveillance," he wrote, "which other federal judges have over those aberrations."[16] His sentiments were pronounced even more strongly in the dissent of Justice Hugo Black.[17]

Those apprehensions were not merited in all three of the cases that resulted in impeachment after the law's implementation. The Ninth Circuit Judicial Council took no action on Claiborne's conviction and, in view of the Nevada supreme court's refusal to disbar him, may well have been sympathetic to his plight. The Eleventh Circuit Judicial Council acted in the Nixon case only in a most passive fashion, serving merely as a vehicle to transmit the findings of the jury through the system to the House of Representatives. In the Hastings case, if one is convinced (as the Senate was) that the jury reached the wrong conclusion, then the Eleventh Circuit Judicial Council acted as the law had anticipated it should. The Judicial Conduct Act was designed to assure that judges would not act as a "priestly tribe" cloaked in the holy vestments of their offices. The "cult of the robe" was not intended to render judges impervious to criticism and surely not to criminal scrutiny.[18]

Judicial Ethics

Corruption in political life in the United States is nothing new, nor is it restricted to judges.[19] The judiciary, however, constitutes a special case where impartiality is not only prized but is also an intrinsic attribute of the position. Indeed, "the goal of insulation and independence is a particularly distinctive and significant feature of the judicial role."[20] Judicial independence, then, involves more than protections from executive or legislative intrusions into judicial decision making. It requires also that judges act independently of financial, partisan, and friendship considerations. Standards of judicial behavior are expected to be higher than others; judges must "avoid impropriety and the appearance of impropriety."[21] Judges are, as the old adage goes, to be like Caesar's wife, beyond reproach. A single misstep by a judge may "have damaging consequences far out of proportion to its intrinsic moral seriousness."[22]

Although the prosecutions of Claiborne, Hastings, and Nixon were flawed, each judge certainly fell short of these expectations. Each argued that he was a victim of a flim-flam man and convicted as a result of perjured and self-serving testimony, but each likely would have rejected such worn-out pleas if offered by defendants in their courtrooms. The perjurers and rainmakers were, moreover, friends or business associates of the judges. Each judge indulged in behavior that invited suspicion: Claiborne cashed checks at casinos, while Hastings more than once played telephone tag from pay telephones. Nixon never questioned why Wiley Fairchild included him in lucrative business transactions. The Claiborne tax case was undeniably treated differently than the average citizen's, but he was, after all, not just the ordinary man on the street. Alcee Hastings alleged that he was a victim of his friends and avowed complete shock at the behavior of William Borders and Hemphill Pride, although the latter was a convicted felon. Hastings's departure from the Washington airport after Borders's arrest, although perhaps not technically "flight," was inconsistent with expectations of proper judicial behavior. Even his choices for legal counsel and the many changes thereof signaled a gamesmanship approach to the legal system. Major phases of the Hastings investigation were bungled, from the decision not to let the bribe money reach the judge to the ill-fated and obviously erroneous wiretap allegation. Hastings's behavior when accused, however, demonstrated a lack of those qualities most prized on the bench: temperament and judgment.

Walter Nixon, unlike Claiborne and Hastings, was not prone to public outbursts. He may not technically have received an illegal gratuity from Wiley Fairchild, but the propriety of a judge asking an influential person to include him in a business deal and never even pausing at the significant profits his oil investment yielded seems dubious. Fairchild likely would not have offered the deal were Nixon not a federal judge and if he could not at some time anticipate some reciprocity. His investment apparently was not wasted, as Nixon was willing to "put in a good word" for his son with District Attorney Holmes. Nixon's denial of any connection with Drew Fairchild's cases before the grand jury may have been an oversight. Nonetheless, a jurist of his experience surely could have attempted to correct the error; even the comical Jerry

Watson sent a telegram to the grand jury investigating Claiborne to rectify an omission in his testimony.

Claiborne's and Nixon's actions drew scrutiny when they each appeared in need of money, finding their judicial salaries too constraining. The need for higher salaries to attract the best to the federal judiciary has been recognized since the Constitutional Convention in 1787.[23] Competition with the significant compensation available in private legal practice has remained an issue throughout American history, and even Justices Benjamin P. Curtis and Samuel Freeman Miller in the nineteenth century were tempted to desert the Supreme Court for the increased income and prestige that could be found in corporate law.[24] The ideal of attracting and compensating federal judges well might foster the sense that judges serve *nec spe nec metu*, without hope and without fear. Federal judicial salaries have been raised but will likely never be on par with the inflated incomes of some private attorneys. Greed and venality, however, might still lead judges astray, whatever the compensation offered.

The specific criminal charges levied against these three judges may not have been fully justified, and the prosecutions stand as no model of investigatory tactics. Actions of the three, nonetheless, marred the image of the federal judiciary. Intelligent and personable judges each, whether through calculated or thoughtless deed, compromised their offices of trust. Courts are, as Alexander Hamilton noted, "the least dangerous branch of government," but they are also undemocratic institutions because they say that "the majority of the people cannot always do what they wish."[25] The legitimacy of courts is consequently more crucial than perhaps that of other powers of government. Legitimacy not only confers prestige, but it is also the fount of judicial power and authority. Legitimacy is not approval, but rather is accorded to the courts when the proper authority allows judges to make decisions and when those pronouncements are "not grossly biased or totally absurd."[26] It is, conversely, forfeited if judges are seen to "take the law in their hands as if there was nothing more to it than having a winning hand."[27]

Ethical standards for judges, although not for legislators, were firmly established in the nineteenth century,[28] and the American Bar Association continues to modernize and clarify the boundaries of acceptable judicial conduct.[29] Corruption on the bench or in other public offices is intolerable, not just because of the moral implications but also because it undermines the norms "indispensable for the maintenance of political democracy."[30]

The Congressional Role

Impeachment is a clumsy, time-consuming, and expensive procedure. Those attributes of the process were recognized in Britain, where no impeachment has been undertaken since 1805. Dissatisfaction with the system in the United States has been expressed by those participating in it from Edmund Randolph after the trial of Samuel Chase in 1805 to Senator Howell Heflin in the 1980s. The American states recognized the limitations of both impeachment and address by the legislature for investigating and correcting judicial misbehavior, and in the decades since 1960 a number of other schemes have been tried for sanctioning errant judges. Measuring the effectiveness of the various schemes is not possible because most, like the federal judicial council procedures, function in private to protect the reputation of the system as a whole and of one who is wrongly accused. The state judicial discipline councils have not, however, been accused of laxness. They have, if anything, been overly zealous, and judges who appeal the sanctions applied to them tend to receive even harsher punishments.[31]

The creaky federal machinery of impeachment, although unused for fifty years, seems once again to be working. The Claiborne case in 1986 was much like the impeachment of John Pickering in 1803, as members of both the House and the Senate felt their way through the proceedings.[32] The fifty-year hiatus meant that virtually no one had any firsthand experience with the system except the brush made before Richard Nixon resigned as president in 1974.

Hastings and Claiborne raised constitutional questions challenging trial in advance of impeachment, a breach of separation of powers, incursions into judicial independence, and the legitimacy of the Judicial Conduct Act. Through Hastings's and Claiborne's attempts, the answers provided by appellate courts were sufficiently settled that Walter Nixon raised none. Nixon, however, later raised constitutional questions about the use of a Senate evidentiary to "try" him.[33] The Supreme Court, reversing its practice of never hearing an impeachment question, granted *certiorari* on February 24, 1992, but did not hear arguments until the next session. The issue raised, however, is quite distinct from those presented in *Isaacs and Kerner,* now supported by decisions on Hastings and Claiborne, and the *Isaacs* case can be treated as settled law.

A routine has likewise been adopted in Congress for handling impeachments of federal judges. The House now seems comfortable in disposing of its obligation to accuse rather promptly. It may, in fact, now discharge its duties as accuser too quickly and too easily, acting much like a grand jury that simply rubber stamps the presentation of the prosecutor with an indictment. The House, in the Nixon and Claiborne cases, predetermined its actions and heard only minimal evidence. The Senate has also adapted to its now all-too-common role as judge and jury. Provisions allowing for a committee, instead of the full Senate, to hear and gather evidence are not new but were first used in the trial of Harry Claiborne. The committees, in each of the three cases, approached their tasks conscientiously and produced volumes of reports, exhibits, transcripts, and even video tapes for the other senators. The evidentiary committees, however, are not permitted to recommend action to the full Senate and may simply construct an objective report. The record in each of these cases is voluminous and would require hours or days for digestion by those senators who did not directly participate in the hearings.

Nixon's post-Senate conviction case challenges the validity of the evidentiary committee system by focusing on the Article 1 provision that gives the Senate "the sole power to try all Impeachments." The district court, hearing his allegations, dismissed the claim as nonjusticiable because the internal procedures of the Senate trial fall into that special category of "political questions" from which judicial countenance is barred.[34] The three-judge appellate panel that reviewed the case, however, saw Nixon's arguments as more multifacited. In fact, each judge filed a separate opinion, although the result of all was a rejection of Nixon's claim. One followed the essential reasoning of the district court and pronounced Nixon's claim to be nonjusticiable; a second agreed to reject the case but preferred not to rely on the political question argument. The third appeals judge found the question raised to be justiciable but, on the merits, found Nixon's arguments to be specious.[35] The varying interpretations of the case at the appellate level probably explain why the Supreme Court decided to hear the case.[36]

The record of committee members voting on articles of impeachment in contrast to the full upper house indicates how participation may color the conclusions reached. A larger proportion of the senators on the twelve-person evidentiary committees consistently voted not guilty than did the whole Senate. Two or three cast their ballots for the acquittal of Harry Claiborne;[37] between four and eight did the same with Alcee Hastings;[38] three to seven voted not guilty on the articles against Walter Nixon.[39] The standard of proof generally required in the Senate is "clear and convincing evidence," and even the number of committee members voting for not guilty would generally sustain convictions using that criteria. These votes seem, nonetheless, to suggest that full Senate trials and the two-thirds majority requirement might have bred different outcomes on one or more articles of impeachment. The problem lies, of course, in justifying the enormous commitment of Senate time to such undertakings, particularly if they occur frequently. Use of written questions from senators after closing presentations, an innovation first used in the Nixon case, appears to be a worthwhile device to enable senators, in addition to those on the evidentiary committee, to participate meaningfully in the trial.

Attendance at the final arguments in Claiborne's case was sparse, with only forty to fifty senators present, and was hardly commensurate with the seriousness that should be expected in impeachment trials. Attendance was notably higher, close to complete, in the trials of Hastings and Nixon. I take that shift as evidence of a renewed recognition of the importance of the task confronting the upper house. The audience increased in the latter two cases, and the deliberations were also lengthened. The questions senators asked in the Nixon case further underscored the heightened significance they attributed to the issues.

Congress, in particular the Senate, appears now to be appropriately prepared and competent to discharge its duties in impeachment proceedings. Individual representatives and senators may rue the time demanded by the procedures, but overall congressional performance must be given high marks. The kinks are out of the system, and a workable routine is in place. The time and energy that are consumed by the task are great, but so is the decision that each house makes. The punishment of those convicted is not only limited to removal from office, but also carries a sentence "of perpetual ostracism from the esteem and confidence, and honors and emoluments of this country."[40]

Frustration with the current system prompted a call for a constitutional amendment to take Congress out of the business of adjudicating judicial wrongdoing. Alabama Senator Howell Heflin proposed a plan that would imitate those now commonly used in the states, with a judicial inquiry commission to investigate complaints against judges and a court of the judiciary to try accused judges. Both bodies would be composed of judges, lawyers, and nonlawyers, and appeals from their decision would be heard by the Supreme Court.[41]

Reforms short of constitutional amendment have also been suggested to streamline the system or simply to avoid retrying judges already convicted of felonies. The least complicated is a statute that would make removal and disqualification automatic if a judge is convicted of a criminal offense. Congress, the argument goes, could retain discretion to consider any specific case if it were politically prudent to do so. Should Congress be wary of an automatic process for removal, it could, in the cases of judges already convicted, accept the convictions as factual findings and, like an appellate court, hear only collateral attacks on the conviction in impeachment proceedings. Another recommendation is that Congress direct some outside agency to conduct an investigation, at least in some cases.[42] All of these proposals are aimed at judges who have already been convicted by a court. Each assumes that convictions are, in all likelihood, sufficient grounds for removal and that Congress should be permitted to discharge its constitutional duties more expeditiously. None, however, would have saved Congress from the prickly situation raised by the Alcee Hastings case.

A Modest Proposal for Reform

The sleaze factor that emerges in the three cases discussed in this book cannot be ignored if the legitimacy of the American judiciary is to be preserved. There are, unfortunately, too many cases of judicial incompetence, disability, and outright corruption on the nation's courts.[43] U.S. District Judge Robert Aguilar of California was convicted on five counts of conspiracy, obstruction of justice, and unlawful disclosure of wiretaps in 1990,[44] and Judge Robert F. Collins of Louisiana was convicted in 1991 of bribery.[45] That bad judges must be removed from office and punished for their deeds is not at issue. The question is how that should be accomplished.

Claiborne, Hastings, and Nixon all alleged prosecutorial misconduct in the investigation and prosecution of their cases. Were there no basis for such claims, at least in two instances, impeachment might have been avoided. Both Claiborne and Nixon sought another forum to correct the miscarriages of justice they claimed colored their prosecutions. Sufficient irregularities were noted by Congress to prompt repeated calls for investigation of the Justice Department's handling of their cases. Allegations of prosecutorial misconduct can be dismissed, as they were by House managers in the Claiborne case, as arguments that the judges should not have been caught. That blithe retort, however, has little place in discussions of the integrity and dignity of the federal judiciary. Judges are expected, it is true, to be above reproach, but some of the investigatory means used against Claiborne, Hastings, and Nixon are highly questionable.

Witness intimidation was clearly demonstrated with Jerry Watson, Claiborne's accountant, and with Bud Holmes and Wiley Fairchild in the Nixon case. Prosecutors used their prerogative to take charges against others to the grand jury or to threaten that action to force reluctant cooperation. Tainted testimony was also a part of each investigation and trial. The testimony of brothel owner Joseph Conforte and his lawyer, Stanley Brown, in the Claiborne case was surely dubious, as the prosecutors themselves must have concluded when they dropped the two from the second trial. William Dredge was hardly the most reliable source of information on Alcee Hastings as he bartered with federal agents to save himself from drug charges, and Steven Clark proved to be untrustworthy in his presentation of the illegal wiretap disclosure attributed to Hastings. Wiley Fairchild and Bud Holmes forfeited their credibility, as each sought favorable treatment from the government, in their testimony against Walter Nixon. The Justice Department's strategy of arresting William Borders and then trying to "flip" him was flawed, and its probe of the wiretap allegations against Hastings was clumsy when guilt was assumed and no other leads pursued. The three cases read together illustrate a pattern of investigatory bungling.

While the last of the impeachments considered in this book was underway, another federal judge, Robert Aguilar, was indicted for racketeering activities, and the bare facts of that case bear striking similarities to those of Claiborne, Hastings, and Nixon. The government dismissed the racketeering charge after a hung jury in the first trial in early 1990, but Aguilar was later convicted on five other counts. Like Hastings and Claiborne, he charged selective prosecution and political motivations because of his liberal Democratic politics and the decisions he had made against the government in several civil cases.[46]

Even if the Justice Department had executed its investigations of each judge with absolute precision, the issue of executive interference in the judiciary would remain. One of the greatest threats to judicial independence occurs when, as Harry Claiborne put it, judges become buddies with the prosecution. Fear of investigation and expensive legal defense has the potential to blur the separation of powers by encouraging judges not to antagonize federal authorities. By the same token, judges, "if they break a law... can be prosecuted."[47]

A similar predicament was faced in deciding how to investigate and prosecute officers of the executive branch, for the Justice Department presumably would be inclined to impede thorough investigations. The problem of proper law enforcement within the executive branch was confronted in the Ethics in Government Act of 1978, which essentially allows for the appointment of independent counsel to investigate allegations of criminality by executive officers.[48] That statute can serve as a model to be imitated in protecting both the integrity of the federal bench and the rights of accused judges. The Ethics in Government Act manages to strike a delicate balance between preservation of the executive branch's law enforcement authority and the need to remove politics from criminal prosecutions involving federal officials. Separation of powers is preserved, while responsibility for investigation and prosecution in potentially political cases is diffused.

The Ethics in Government Act provides that when any criminal violation is alleged, the attorney general must conduct a preliminary investigation, an obligation generally discharged by the Public Integrity Section. When that investigation is complete, or when ninety days have passed since the initial accusation, the attorney general is required to report to the Special Division Court authorized by the law. The Special Division Court is part of the Court of Appeals for the District of Columbia and composed of three appellate judges, one of whom must be on the District of Columbia Court of Appeals and the other two from different circuits. All are appointed by the chief justice of the Supreme Court and serve two-year terms. The fixed-term requirement explicitly forestalls charges that judges can be handpicked for a specific investigation. The attorney general may report that there is no foundation for further investigation, and, if he does, the matter is dropped. Conversely, if the attorney general finds evidence to support additional inquiry, the Special Division is authorized to name a special counsel to pursue the issue. A special counsel, once appointed, is given all of the powers that a regular employee of the Justice Department would enjoy, including the ability to take a case before a grand jury. The expenses of special counsels are paid by the Justice Department, and an accounting must be made to Congress.

The Ethics in Government Act's constitutionality was challenged for violating the doctrine of separation of powers by interfering in the executive branch's power to take care that the laws be faithfully executed. However, the Supreme Court, in *Morrison v. Olson* (1988), upheld the law by a seven to one majority.[49] The majority opinion by Justice William Rehnquist held that the law did not violate the appointments clause by placing the authority to name a special counsel in the Special Division, because the office is an inferior and temporary one, not subject to presidential appointment and senatorial confirmation. Separation of powers, more importantly, is not breached because Congress does not increase its own powers at the expense of the executive. The executive branch, furthermore, retains some degree of control over the law enforcement activities of a special counsel.

A similar provision for investigation and prosecution of criminality by judicial officers has the advantage of removing any hint of partisan politics from probes of judges. Only accusations that are strictly criminal could be pursued. The Special Division, although staffed by judges, is limited in its authority and can overcome the charge that judges are simply hazing other judges. The Public Integrity Section of the Justice Department that acted in the Claiborne, Hastings, and Nixon cases would remain critical at the inception of investigations and the receipt of allegations, but that body would not be in a position to proceed further against a judge if the original charges, as they did with Claiborne and Nixon, dissolved. Use of a special counsel could guarantee the appearance of impartiality.

The problem that inheres in a special counsel system is the same one that seems intrinsic to the prosecutorial role. "A conviction is the overriding goal of a government attorney" once a prosecution has commenced.[50] That motive can allow prosecutors, with the sympathy of the presiding judge, to cross the line of acceptable ethical behavior.[51] Reputations are made on convictions, not on investigations that are dropped. Justice Antonin Scalia, in his dissent in *Morrison v. Olson,* touched on that concern, heightened in his view because there is "no one accountable to the public to whom the blame could be assigned."[52] Scalia's argument, however, rests on the assumption that the check against prosecutorial abuse lies in politics, because "the prosecutors who exercise this awesome discretion are selected and can be removed by a President."[53] That so little Justice Department control was apparently exercised in the tenacious prosecutions against Claiborne and Nixon argues that the check is minimal at best in all but the most celebrated cases. Aggressive investigative techniques in federal prosecutions are becoming more common, and a weakening of ethical standards may even be officially sanctioned.[54]

The peculiar problem with special prosecutors is that highlighted in an *amicus curiae* brief in *Morrison v. Olson* that was submitted by three former attorneys general, Edward Levi, Griffin Bell, and William French Smith. The three, as former chief law enforcement officers, underscored the "occupational hazards of the dedicated prosecutor" and argued that the inclination toward a narrow focus, or the tendency to pursue a single suspect while ignoring other possibilities, would be heightened outside the atmosphere of the Justice Department.[55] The solution is to name only established professionals who have a reputation and no need to create one and who have the balanced perspective that comes with experience. A novice, an assistant U.S. attorney such as Steven Shaw, Reid Weingarten, or Roberto Martinez, may be motivated by career enhancement or simply lack the experience that enables the seasoned practitioner to view the larger picture.

Archibald Cox and Leon Jarworski served as independent counsel in the Watergate investigations, and individuals of their stature must also be tapped for inquiries into the behavior of judges. The appointment of John Doar by the judicial council investigating Alcee Hastings undoubtedly did much to deflect charges of racism or political targeting in the judicial investigation. Although the third branch of government may be populated by almost a thousand people, the power and place of the judiciary and the need for honesty and objectivity in that branch are at least as important as integrity in the Oval Office. The prestige of the judicial office has impartiality and respect for the law at its base, and public confidence in those attributes must be preserved. Well-qualified judges, by the same token, should not be forced to look over their shoulders at ambitious prosecutors anxious to make a name.

Finding that delicate balance between judicial independence and accountability has challenged lawmakers in all western democracies, and various approaches have been tried. A superior council of the magistrature that oversees recruitment, promotion, and discipline of both prosecutors and judges has been tried in civil law systems but is not without its detractors. Judges and prosecutors, as the three cases treated in this book illustrate too well, are human and subject to the failings of pride, avarice, and greed. The federal system of impeachment, supplemented by the 1980 Judicial Conduct Act, seemed to work reasonably well in handling the cases of Claiborne, Hastings, and Nixon. The lengthy, costly, and tedious nature of the process draws criticism, but expediency cannot override concerns for fairness and justice. Had the original prosecutions not been tainted, the awkward procedure of impeachment might have been avoided, at least in the Claiborne and Nixon cases. The nation obviously cannot tolerate criminal behavior from officers of the court and, indeed, can rightly expect judges to adhere to an even higher standard of ethics than the rest of the population. Apprehension of lawbreakers, whether they be judges or laypeople, must also follow the rules. "To declare that in the administration of criminal law the end justified the means—to declare that the government may commit crimes in order to secure the conviction of a private criminal would bring terrible retribution," wrote Louis Brandeis in his dissent in the *Olmstead* case in 1928.[56] Cleaner prosecution tactics might obviate the need for impeachment and better preserve the notion of judicial independence.

Judicial independence should not be confused with the personal independence of the individual judges to act capriciously and decide cases on any basis other than the laws that are applicable and the facts as they are known. Judicial legitimacy is predicated on the notion that "the greater the perceived legitimacy of the court, the greater the probability that its policies will be accepted and faithfully implemented."[57] An independent judiciary, along with independent political opinion, are the hallmarks of democracy and the bulwarks against despotism. When either is compromised, the legitimacy of the state is at peril and prone to asphyxiation.[58]

Notes

1. Madison, *The Federalist, No. 51*, 337.
2. As Blackstone put it: "in order to maintain both the dignity and independence of the judges in the superior courts, it is enacted by the Statute 13 W.III c.2 that their commissions shall be made (not as formerly, *durante bene placito*, but) *quam diu bene se ges serint*." *Commentaries*, 4:121.

3. Hamilton, *The Federalist, No. 78*, 503.

4. Volcansek and Lafon, *Judicial Selection*, 18–19.

5. *Congressional Record*, May 10, 1989, H-1811.

6. Exceptions appear to be Taft and Hoover, who sought professional competence, and Harding and Coolidge, who resorted to patronage. Solomon, "The Politics of Appointment," 285.

7. Simon, *In His Own Image*.

8. O'Brien, *Judicial Roulette*, 95. The Reagan tradition appears to be followed by George Bush. Goldman, "The Bush Imprint on the Judiciary," 294–306.

9. Hamilton, *Federalist, No. 65*, 424.

10. *Congressional Record*, May 10, 1989, H-1809.

11. Blackstone, *Commentaries*, 4:140.

12. *Congressional Record*, November 3, 1989, S-14367.

13. Hamilton, *Federalist, No. 65*, 426.

14. The Dade County bar poll that rates all local judges confirms a decline in perceptions of Hastings's competence. In the 1983 poll, taken after his acquittal, more than 53 percent of the lawyers polled rated him as unqualified. The 1985 poll indicated some improvement, with 39 percent voting for an unqualified rating. In the 1987 poll, 37 percent voted him unqualified. Hastings was not the judge who received the lowest ratings in those last two years. "Dade County Bar Association, Judicial Polls."

15. Holloman, "The Judicial Reform Act," 144.

16. *Chandler v. Judicial Council*, 398 U.S. 74 at 139 (1970).

17. "They [the constitutional framers] knew that judges of the past—good, patriotic judges—had occasionally lost not only their offices," Black wrote, "but had also sometimes lost their freedom and their heads because of the actions and decrees of other judges." Ibid., at 141.

18. This characterization of the bench is from Frank, *Court on Trial*, 254.

19. Berg, Hahn, and Schmidhauser, *Corruption in the American Political System*, 1–27.

20. Glick and Vines, *State Court Systems*, 65.

21. *Model Code of Judicial Conduct*, Canon 2.

22. Braithwaite, *Who Judges the Judges?*, 9.

23. General Pickering, at the Constitutional Convention, noted that "the importance of the Judiciary will require men of first talents: large salaries will therefore be necessary, larger than the U.S. can allow in the first instance." Farrand, *Records of the Federal Convention of 1787*, 2:429.

24. Berg, Hahn, and Schmidhauser, *Corruption in the American Political System*, 19–20.

25. Garvey, "Foreword," 633.

26. Johnson and Canon, *Judicial Policies*, 191.

27. Sartori, *The Theory of Democracy Revisited*, 2:326.

28. Berg, Hahn, and Schmidhauser, *Corruption in the American Political System*, 21.

29. Shaman, Lubet, and Alfini, "The 1990 Code of Judicial Conduct," 21–27.

30. Berg, Hahn, and Schmidhauser, *Corruption in the American Political System*, 3.

31. Brooks, "Penalizing Judges Who Appeal Disciplinary Sanctions," 95–102.

32. For a discussion of Pickering's case, see Bushnell, *Crimes, Follies, and Misfortunes*, 43–57.

33. *Nixon v. U.S.*, 744 F.Supp. 9 (1990).

34. Ibid.

35. *Nixon v. U.S.*, 938 F.2d 239 (1991).

36. Before the Supreme Court could review Nixon's challenge to the use of an evidentiary committee, U.S. District Judge Stanley Sporkin overturned the Senate's conviction of Alcee Hastings. Sporkin cited the use of a committee as violating Hastings's rights. Lewis, "2 Branches Entangled," A-1.

37. *Congressional Record*, October 6, 1989, S-15760–1.

38. *Congressional Record*, October 20, 1989, S-13782–5.

39. *Congressional Record*, November 3, 1989, S-14635–6.

40. Hamilton, *Federalist No. 65*, 426.

41. Heflin, "The Impeachment Process," 125.

42. Gerhardt, "The Constitutional Limits to Impeachment and Its Alternatives," 102-3.

43. See, for example, Baum, *American Courts*, 154–58; Braithwaite, *Who Judges the Judges?*; and Goulden, *The Benchwarmers*.

44. "Judge Found Guilty in Obstruction of Justice," A-18. Aguilar received a minimal sentence of six months in prison, a thousand hours of community service, and a $2,000 fine. Bishop, "Federal Judge Is Given Reduced Sentence," A-12.

45. Marcus, "Federal Judge Is Found Guilty in Bribery Trial," Y-14.

46. Bishop, "Racketeering Count Against Judge Dropped," A-13.

47. *Chandler v. Judicial Council*, at 139.

48. Public Law 95–521, 92 Stat. 1867, was passed in 1978 and has been reenacted with amendments twice. 28 U.S.C.A. Section 599.

49. *Morrison v. Olson*, 108 S.Ct. 2597 (1988). Justice Kennedy did not participate in the decision.

50. Norton, "Government Attorneys' Ethics in Transition," 299.

51. Alschuler, "Courtroom Misconduct by Prosecutors and Trial Judges," 642.

52. *Morrison v. Olson*, at 2639.

53. Ibid., at 2638.

54. Norton, "Ethics and the Attorney General," 203–7. That piece prompted a direct response from the attorney general. Thornberg, "Ethics and the Attorney General: The Attorney General Responds," 290–91, 336. Thornburg said that "the controversy, it seems to me, is not that we have developed our policy, but that we have articulated it."

55. *Morrison v. Olson*, at 2640.

56. *Olmstead v. U.S.*, 277 U.S. 438 (1928).

57. Johnson and Canon, *Judicial Policies*, 194.

58. Paul Ricoeur, "The Political Paradox," in *Legitimacy and the State*, ed. Connolly, 270.

References

Books

Abraham, Henry J. *The Judicial Process.* New York: Oxford University Press, 1986.

Baum, Lawrence. *American Courts: Process and Policy.* Boston: Houghton Mifflin Company, 1990.

Becker, Theodore L. *Comparative Judicial Politics: The Political functionings of Courts.* Chicago: Rand McNally, 1970.

Berg, Larry L., Harlan Hahn, and John R. Schmidhauser. *Corruption in the American Political System.* Morristown, N.J.: General Learning Press, 1976.

Berger, Raoul. *Impeachment: The Constitutional Problems.* Cambridge: Harvard University Press, 1974.

Black, Charles. *Impeachment: A Handbook.* New Haven: Yale University Press, 1974.

Blackstone, William. *Commentaries on the Laws of England,* 8th edition. Oxford: Clarendon Press, 1778.

Borkin, Joseph. *The Corrupt Judge: An Inquiry into Bribery and Other Crimes and Misdemeanors in Federal Courts.* New York: Clarkson N. Potter, 1962.

Braithwaite, William Thomas. *Who Judges the Judges?* Chicago: American Bar Foundation, 1971.

Bushnell, Eleanore. *Crimes, Follies, and Misfortunes: The Federal Impeachment Trials.* Urbana: University of Illinois Press, 1992.

Comisky, Marvin, and Philip C. Patterson. *The Judiciary—Selection, Compensation, Ethics, and Discipline.* New York: Quorum Books, 1987.

Connolly, William, ed. *Legitimacy and the State.* New York: New York University Press, 1984.

Directory of Florida Judges, 1985. Miami: South Publishing Company, 1985.

Dubois, Philip L., ed. *The Analysis of Judicial Reform.* Lexington: D.C. Heath, 1982.

Farrand, Max, ed. *The Records of the Federal Convention of 1787.* New Haven: Yale University Press, 1911.

Fish, Peter Graham. *Federal Judicial Administration.* Princeton: Princeton University Press, 1973.

Frank, Jerome. *Courts on Trial: Myth and Reality in American Justice.* Princeton: Princeton University Press, 1973.

Glick, Henry R., and Kenneth N. Vines. *State Court Systems.* Englewood Cliffs, N.J.: Prentice-Hall, 1973.

Goulden, Joseph C. *The Benchwarmers: The Private World of the Powerful Federal Judges.* New York: Ballantine Books, 1974.

Haynes, Evan. *The Selection and Tenure of Judges.* Littleton, Colo.: Fred B. Rothman, 1944.

Hoffer, Peter Charles, and N. E. H. Hull. *Impeachment in America, 1635–1805.* New Haven: Yale University Press, 1984.

Jay, John, Alexander Hamilton, and James Madison. *The Federalist.* New York: Modern Library.

Johnson, Charles A., and Bradley C. Canon. *Judicial Policies: Implementation and Impact.* Washington, D.C.: CQ Press, 1984.

Johnson, Herbert A. *Foundations of Power: John Marshall, 1801–1815.* New York: Macmillan, 1981.

Lipset, Seymour Martin. *Political Man: The Social Bases of Politics.* Garden City: Anchor Books, 1963.

Lummis, Henry T. *The Trial Judge.* Chicago: Foundation Press, 1937.

Model Code of Judicial Conduct. Chicago: American Bar Association, 1972.

Montesquieu, Baron de. *The Spirit of the Laws.* New York: Hafner Publishing, 1949.

Murphy, Bruce Allen. *Fortas: The Rise and Ruin of a Supreme Court Justice.* New York: William Morrow, 1988.

O'Brien, David M. *Judicial Roulette: Report of the Twentieth Century Fund Task Force on Judicial Selection.* New York: Priority Press Publications, 1988.

Poore, Ben Perley. *The Federal and State Constitutions, Colonial Charters, and Other Organic Laws of the United States.* New York: Burt Franklin, 1877.

Ryan, John Paul, Allan Ashman, Bruce D. Sales, and Sandra Shane-DuBow. *American Trial Judges: Their Work Styles and Performance.* New York: Free Press, 1980.

Sartori, Giovanni. *The Theory of Democracy Revisited.* Chatham, N.J.: Chatham House Publishers, 1987.

Shaman, Jeffrey M., Steven Lubet, and James J. Alfini. *Judicial Conduct and Ethics*. Charlottesville: Michie Company, 1990.
Shapiro, Martin. *Courts: A Comparative and Political Analysis*. Chicago: University of Chicago Press, 1981.
Simon, James F. *In His Own Image: The Supreme Court in Richard Nixon's America*. New York: David McKay, 1973.
The Trial of Samuel Chase, an Associate Justice of the Supreme Court of the United States. Washington, D.C.: Samuel H. Smith, 1805.
Volcansek, Mary L., and Jacqueline Lucienne Lafon. *Judicial Selection: The Cross-Evolution of French and American Practices*. Westport: Greenwood Press, 1988.
White, Theodore H. *Breach of Faith: The Fall of Richard Nixon*. New York: Atheneum, 1975.
Wise, David. *The American Police State*. New York: Random House, 1976.

Articles

Alschuler, Albert. "Courtroom Misconduct by Prosecutors and Trial Judges." *Texas Law Review* 50 (1972): 642–54.
Berger, Raoul. "Impeachment for High Crimes and Misdemeanors." *Southern California Law Review* 44 (1971): 395–460.
Brooks, Daniel J. "Penalizing Judges Who Appeal Disciplinary Sanctions: The Unconstitutionality of 'Upping the Ante.'" *Judicature* 69 (August–September 1985): 95–102.
Burbank, Stephen B. "Politics and Progress in Implementing the Federal Judicial Discipline Act." *Judicature* 71 (June–July 1987): 13–28.
Drinan, Robert F. "Judicial Appointments for Life by the Executive Branch of Government: Reflections on the Massachusetts Experience." *Texas Law Review* 44 (June 1966): 1103.
Fitzpatrick, Collins T. "Misconduct and Disability of Federal Judges: The Unreported Informal Responses." *Judicature* 71 (February-March 1988): 282–83.
Gardiner, John A. "Preventing Judicial Misconduct: Defining the Role of Conduct Organizations." *Judicature* 70 (August–September 1986): 113–21.
Garvey, John H. "Foreword: Judicial Discipline and Impeachment." *Kentucky Law Journal* 76 (1988): 633–41.
Gerhardt, Michael J. "The Constitutional Limits to Impeachment and Its Alternatives." *Texas Law Review* 68 (November 1989): 1–104.
Goldman, Sheldon. "The Bush Imprint on the Judiciary: Carrying on the Tradition." *Judicature* 74 (April-May 1991): 294–306.

———. "Carter's Judicial Appointments: A Lasting Legacy." *Judicature* 64 (March 1981): 344–55.

———. "Reagan's Judicial Legacy: Completing the Puzzle and Summing Up." *Judicature* 72 (April-May 1989): 318–30.

Heflin, Howell. "Additional Views of Senator Howell Heflin on the Judicial Conduct and Disability Act of 1979." *U.S. Code and Administrative News* (1980): 4334.

———. "The Impeachment Process: Modernizing an Archaic System." *Judicature* 71 (August-September 1987) 123–25.

Holloman, John H., III. "The Judicial Reform Act: History, Analyses and Comment." *Law and Contemporary Problems* 35 (1970): 128–50.

Humphrey, Alexander Pope. "The Impeachment of Samuel Chase." *American Law Review* 33 (1899).

"Impeaching Federal Judges: Where We Are and Where We Are Going." *Judicature* 72 (1989): 359–65.

Jones, Elaine R., and Janice King-Robinson. "Choices: Appointing Blacks to the Federal Judiciary." *National Bar Association Magazine* (July 1988): 17–39.

Laxalt, Paul. "Additional Views of Senator Paul Laxalt on the Judicial Conduct and Disability Act of 1979." *U.S. Code and Administrative News* (1980): 4342.

Mathias, Charles. "Additional Views of Senator Charles Mathias, Jr., on the Judicial Conduct and Disability Act of 1979." *U.S. Code and Administrative News* (1980): 4336–37.

Neisser, Eric. "The New Federal Judicial Discipline Act: Some Questions Congress Didn't Answer." *Judicature* 65 (September 1981): 142–60.

Norton, Jerry E. "Ethics and the Attorney General." *Judicature* 74 (December-January 1991): 203–7.

———. "Government Attorneys' Ethics in Transition." *Judicature* 72 (February-March, 1989): 299–303.

Shaman, Jeffrey M., Steven Lubet, and James J. Alfini. "The 1990 Code of Judicial Conduct." *Judicature* 70 (June-July 1990): 21–27.

Solomon, Raymond L. "The Politics of Appointment and the Federal Courts' Regulating America: U.S. Courts of Appeals Judgeships from T. R. to F. D. R." *American Bar Foundation Research Journal* 1984 (1984): 285–343.

Ten Broek, Jacobus. "Partisan Politics and Federal Judgeship Impeachment since 1903." *Minnesota Law Review* 23 (1939): 185–204.

Thornburg, Dick. "Ethics and the Attorney General: The Attorney General Responds." *Judicature* 74 (April-May 1991): 290–91, 316.

Volcansek, Mary L. "British Antecedents for U.S. Impeachment Practices: Continuity and Change." *Justice System Journal* 14 (1990): 40–62.

Ware, Gilbert. "A Sense of History." *National Bar Association Magazine* (July 1988): 35–37.

Government Documents

Annual Report of the Director of the Administration Office of the U.S. Courts. Washington, D.C.: U.S. Government Printing Office, 1988.

Annual Report of the Director of the Administrative Office of the U.S. Courts. Washington, D.C.: U.S. Government Printing Office, 1989.

Conduct of Harry E. Claiborne, United States District Judge, District of Nevada. Hearings before the Subcommittee on Courts, Civil Liberties and the Administration of Justice, Committee on the Judiciary, House of Representatives, 99th Cong. Washington, D.C.: U.S. Government Printing Office, 1986.

Hearings before the Senate Impeachment Trial Committee, U.S. Senate. 101st Cong. Washington, D.C.: U.S. Government Printing Office, 1989.

Hearings before the Subcommittee on Civil and Constitutional Rights, Judge Walter L. Nixon, Jr., Impeachment Inquiry. 100th Cong. Washington, D.C.: U.S. Government Printing Office, 1989.

Hearings before the Subcommittee on Courts, Civil Liberties and the Administration of Justice, Committee on the Judiciary. House of Representatives, 99th Cong. Washington, D.C.: U.S. Government Printing Office, 1986.

Hearings before the Subcommittee on Criminal Justice of the Committee on the Judiciary. House of Representatives, 100th Cong. Washington, D.C.: U.S. Government Printing Office, 1987.

Hearings before the Subcommittee on Criminal Justice of the Committee on the Judiciary, House of Representatives: Materials Relating to Wiretap Disclosure. Washington, D.C.: U.S. Government Printing Office, 1988.

Impeachment Inquiry Hearings before the Committee on the Judiciary, House of Representatives, 93d Cong. Washington, D.C.: U.S. Government Printing Office, 1975.

Impeachment Inquiry, Hearings before the Subcommittee on Criminal Justice of the Committee on the Judiciary, House of Representatives. 100th Cong. Washington, D.C.: U.S. Government Printing Office, 1988.

In the Matter of the Impeachment Inquiry Concerning U.S. District Judge Alcee L. Hastings, Hearings before the Subcommittee on Criminal

Justice of the Committee on the Judiciary, House of Representatives. Washington, D.C.: U.S. Government Printing Office, 1987.

Markup of House Resolution 461, Impeachment of Judge Harry E. Claiborne. Committee on the Judiciary, House of Representatives, 99th Cong. Washington, D.C.: U.S. Government Printing Office, 1986.

Nomination of Walter L. Nixon, Jr., Hearing before a Special Subcommittee of the Committee on the Judiciary, United States Senate. 90th Cong. Washington, D.C.: U.S. Government Printing Office, 1968.

Report of the Senate Impeachment Trial Committee on the Articles against Judge Alcee Hastings. Washington, D.C.: U.S. Government Printing Office, 1989.

Report of the Senate Impeachment Trial Committee on the Articles against Judge Alcee L. Hastings, Hearings, Senate Impeachment Trial Committee. United States Senate. Washington, D.C.: U.S. Government Printing Office, 1989.

Report of the Proceedings of the Judicial Conference of the United States. March 17, 1987.

Report of the Senate Impeachment Trial Committee on the Articles against Judge Alcee Hastings. 101st Cong. Washington, D.C.: U.S. Government Printing Office, 1989.

Report of the Senate Impeachment Trial Committee on the Articles against Judge Alcee Hastings, Exhibits Admitted into Evidence. Washington, D.C.: U.S. Government Printing Office, 1989.

Report of the Senate Impeachment Trial Committee on the Articles against Judge Walter L. Nixon, Jr. Washington, D.C.: U.S. Government Printing Office, 1989.

Report of the Senate Trial Committee on the Articles against Judge Walter L. Nixon, Jr., U.S. Senate. 101st Cong. Washington, D.C.: U.S. Government Printing Office, 1989.

Senate Impeachment Trial Committee. U.S. Senate, 99th Cong. Washington, D.C.: U.S. Government Printing Office, 1986.

Trial of John Pickering, Judge of the New Hampshire District Court, a Charge Exhibited to the Senate of the United States for High Crimes and Misdemeanors. S. Doc. 876.

Court Cases

Borders v. Reagan, 518 F. Supp 250 (1981).
Borders v. U.S., 461 U.S. 905 (1983).
Burton v. U.S., 202 U.S. 344 (1906).
Chandler v. Judicial Council, 398 U.S. 74 (1970).
Claiborne v. U.S., 469 U.S. 829 (1984).

Claiborne v. U.S., 475 U.S. 1120 (1986).
Hastings v. Judicial Conference of the United States, 593 F.Supp. 1371 (1984).
Hastings v. Judicial Conference, 770 F.2d 1093 (1985).
In re Certain Complaints under Investigation by an Investigating Committee of the Judicial Council of the Eleventh Circuit, 610 F.Supp. 169 (1985).
In re Grand Jury Proceedings, 669 F.Supp. 1072 (1987).
In re Grand Jury Proceedings, 841 F.2d 1948 (1988).
In re Petition to Inspect and Copy Grand Jury Materials, 576 F.Supp. 1275 (1983).
In re Request for Access to Grand Jury Materials, 833 F.2d 1438 (1987).
LaBuy v. Howes Leather Company, 325 U.S. 249 (1956).
Morrison v. Olson, 108 S. Ct. 2597 (1988).
Nixon v. U.S., 744 F.Supp. 9 (1990).
Nixon v. U.S., 938 F.2d 239 (1991).
O'Donoghue v. U.S., 289 U.S. 516 (1932).
Olmstead v. U.S., 277 U.S. 438 (1928).
O'Shea v. Littleton, 414 U.S. 488 (1974).
U.S. v. Borders, 693 F.2d 1318 (1982).
U.S. v. Claiborne, 727 F.2d 842 (1984).
U.S. v. Claiborne, 765 F.2d 784 (1985).
U.S. v. Claiborne, 781 F.2d 1327 (1985).
U.S. v. Conforte, 624 F.2d 869 (1980).
U.S. v. Hastings, 681 F.2d 706 (1982).
U.S. v. Hastings, 689 F.2d 706 (1982).
U.S. v. Hastings, 695 F.2d 1278 (1983).
U.S. v. Hastings, 704 F.2d 559 (1983).
U.S. v Hastings, 459 U.S. 1094 (1983).
U.S. v. Hastings, 459 U.S. 1203 (1983).
U.S. v. Isaacs and Kerner, 493 F.2d 1124 (1973).
U.S. v. Martino, 648 F.2d 367 (1981).
U.S. v. Marubeni America Corp., 611 F.2d 763 (1980).
U.S. v Nixon, 816 F.2d 1022 (1987).
U.S. v. Nixon, 827 F.2d 1019 (1987).
U.S. v. Nixon, 881 F.2d 1305 (1989).
U.S. v. Peacock, 654 F.2d 339 (1981).

Newspaper Articles

Anderson, Paul. "Hastings Opens Campaign for Governor." *Miami Herald*, October 24, 1989, A-16.

Bishop, Karen. "Federal Judge Is Given Reduced Prison Sentence in Corruption Case." *New York Times,* November 2, 1990, A-12.

———. "Racketeering Count against Judge Dropped; New Trial Is Set." *New York Times,* May 9, 1990, Y-13.

"Claiborne Impeached, Stripped of Judgeship." *Congressional Quarterly Almanac,* 1986.

Eisler, Kim I. "Claiborne Gets His Point Across." *Legal Times,* September 9, 1986, 80.

Fiedler, Tom. "Hastings Briefly Explored Deal to Avoid Senate Trial." *Miami Herald,* May 4, 1989, B-3.

Friend, Tad. "Peer Pressure." *American Lawyer,* November 8, 1986, 82.

Greenhouse, Linda. "Judge Impeachment Process Assailed." *New York Times,* October 11, 1986, Y-24.

———. "U.S. Judge Ousted by Impeachment, First in 50 Years." *New York Times,* October 10, 1986, Y-23.

"Hastings: Heart Ailment May Delay Senate Trial." *Miami Herald,* January 6, 1989, D-1.

Hedges, Stephen J. "Judge Calls Report 'Slopped-Up Ink.' " *Miami Herald,* October 8, 1987, A-1.

Hiaasen, Carl. "Hastings Race Will Be Fun, but Not Real." *Miami Herald,* October 23, 1989, B-1.

"Judge Found Guilty in Obstruction of Justice." *New York Times,* August 23, 1990, A-18.

Kilpatrick, James J. "Impeachable Character or Not, It's Double Jeopardy." *Miami Herald,* March 23, 1989, A-31.

Lewis, Neil A., "2 Branches Entangled." *New York Times,* September 19, 1992, A-1.

Liff, Robert A. "Hastings Trial Stirs Nest of Ethical Legal Questions." *Orlando Sentinel,* February 6, 1983, 1.

Lowe, Bob. "City Officials Bullied Developers while Cashing in on Mango Hill." *Miami Herald,* January 29, 1985, A-1.

———, and Marie Betancourt. "Hialeah Officials Mix Votes, Private Deals." *Miami Herald,* January 27, 1985, A-1.

Marcus, Frances Frank. "Federal Judge Is Found Guilty in Bribery Trial." *New York Times,* June 30, 1991, Y-14.

Marcus, Noreen. "Congress Reluctantly Takes up Hastings' Ouster." *Legal Times,* March 30, 1987, 1.

———. "Now the Fate of Lawyer Hastings." *Miami Review,* October 31, 1989, 4.

McGarrahan, Ellen. "Hastings Quits Governor's Race, Begins Run for Secretary of State." *Miami Herald,* April 1, 1990, B-4.

"Parole Panel Rejects Bid by Convicted Judge." *New York Times*, October 29, 1986, Y-23.

Shenon, Philip. "Judge Acquitted in 1983 Says Panel Wants Him Impeached." *New York Times*, August 27, 1986, Y-14.

———. "Judge Suggests Racism Is Motivating Inquiry." *New York Times*, January 20, 1987, Y-13.

Skene, Neil. "Alcee Hastings Faces His Next 'Trial.'" *St. Petersburg Times*, February 6, 1983, A-14.

Slevin, Peter. "Judge Vows to Return to Federal Bench." *Miami Herald*, February 6, 1983, A-6.

Solov, Dean. "Judge Nixon Refuses to Resign, Vows to Fight Impeachment." *Clarion Ledger*, January 21, 1988, 1.

Strasser, Fred. "A Judge's Fall from Grace." *National Law Journal*, April 4, 1988, 24.

Stuart, Reginald. "Judge Expects New Attacks after Acquittal in Bribe Plot." *New York Times*, February 6, 1983, Y-15.

Thompson, Gary, and Jeff German. "The Impeachment of Judge Harry Claiborne." *Las Vegas Sun*, August 24, 1986, special report.

———. "The Swanson Sting." *Las Vegas Sun*, August 24, 1986, special report, 14.

Turner, Wallace. "Jailed U.S. Judge Resists Resigning." *New York Times*, June 16, 1986, Y-17.

Wallace, Richard. "Clark Says Books Back Him on 'Spook' Meaning." *Miami Herald*, June 12, 1988, B-1.

Wines, Michael. "Shaking Up Justice." *New York Times Magazine*, May 21, 1989, 48.

Zaldivar, R. A. "Hastings Asks D.C. Radio Listeners to Pack Galleries." *Miami Herald*, March 15, 1989, A-9.

———. "Hastings' Senate Fight Begins." *Miami Herald*, March 16, 1989, A-1.

———. "Impeachment Saga Nears Finish." *Miami Herald*, June 10, 1988, A-6.

———, and Stephen J. Hedges. "Lawyer: I Told Hastings Not to Involve Me." *Miami Herald*, May 20, 1988, A-13.

Unpublished Materials

Carter Presidential Library, Document FG53/ST9/A.

Carter Presidential Library, Document FG53/ST28/A.

"Dade County Bar Association, Judicial Polls (1983, 1985, 1987)." Miami: Arthur Young Associates.

U.S. v. Borders and Hastings, Case no. 81-00596-CR-ETG (Docket Sheets).

U.S. v. Claiborne, Case no. 83-00057 (1984), Trial Transcript.

U.S. v. Claiborne, Case no. CR-R-83-57 (1984), Trial Transcript.

U.S. v. Dredge and Nodolski et al., Case no. K-81-0209.

U.S. v. Hastings, Case no. 81-00596-ETG (1981).

U.S. v. Nixon, Case no. H85-00012 (1986).

Index

MARY L. VOLCANSEK is a professor of political science at Florida International University, where she has also served as associate dean of arts and sciences and as acting assistant vice president for academic affairs. She has also written *Judicial Politics in Europe: An Impact Analysis*, edited *Judicial Politics and Policymaking in West Europe*, and co-authored *Judicial Selection: The Cross-Evolution of French and American Practices*. Her articles have appeared in *Western Political Quarterly*, *West European Politics*, *Judicature*, and *Policy Studies Journal*, among others.